Hands-On Activities With Scripture Values

LEVEL C

TEACHER GUIDEBOOK

ISBN #1-58938-148-3

Published by The Concerned Group, Inc.
700 East Granite • PO Box 1000 • Siloam Springs, AR 72761

Authors	**Dave & Rozann Seela**
Publisher	**Russ L. Potter, II**
Senior Editor	**Bill Morelan**
Project Coordinator	**Rocki Vanatta**
Creative Director	**Daniel Potter**
Proofreader	**Renee Decker**
Step Illustrations	**Steven Butler**
Character Illustrations	**Josh Ray**
Colorists	**Josh & Aimee Ray**

Printed on recycled paper in the United States

For more information about **A Reason For**® curricula,
write to the address above, call, or visit our website.

www.areasonfor.com
800.447.4332

TABLE OF CONTENTS

Overview

How To Use This Guidebook

Weekly Lessons

Assessment

"A sound grounding in science strengthens many of the skills that people use every day, like solving problems creatively, thinking critically, working cooperatively in teams, using technology effectively, and valuing life-long learning."

*National Science Education Standards, 1999 Washington, D.C.: National Academy Press. (p. ix)

A NEW PARADIGM

A Reason For® Science was designed for children, the handiwork of an infinite God — young minds created with an unlimited capacity to think, to learn, and to discover!

Because of this emphasis on children and how they learn, *A Reason For® Science* is based on a different paradigm from the traditional textbook approach. Why? In an effort to address standards and accountability, many of today's science textbooks seem to get learning backwards. They focus primarily on building a knowledge base, assuming students will later attach meaning to memorized facts. The problem is that few elementary students master information presented this way because they simply never become engaged with the material.

By contrast, *A Reason For® Science* is based on the premise that learning science is an *active* process. It's "something children do, not something done to them." [2]

According to the **National Science Education Standards**, ". . . active science learning means shifting emphasis away from teachers presenting information and covering science topics. The perceived need to include all the topics and information . . . is in direct conflict with the central goal of having students learn scientific knowledge with understanding." [3]

To paraphrase William Butler Yeats, "Teaching is not filling a pail. It's lighting a fire!"

INQUIRY-BASED LEARNING

A Reason For® Science is designed to teach basic Life, Earth, and Physical Science concepts through fun, hands-on activities. Its focus is to make learning both fun and meaningful.

But hands-on activities by themselves are not enough. To truly master a concept, students must have "minds-on" experiences as well! This means actively engaging the material through a variety of activities such as group discussion, problem solving, and journaling. It also requires thought-provoking questions that help develop higher-level cognitive skills. The weekly format of *A Reason For® Science* is designed to reflect this inquiry-based model.

According to the **National Science Education Standards**, "Inquiry is central to science learning. When engaging in inquiry, students describe objects and events, ask questions, construct explanations, test those explanations against current scientific knowledge, and communicate their ideas to others . . . In this way, students actively develop their understanding of science by combining scientific knowledge with reasoning and thinking skills." [4]

Since different students achieve understanding in different ways and to different degrees, the flexible format of *A Reason For® Science* also encourages multiple learning styles and allows for individual differences. Activities challenge students to develop their own unique skills, and encourage them to come up with creative solutions.

NATIONAL STANDARDS

National standards referred to in **A Reason For® Science** come from the **National Science Education Standards**[1]. More specifically, they reflect the "K-4 Science Content Standards" (p.121 - 142) and "5-8 Science Content Standards" (p. 143 - 172).

The Teacher Guidebook includes a list of content standards that relate to each individual lesson. References are based on the NSES alphabetic format, plus a numeric code to indicate the bulleted sub-topic. For example, **C1** in a fourth grade lesson would indicate Content Standard **C** and sub-topic **1**. (A detailed description of this content standard can be found on pages 127 - 229 of the **Standards**.)

As noted above, lower grade and upper grade standards are found in different sections of the book. A **C1** reference for a third grade lesson, for example, would be found on page 127 (characteristics of organisms). By contrast, a **C1** reference for a seventh grade lesson would be found on page 155 ("structure and function in living systems").

METHODOLOGY

Master teachers know that a science curriculum is much more than information in a textbook. It has to do with the way content is organized and presented in the classroom. It is driven by underlying principles, and by attitudes and beliefs about how learning occurs. It is expressed in the practices and procedures used in its implementation.

In other words, textbooks don't teach science — *teachers* do!

That's why it's important for you to understand how this curriculum is designed to be used, and how you can enhance the learning process in your classroom.

Concepts, Not Content

The needs of children in elementary school are very different from high school students, especially when it comes to science education. The presentation of the Periodic Table provides a good example. High school students may find it useful to memorize each element, its atomic weight, and its position on a chart. By contrast, elementary school students must first understand the concept of such a table. What is it? How is it used? Why is it arranged this way? Has it always looked like this? How (and why) has it changed over time? Such an approach leads to a foundational understanding of a concept, rather than a body of memorized "facts" that may change over time.*

As Nobel prize winner, Dr. Richard Feynman, once said, "You can know the name of a bird in all the languages of the world, but when you're finished, you'll know absolutely nothing whatever about the bird . . . (that's) the difference between knowing the name of something and knowing something!"

---

* For example, less than 30 years ago many students were still being taught the "fact" that matter only has three states (solid, liquid, gas). But in 1970, Hannes Alfven won the Nobel prize for identifying a fourth state of matter (plasma). There are many such examples in education — including Periodic Table charts themselves, which are being replaced in many colleges by a new 3D computer model that offers new insights into relationships between elements.

Multi-Sensory Learning

In addition to focusing on concepts instead of just content, **A Reason For® Science** uses a multi-sensory approach to learning that supports multiple learning styles.

Visual events include watching teacher demonstrations, studying diagrams and illustrations, and reading summaries. **Auditory** events include participating in group discussions with team members, listening to teacher directions and explanations, and hearing the unique sounds associated with the activities. **Kinesthetic** events include tactile interaction with activity materials, hands-on experimentation, and taking notes, writing answers, and drawing diagrams in individual Student Worktexts.

Omitting any of these components can significantly weaken the learning process, especially for children with specific learning disabilities.

Student-Driven, Teacher-Directed

As long-time educators, the authors of this series recognize that many elementary teachers don't consider themselves "science people." Therefore, this series avoids unnecessary technical jargon, and deals with complex interactions in simple, easy-to-understand language that's reinforced with concrete, hands-on activities.

The Teacher Guidebook is designed to give you the confidence that you need to teach science effectively. In addition to the usual answer keys and explanations, it includes several sections just for teachers.

"Additional Comments" offers tips and techniques for making each lesson run smoothly. "Teacher to Teacher" provides expanded science explanations to increase your understanding. "Extended Teaching" presents a variety of extension ideas for those who wish to go further.

During the first year, we strongly recommend that you try every activity a day or two in advance. Although most activities are relatively simple, this added practice will give you a better feel for any potential problems that might arise.

Most of all, remember that one of the primary goals of this series is to make science FUN for the participants. And that includes you, too!

COMPONENTS

The following are some of the key components in this series:

Letter to Parents

Positive communication between home and school is essential for optimum success with any curriculum. The "Letter to the Parents" (page 3, Student Worktext) provides a great way to introduce **A Reason For® Science** to parents. It covers the lesson format, safety issues, connections with national standards, and the integration of Scripture. Along with the opening sections of this Guidebook, the parent letter provides information you need to answer common questions about the series.

Student Research Teams

A Reason For® Science was created to model the way scientific study works in the adult world. Students are divided into "research teams" to work through activities cooperatively. Ideally, each research team should be composed of three to five students. (Fewer students per team makes monitoring more difficult; more students per team minimizes participation opportunities.) The best groupings combine students with different "gifts" (skills or abilities), complimentary personalities, etc. — the same kinds of combinations that make effective teams in the corporate or industrial world.

In addition, *A Reason For® Science* encourages collaboration between the different teams, again modeling the interactions found in the scientific community.

Individual Student Worktexts

Although students collaborate on activities and thought questions, the Student Worktexts provide opportunities for individual reaction and response. The importance of allowing students to write their own response to questions, keep their own notes, and journal about their individual experiences cannot be underestimated. (While collaboration is essential in the scientific community, no true scientist would neglect to keep his/her own personal notes and records!)

Individual Student Worktexts also provide teachers with an objective way to monitor student participation and learning throughout the school year.

Materials Kits

Quality materials are an integral part of any "hands-on" curriculum. *A Reason For® Science* offers complete, easy-to-use materials kits for every grade level. With some minor exceptions*, kits contain all the materials and supplies needed by one research team for an entire school year. Materials for each team come packaged in an attractive, durable storage container. You can choose to restock consumable portions of the kit from local materials, or purchase the convenient refill pack.

Personal Science Glossary

A glossary is a common component in many science textbooks, yet students rarely use traditional glossaries except when assigned to "look up" a word by the teacher. Since words and terms used in elementary science are not highly technical, this activity is better served by referring students to a standard dictionary.

A more effective approach to helping students learn science words at this level is to encourage them to develop and maintain a **personal science glossary**. This can be a plain spiral-bound notebook with one page (front and back) dedicated to each letter of the alphabet. Throughout the school year, students continually add new words and definitions — not only from their own reading and research, but from the findings of their team members as well. (For your convenience, a black-line master for a glossary cover is included in Appendix A.)

---

* To help minimize expenses, kits do not include common classroom supplies (pencils, paper, etc.) and a few large items (soft drink bottles, tin cans, etc.) that are easily obtained by the teacher. Kit and non-kit materials needed for each lesson are clearly marked in this Teacher Guidebook.

SAFETY ISSUES

When using hands-on science activities, teachers must be constantly aware of the potential for safety problems. Even the simplest activities using the most basic materials can be dangerous when used incorrectly. **Proper monitoring and supervision is required at all times!**

Although the publisher and authors have made every reasonable effort to ensure that all science activities in *A Reason For® Science* are safe when conducted as instructed, neither the publisher nor the authors assume any responsibility for damage or injury resulting from implementation.

It is the responsibility of the school to review available science safety resources and to develop science safety training for their teachers and students, as well as posting safety rules in every classroom.

An excellent source of science safety information is the Council of State Science Supervisors at: http://csss.enc.org/safety. The CSSS website offers a FREE, downloadable safety guide, "Science and Safety, Making the Connection." This booklet was created with support from the American Chemical Society, the Eisenhower National Clearinghouse for Mathematics and Science Education, the National Aeronautics and Space Administration, and the National Institutes of Health.

To support appropriate safety instruction, every *A Reason For® Science* Student Worktext includes a special section on safety. In addition to the safety precautions above, it is strongly recommended that *every* teacher verify all students clearly understand this information *before* beginning any science activities.

ASSESSMENT METHODS

Authentic assessment is an important part of any quality curriculum. *A Reason For® Science* offers a duel approach to assessment. First, participation, understanding, and higher-level thinking skills and can be assessed by periodically collecting and reading students' responses to the essay-style questions in the Student Worktext.

Second, this Teacher Guidebook provides black-line masters for a "weekly quiz" (see page 163). These quizzes offer a more traditional assessment based on fact acquisition. Questions are similar to the type that students might face on any standardized test.

In addition, you can use both these methods to create a customized quarterly or yearly assessment tool. Simply select a combination of true/false and multiple choice questions from the quizzes and essay-style questions from the Student Worktext.

SCRIPTURE CONNECTION

Integrating faith and learning is an essential part of a quality religious education. A unique component of *A Reason For® Science* is the incorporation of Scripture Object Lessons into every unit. As students discover basic science principles, they are encouraged to explore various spiritual connections through specific Scripture verses.

Since some school systems may prefer one Scripture translation to another, Scriptures are referenced by chapter and verse only, rather than direct quotations in the text.

CREATIONISM

Many people (including many notable scientists) believe that God created the universe and all the processes both physical and biological that resulted in our solar system and life on Earth.

However, advocates of "creation science" hold a variety of viewpoints. Some believe that Earth is relatively young, perhaps only 6,000 years old. Others believe that Earth may have existed for millions of years, but that various organisms (especially humans) could only be the result of divine intervention since they demonstrate "intelligent design."

Within the creation science community, there are dozens of variations on these themes, even within the specific denominational groups. Instead of promoting a specific view, the authors of this series have chosen to focus on the concept that "God created the Heavens and the Earth," and leave the specifics up to the individual school. Creationism is a faith-based issue.* As such, schools are strongly urged to have a clear position on this topic, and an understanding of how that belief is to be conveyed to their students.

For that matter, so is the theory of evolution.

[1] *National Science Education Standards*, 1999 Washington, D.C.: National Academy Press. (p. ix)
[2] *Ibid.* (p. 2)
[3] *Ibid.* (p. 20)
[4] *Ibid.* (p. 2)

This Teacher Guidebook . . .

is based on a simple, easy-to-understand format. Lessons throughout the series follow the same pattern, so once you're familiar with the format for one lesson, you can find information quickly for any other lesson. The samples on the following pages explain the purpose of each section.

Category
Life Science

Focus
Germination

Objective
To explore growth in plants

National Standards [1]
A1, A2, B1, B2, B3, C1, C2, C3, E3, F2, F3, F4, G1

Materials Needed [2]
petri dishes (3)
pipette
seeds (assorted)
water
paper towels
tape
scissors

Safety Concerns
4. Sharp Objects
Remind students to be careful using scissors.

[1] See page xx for a description of standards source and code.

[2] Bold-face type indicates items included in Materials Kit.

Additional Comments
Seeds provided for this activity are common American grain crops: oats, corn, wheat, and soybeans. If students wish to repeat this activity, have them try seeds like alfalfa, radish, sunflower, or pumpkin. Be sure to clean petri dishes thoroughly after each use to sterilize.

Overview
Read the overview aloud to your students. The goal is to create an atmosphere of curiosity and inquiry.

Here's a great way to point straight down. introduce this activity: Seat two students at the front of the class. Ask them both to point straight down. Praise their accuracy. Now blindfold them. Repeat your request to point down. Praise their ability again, remove their blindfolds, and have them return to their seats. Ask the class, "Do you think animals might have this same ability?" Follow this by asking, "What about fish?" Then ask, "What about living things with no brains, like plants? Do they have this ability, too?" Many students respond "no" to this last question, setting the stage to explore the answer.

LIFE **15**

Category
All lessons are divided into one of three primary categories — Life Science, Earth Science, or Physical Science. Physical Science is further divided into two parts — Forces or Energy/Matter.

Focus
"Focus" states the topic of the lesson.

Objective
"Objective" describes the purpose of the lesson.

National Standards
"National Standards" refers to content standards found in the **National Science Education Standards**. (For details on standards, see page 6.)

Materials Needed:
"Materials Needed" is a comprehensive list of materials used in the lesson. **Bold-faced** words indicate items provided in the Materials Kit.

Safety Concerns:
"Safety Concerns" provides details about potential safety hazards. (For more on Safety, see page 9.)

Additional Comments: "Additional Comments" offers tips and techniques for making each lesson run more smoothly.

Overview: The "Overview" provides lesson summaries, thoughts on introducing the lesson, ideas for dealing with materials, and other valuable lesson-specific tips.

What To Do

"What to Do" expands on the Steps found in the Student Workbook. It outlines potential problems, offers alternative procedures, and explains ways to enhance the lesson.

WHAT TO DO

Monitor student research teams as they complete each step.

Step 2

Grouping instructions are purposely ambiguous to allow several options. Depending on class size and materials available, 1) have each research team create their own set of three, 2) have each team create only one dish, then combine dishes to create groupings, 3) create a unique combination to meet your specific classroom needs. Regardless of the total number of dishes, at least one dish must lie flat, one must be on edge with seeds up, and one must be on edge with seeds down. These three environments are necessary for the primary comparisons.

Step 4

Emphasize the instruction, "*Don't change their position in any way!*" If dishes are moved, the results will be invalid.

Teacher to Teacher

Another name for the energy stored in seeds is endosperm. Humans and animals use plant endosperm as a food source, too. For instance, flour is ground-up wheat endosperm!

Be sure students realize the two phases of a plant's life cycle that are involved: sprouting and growing. The sprouting process only requires warmth and water. A seed soaks up moisture, swells, splits, and a new plant emerges. But light is needed for the next stage. Light stimulates the new plant into producing the chemical chlorophyll (the green in plants). Without chlorophyll, plants have no way to make food once they've used up the energy in the endosperm. The process of using chlorophyll to direct more food is called photosynthesis.

Teacher To Teacher

"Teacher to Teacher" offers expanded science explanations designed to increase teacher understanding.

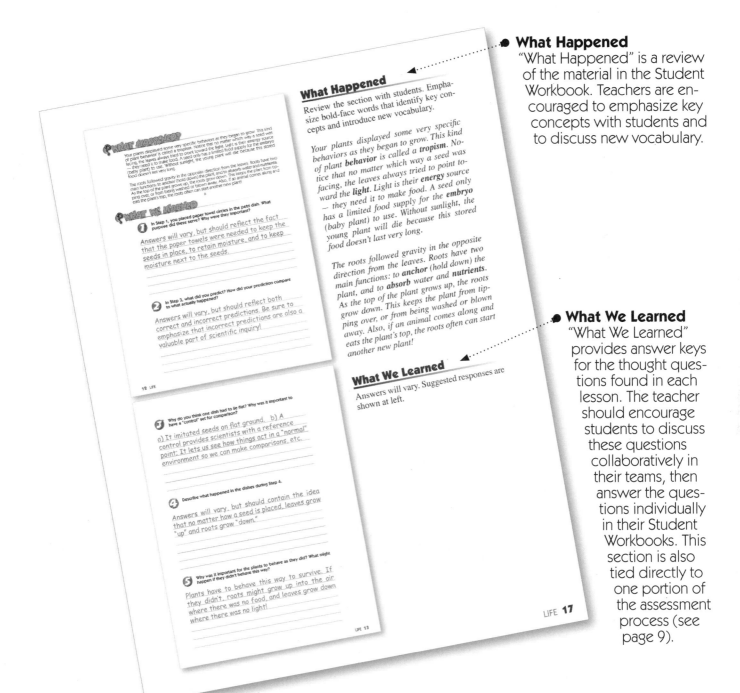

What Happened

Review the section with students. Emphasize bold-face words that identify key concepts and introduce new vocabulary.

*Your plants displayed some very specific behaviors as they began to grow. This kind of plant **behavior** is called a **tropism**. Notice that no matter which way a seed was facing, the leaves always tried to point toward the **light**. Light is their **energy** source — they need it to make food. A seed only has a limited food supply for the **embryo** (baby plant) to use. Without sunlight, the young plant will die because this stored food doesn't last very long.*

*The roots followed gravity in the opposite direction from the leaves. Roots have two main functions: to **anchor** (hold down) the plant, and to **absorb** water and **nutrients**. As the top of the plant grows up, the roots grow down. This keeps the plant from tipping over, or from being washed or blown away. Also, if an animal comes along and eats the plant's top, the roots often can start another new plant!*

What We Learned

Answers will vary. Suggested responses are shown at left.

What Happened

"What Happened" is a review of the material in the Student Workbook. Teachers are encouraged to emphasize key concepts with students and to discuss new vocabulary.

What We Learned

"What We Learned" provides answer keys for the thought questions found in each lesson. The teacher should encourage students to discuss these questions collaboratively in their teams, then answer the questions individually in their Student Workbooks. This section is also tied directly to one portion of the assessment process (see page 9).

Conclusion
The "Conclusion" is a summary of the key concepts presented in the lesson.

Food for Thought
"Food for Thought" suggests ways to enhance the Scripture Object Lesson. This section provides an important tool for integrating faith and learning.

Journal
"Journal" suggests ways to expand journaling opportunities related to the lesson. The teacher should encourage the students not only to take notes and keep records, but also to make sketches, draw diagrams, and create charts and lists as needed.

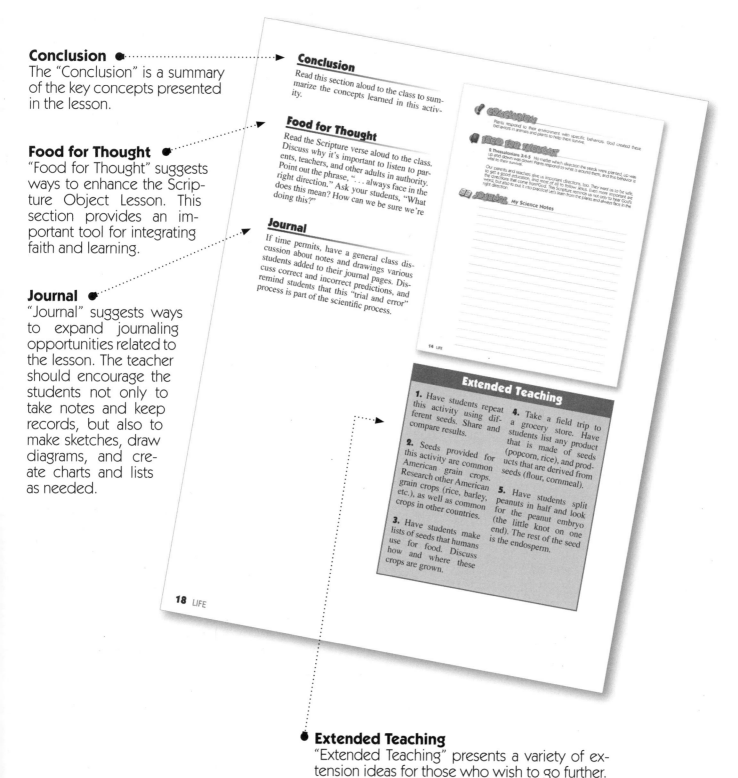

Conclusion
Read this section aloud to the class to summarize the concepts learned in this activity.

Food for Thought
Read the Scripture verse aloud to the class. Discuss why it's important to listen to parents, teachers, and other adults in authority. Point out the phrase, ". . . always face in the right direction." Ask your students, "What does this mean? How can we be sure we're doing this?"

Journal
If time permits, have a general class discussion about notes and drawings various students added to their journal pages. Discuss correct and incorrect predictions, and remind students that this "trial and error" process is part of the scientific process.

Extended Teaching

1. Have students repeat this activity using different seeds. Share and compare results.

2. Seeds provided for this activity are common American grain crops. Research other American grain crops (rice, barley, etc.), as well as common crops in other countries.

3. Have students make lists of seeds that humans use for food. Discuss how and where these crops are grown.

4. Take a field trip to a grocery store. Have students list any product that is made of seeds (popcorn, rice), and products that are derived from seeds (flour, cornmeal).

5. Have students split peanuts in half and look for the peanut embryo (the little knot on one end). The rest of the seed is the endosperm.

Extended Teaching
"Extended Teaching" presents a variety of extension ideas for those who wish to go further.

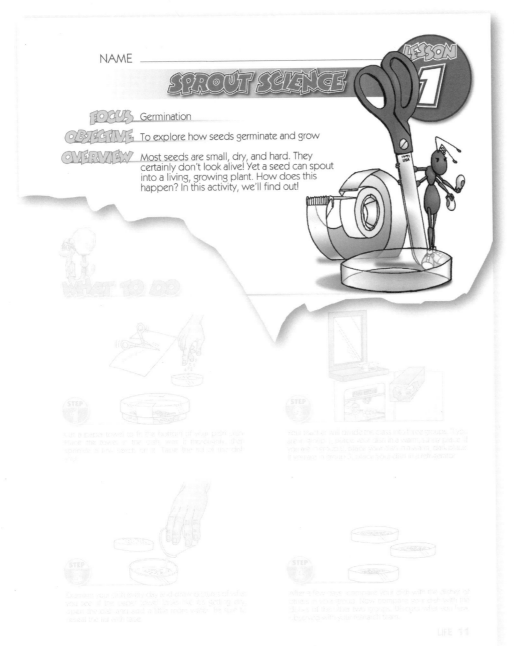

Category

Life Science

Focus

Germination

Objective

To explore how seeds germinate and grow

National Standards [1]

A1, A2, B1, B2, B3, C1, C2, C3, E3, F2, F3, F4, G1

Materials Needed [2]

petri dish
seeds
paper towel
water
tape
scissors
refrigerator

Safety Concerns

4. Sharp Objects
Remind students to be careful when using the knife.

Additional Comments

Be sure to use quality seeds to ensure a high germination rate. Suitable seeds include alfalfa, radish, sunflower, and pumpkin. Remember, it may take several days for a seed to sprout. Clean petri dishes thoroughly after this activity to sterilize.

[1] *See page 6 for a description of standards source and code.*

[2] *Bold-face type indicates items included in Materials Kit.*

Overview

Read the overview aloud to your students. The goal is to create an atmosphere of curiosity and inquiry.

WHAT TO DO

Monitor student research teams as they complete each step.

Step 2

Make certain at least one team is assigned to each environment.

Step 4

Have students first compare petri dishes from the same environment, then have them compare petri dishes from different environments. Results from the same environment should be similar; results from the different environments should be quite different.

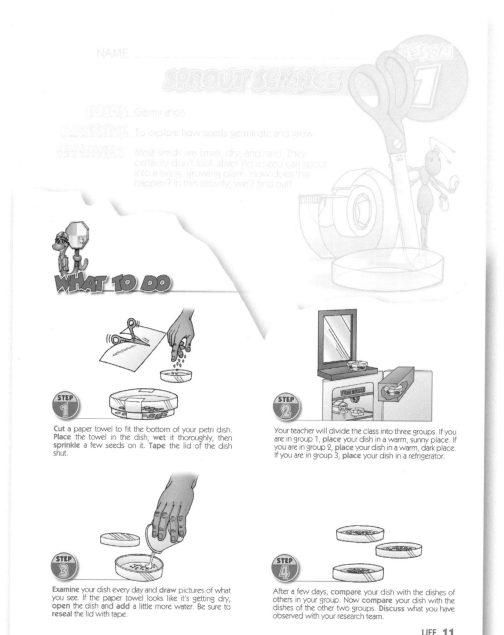

Teacher to Teacher

Another name for the energy stored in seeds is endosperm. Humans and animals use plant endosperm as a food source, too. For instance, flour is ground-up wheat endosperm!

Be sure students realize the two plant life phases involved: sprouting and growing. The sprouting process only requires warmth and water. A seed soaks up moisture, swells, splits, and a new plant emerges. But light is needed for the next stage. Light stimulates the new plant into producing the chemical chlorophyll (the green in plants). Without chlorophyll, plants have no way to make food once they've used up the energy in the endosperm. The process of using chlorophyll to produce more food is called photosynthesis.

⑨WHAT HAPPENED?

Nothing on earth lives forever. For life to continue, every living thing must **reproduce** (make more of itself). Most plants reproduce using **seeds**. Seeds contain two basic parts: an **embryo** (baby plant) and an **energy source** (food).

When seeds **sprout** (begin to grow), scientists call it **germination**. As we saw in this activity, germination requires the correct **environment**.

American farmers produce huge amounts of food. Since many crops begin as seeds, proper germination is very important. Farmers use expensive machinery to prepare the soil and plant seeds just so. Then, as long as the weather cooperates, the seeds will grow — producing plenty of food to eat!

⑨WHAT WE LEARNED

1 Why was the paper towel in the bottom of the dish important? Why was it important to tape the lid shut?

a) answers should reflect the fact that the paper towel was needed to keep the seeds in place and to retain moisture

b) to keep the lid tight; to lock the moisture in the dish, etc.

2 In Step 2, what things were the same between groups?

a) the dish, the towel, the seeds, the amount of moisture, etc.

3 In Step 2, what things were different between groups?

a) light, temperature, etc.

4 When the activity was completed, how were the results different between groups?

warm/sunny = bright green sprouts
warm/dark = some growth, but little or no green in sprouts
cold/dark = almost no growth or change

5 Based on what you've learned, what are some things that plants need in order to germinate?

moisture, warmth, light

What Happened

Review the section with students. Emphasize bold-face words that identify key concepts and introduce new vocabulary.

Nothing on earth lives forever. For life to continue, every living thing must **reproduce** *(make more of itself). Most plants reproduce using* **seeds**. *Seeds contain two basic parts: an* **embryo** *(baby plant) and an* **energy source** *(food).*

When seeds **sprout** *(begin to grow), scientists call it* **germination**. *As we saw in this activity, germination requires the correct* **environment**.

American farmers produce huge amounts of food. Since many crops begin as seeds, proper germination is very important. Farmers use expensive machinery to prepare the soil and plant seeds just so. Then, as long as the weather cooperates, the seeds will grow — producing plenty of food to eat!

What We Learned

Answers will vary. Suggested responses are shown at left.

Conclusion

Read this section aloud to the class to summarize the concepts learned in this activity.

Food for Thought

Read the Scripture aloud to the class. Talk about the wonderful things that God has created. Discuss our responsibility to take care of the world God made for us.

Journal

If time permits, have a general class discussion about students' journal entries. Share and compare observations. Be sure to emphasize that "trial and error" is a valuable part of scientific inquiry!

! CONCLUSION

Seeds contain an embryo and food for the embryo to use until it grows. To germinate, seeds need proper amounts of warmth, moisture, and sunlight. If any one of these is missing, the growing plant may not survive.

FOOD FOR THOUGHT

Genesis 1:11 Sometimes we forget that signs of God's love are everywhere. Scripture tells us God blessed the Earth with fruitful plants and good things to eat. If you're feeling sad or lonely, think about these blessings.

Sprouting seeds and growing plants are miracles that happen every day — providing a constant reminder of how much God loves you!

JOURNAL My Science Notes

Extended Teaching

1. Have students repeat this activity using different seeds. Share and compare results.

2. Explore U.S. agriculture by watching films, reading books, visiting a farm, etc. Have students make a bulletin board based on what they learn.

3. Have students make a list of seeds humans use for food. Discuss how and where these crops are grown.

4. Take a field trip to a grocery store. Have students list any product that contains seeds (popcorn, rice) or is derived from seeds (cornmeal, flour).

5. Have students carefully examine shell peanuts and examine the "seeds." Now have them split the seeds in half and look for the embryo (the little knot at one end). The rest of the seed is the endosperm.

Focus
Water Conservation

Objective
To explore how body coverings conserve water

National Standards
A1, A2, B1, B2, B3, C1, C3, D1, E3, F1, F4, G1

Materials Needed
small sponges - 2
plastic wrap
water
aluminum pie plate

Safety Concerns
4. Slipping
There is a potential for spills with this activity. Remind students to exercise caution.

Additional Comments

Define and discuss the word "saturation" from the lesson title. Let students have fun with this challenging new vocabulary word! Also, if you don't have a sunny window available, a heat lamp is a reasonable substitute. Exercise all safety precautions if you choose this option.

Overview

Read the overview aloud to your students. The goal is to create an atmosphere of curiosity and inquiry.

WHAT TO DO

Monitor student research teams as they complete each step.

Step 2

Check each team's work to make sure the plastic wrap is completely sealed. Even a small opening will impact the final results.

SATURATION SITUATION

LESSON 2

Water Conservation

To explore how body coverings conserve water.

Living things need water to survive. How do living things protect the water inside them? In this activity, we'll explore how water is conserved.

WHAT TO DO

STEP 1 Dip two sponges in water until they are soaked all the way through. Make sure they are soaked equally.

STEP 2 Completely wrap one sponge in plastic wrap. Carefully check to make sure there are no openings anywhere in the plastic.

STEP 3 Lay the sponges side by side in a pie pan or tray. Place the pan in a warm, sunny place. Predict what you think will happen to the two sponges.

STEP 4 Wait two days, then check your sponges to see what's happened. Record the results in your journal. Review each step in this activity. Discuss what you've observed with your research team.

LIFE **15**

Teacher to Teacher

What is your body's largest organ? It's your skin! This amazing organ not only helps conserve water, it protects you from disease and harmful solar radiation. Your skin serves as a major sensory organ, detecting such things as temperature, pain, and pressure. It also regulates body temperature through sweating. It produces its own oil (sebum) to stay soft and waterproof. It contains blood vessels, nerves, and glands. Human skin is also very elastic, allowing for easy movement. These are just a few of the many ways your skin supports your overall health.

❓WHAT HAPPENED?

The plastic wrap **modeled** one function of your **skin** — conserving water. The covered sponge kept its water. The sponge with no covering dried out.

Although you used only one **layer** of material for this activity, human skin has several layers. Each of these layers has its own unique **structure** (how it's built) and **function** (purpose). Together they provide many different kinds of protection.

For instance, to protect against damage from sunlight, your skin produces a chemical called **melanin**. The amount of melanin in your skin determines your skin color. Darker skin has higher levels of melanin, providing more protection. Lighter skin has lower levels of melanin. When exposed to sunlight, lighter skin produces additional melanin, creating a "tan." As you can see, skin is a complex and amazing protective device.

❓WHAT WE LEARNED

1 What does the sponge represent in this activity? What does the water represent?

a) your body

b) the fluids or "water" in your body

2 What does the plastic wrap represent? Why was it important to make sure there were no openings?

a) your skin

b) so that the sponge was completely sealed

3 What did you predict in Step 3? How did this prediction reflect what actually happened?

a) answers will vary

b) answers will vary, but should be logical

4 Skin color varies not only from person to person, but even on the same person over time. What causes this?

skin color changes based on the amount of melanin in your skin

5 Based on what you've learned, explain why body coverings are important. What might happen to a living thing that lost its body covering?

a) to help keep our bodies from drying out

b) it would probably die

What Happened

Review the section with students. Emphasize bold-face words that identify key concepts and introduce new vocabulary.

The plastic wrap **modeled** *one function of your* **skin** *— conserving water. The covered sponge kept its water. The sponge with no covering dried out.*

Although you used only one **layer** *of material for this activity, human skin has several layers. Each of these layers has its own unique* **structure** *(how it's built) and* **function** *(purpose). Together they provide many different kinds of protection.*

For instance, to protect against damage from sunlight, your skin produces a chemical called **melanin**. *The amount of melanin in your skin determines your skin color. Darker skin has higher levels of melanin, providing more protection. Lighter skin has lower levels of melanin. When exposed to sunlight, lighter skin produces additional melanin, creating a "tan." As you can see, skin is a complex and amazing protective device.*

What We Learned

Answers will vary. Suggested responses are shown at left.

Conclusion

Read this section aloud to the class to summarize the concepts learned in this activity.

Food for Thought

Read the Scripture aloud to the class. Talk about how God's love covers and protects us.

Journal

If time permits, have a general class discussion about students' journal entries. Share and compare observations. Be sure to emphasize that "trial and error" is a valuable part of scientific inquiry!

CONCLUSION

Living things need water to survive. A body covering (like skin) helps living things conserve water.

FOOD FOR THOUGHT

Psalm 40:11, 12 This activity demonstrates one amazing ability of human skin — conservation of water. Without the protective covering of our skin, we'd dry out like an uncovered sponge! Skin helps keep essential water inside, protecting us from harm.

Sometimes people think they can make it entirely on their own. They use the gifts God has given them for their own personal pleasure. But without the protective covering of God's love and faithfulness, their hearts soon become barren and dry.

Wrap yourself in God's love — the only real protection!

JOURNAL My Science Notes

Extended Teaching

1. Invite a nurse to visit your classroom. Discuss common skin problems, their causes, and their cures.

2. Teach students to identify Poison Ivy and Poison Oak. Make a bulletin board illustrating these plants. Challenge students to find pictures of the affect these plants can have on human skin.

3. Discuss ways to keep healthy and attractive skin. Research diet, sleep, and other suggestions for healthy skin.

4. Research "electrolytes." Find out what they are, why your body needs them, and what your skin does with them. Have each team compile an "electrolyte report" to share with the class.

5. Research how desert animals and plants conserve moisture. Have students make a bulletin board showing some of these creatures and their special adaptations.

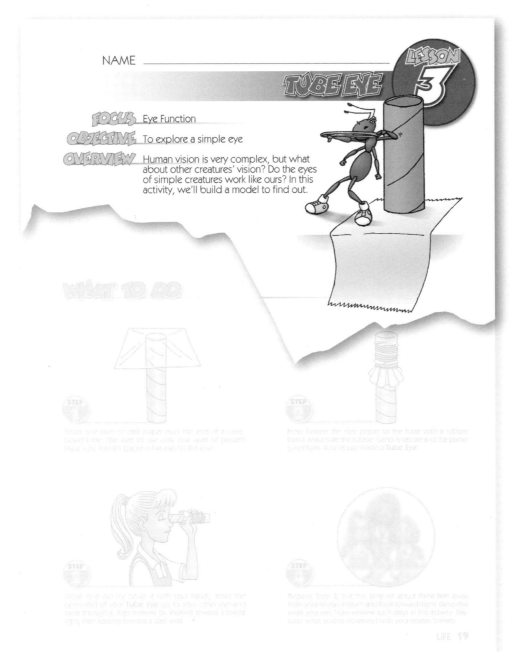

Category

Life Science

Focus

Eye Function

Objective

To explore a simple eye

National Standards

A1, A2, B1, B3, C1, E1, E2, E3, F1, F5, G1

Materials Needed

deli paper
rubber band
cardboard tube

Safety Concerns

Additional Comments

To avoid tripping accidents, don't let students walk around while looking through the tube eye!

Overview

Read the overview aloud to your students. The goal is to create an atmosphere of curiosity and inquiry.

WHAT TO DO

Monitor student research teams as they complete each step.

Step 2
Some teams may require help with this step. The deli paper must be flat across the end (no wrinkles), and the rubber band just tight enough to hold it firmly. Trying to make the rubber band too tight will crush the tube.

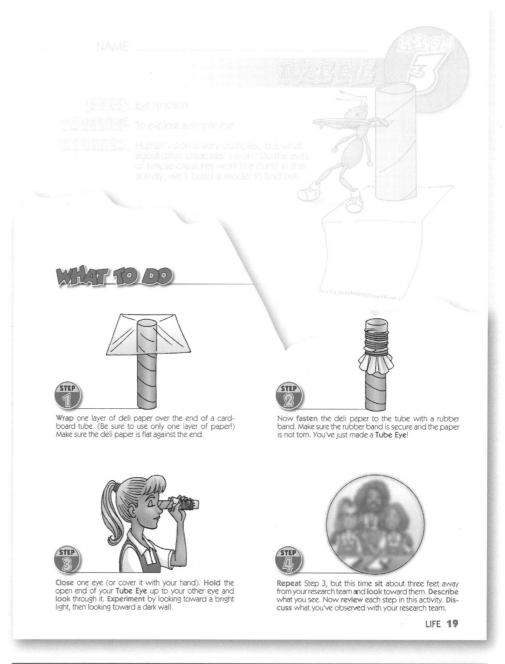

NAME _____

Eye Function
To explore a simple eye

Human vision is very complex, but what about other creatures' vision? Do the eyes of simple creatures work like ours? In this activity, we'll build a model to find out.

WHAT TO DO

STEP 1
Wrap one layer of deli paper over the end of a cardboard tube. (Be sure to use only one layer of paper!) Make sure the deli paper is flat against the end.

STEP 2
Now **fasten** the deli paper to the tube with a rubber band. Make sure the rubber band is secure and the paper is not torn. You've just made a **Tube Eye!**

STEP 3
Close one eye (or cover it with your hand). **Hold** the open end of your **Tube Eye** up to your other eye and **look** through it. **Experiment** by looking toward a bright light, then looking toward a dark wall.

STEP 4
Repeat Step 3, but this time **sit** about three feet away from your research team and **look** toward them. **Describe** what you see. Now **review** each step in this activity. **Discuss** what you've observed with your research team.

LIFE **19**

Teacher to Teacher

Scientists call the brightness of light, "intensity." Intensity depends on how much energy is being received. It also depends on the distance to the light source. (Imagine how intense the sun is on Mercury versus how intense it is on Pluto.) Our eyes adapt remarkably to different levels of intensity. When light is too intense, eyelids close tighter and pupils shrink. With too little intensity, eyelids open wider and pupils enlarge. In low light situations, the body also manufactures a special chemical (called visual purple) to enhance vision. A deficiency in visual purple can result in night blindness.

?WHAT HAPPENED?

The simple eye you created could only detect the difference between **light** and **dark** and maybe sense a few rough shapes. Since simple creatures usually feed in very dark places, this type of **vision** is really all they need.

Human vision is much more complex. The human eye uses a **lens** to bend (**focus**) light. This gathers the light together, allowing us to see detail (not just shapes), and gives the brain the information it needs to understand complex **images**.

Just imagine how restricted your life would be if you could only see the world through simple eyes!

?WHAT WE LEARNED

1 Why was it important to use only one layer of deli paper in Step 1?

answers will vary, but should reflect the fact that more layers would block more light making it even harder to see

2 How is the device you built similar to a telescope? How is it different?

a) similar: both tube shaped, both involve sight, etc.

b) different: a telescope magnifies things, a telescope view is clearer, etc.

20 LIFE

3 Describe what you saw when you looked through the Tube Eye in Step 3.

answers will vary, but should be something like: "not much light," "could only see a bright patch," "everything was very blurry," etc.

4 Describe what you saw in Step 4. What difference did it make if light was behind or in front of your team members?

a) answers will vary, but should reflect that the team was hard to see

b) light behind helped show outline of team

5 How is human vision different from the vision of simple creatures? What makes our eyes more complex?

a) we can see much more clearly in color

b) the human eye has a lens, very simple creatures do not have a lens

LIFE **21**

What Happened

Review the section with students. Emphasize bold-face words that identify key concepts and introduce new vocabulary.

*The simple eye you created could only detect the difference between **light** and **dark** and maybe sense a few rough shapes. Since simple creatures usually feed in very dark places, this type of **vision** is really all they need.*

*Human vision is much more complex. The human eye uses a **lens** to bend (**focus**) light. This gathers the light together, allowing us to see detail (not just shapes), and gives the **brain** the information it needs to understand complex **images**.*

Just imagine how restricted your life would be if you could only see the world through simple eyes!

What We Learned

Answers will vary. Suggested responses are shown at left.

Conclusion

Read this section aloud to the class to summarize the concepts learned in this activity.

Food for Thought

Read the Scripture aloud to the class. This is a great lesson to discuss the concept of trust! Talk about ways we can learn to trust God more completely.

Journal

If time permits, have a general class discussion about students' journal entries. Share and compare observations. Be sure to emphasize that "trial and error" is a valuable part of scientific inquiry!

! CONCLUSION

All kinds of eyes gather light to help living things make sense of the world around them. God gave different creatures different kinds of eyes to meet their specific needs.

FOOD FOR THOUGHT

Proverbs 3:5, 6 Imagine spending an entire school day using only a **Tube Eye** for vision! You'd really have to trust your friends and depend on them to help you make it through the day.

God sees and knows so much more than we do. By comparison we're almost blind! But this Scripture reminds us that we can always depend on God's guidance. Learn to trust God completely. Put God first in everything you do, and you can walk through this world with confidence!

JOURNAL My Science Notes

_____
_____
_____
_____
_____
_____
_____
_____
_____
_____
_____
_____
_____
_____
_____
_____
_____

22 LIFE

Extended Teaching

1. Research animals that have eyes that provide vision similar to the tube eye. Have each team choose an animal to study, then share their findings with the class (where the animal lives, how it finds food, etc.).

2. Research animals that have keener eyesight than humans. Find out how their eyes are different and how this helps them survive. Have students make a bulletin board of these animals.

3. Invite a biologist or spelunker to visit your classroom. Discuss the vision of creatures found in caves. How is it different from similar creatures that live above ground?

4. Research types of artificial light. Compare street lights, gym lights, classroom lights, home lighting, etc. Find out how colors look different in each kind of light. Challenge students to share their findings with the class.

5. Invite someone connected with laser eye surgery to visit your class. Ask them to describe this process and how it improves people's vision.

Category

Life Science

Focus

Seed Dispersal

Objective

To explore ways plants spread seeds

National Standards

A1, A2, B1, B2, C1, C2, C3, E3, F2, F3, G1

Materials Needed

seed bag with seeds - 2
apple
knife (teacher only)

Safety Concerns

3. Poison
Potential for allergic reactions (especially to peanuts). Take necessary precautions.

4. Sharp Objects
Remind students to be careful around the knife.

Additional Comments

Feel free to substitute seeds of local origin that students may be familiar with. Remind students that good scientists don't eat their experiments! (The temptation will be strong for some, especially with the nuts and the apple.)

Overview

Read the overview aloud to your students. The goal is to create an atmosphere of curiosity and inquiry. Help students understand that seeds use a variety of methods to spread.

WHAT TO DO

Monitor student research teams as they complete each step.

Step 4

Check packages to make sure students have returned all materials. Seeds may be reused from year to year if they are kept completely dry.

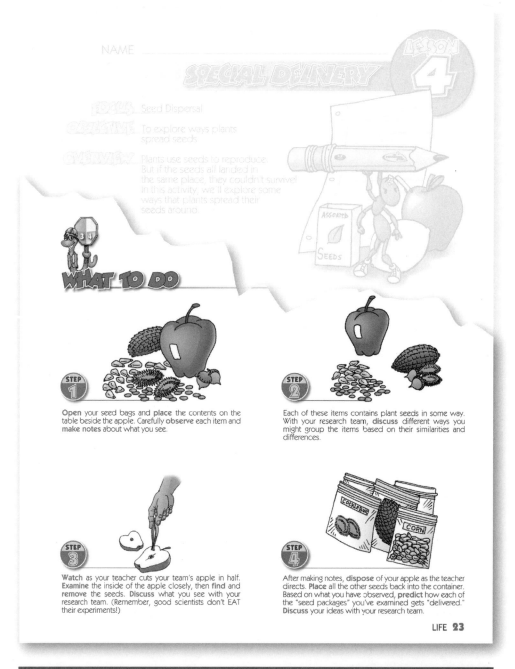

NAME

SPECIAL DELIVERY

LESSON 4

TOPIC Seed Dispersal

OBJECTIVE To explore ways plants spread seeds

OVERVIEW Plants use seeds to reproduce. But if the seeds all landed in the same place, they couldn't survive. In this activity, we'll explore some ways that plants spread their seeds around.

WHAT TO DO

STEP 1
Open your seed bags and **place** the contents on the table beside the apple. Carefully **observe** each item and **make notes** about what you see.

STEP 2
Each of these items contains plant seeds in some way. With your research team, **discuss** different ways you might group the items based on their similarities and differences.

STEP 3
Watch as your teacher cuts your team's apple in half. **Examine** the inside of the apple closely, then **find** and **remove** the seeds. **Discuss** what you see with your research team. (Remember, good scientists don't EAT their experiments!)

STEP 4
After making notes, **dispose** of your apple as the teacher directs. **Place** all the other seeds back into the container. Based on what you have observed, **predict** how each of the "seed packages" you've examined gets "delivered." **Discuss** your ideas with your research team.

LIFE **23**

Teacher to Teacher

Scientists have identified over 300,000 different seed plants. The two basic groups are gymnosperms and angiosperms. Gymnosperms (a term meaning "naked seed") include most conifers. The seeds of most gymnosperms have little protection and contain very little food. By contrast angiosperm seeds have both abundant protection and food. Some angiosperms surround their seeds with a thick layer we call fruit. Others create seeds we call grain. Some angiosperms make a lot of seeds. Modern agriculture is constantly searching for ways to increase both the amount and quality of these seeds which make up most of the world's food supply.

What Happened

Review the section with students. Emphasize bold-face words that identify key concepts and introduce new vocabulary.

*If a plant's **seeds** all landed in the same place, there wouldn't be enough **water**, **nutrients**, or **light** to go around. Most would die! That's why plants use many different methods to spread their seeds. This gives the **embryo** (baby plant) in each seed a much better chance of becoming a mature plant.*

*Some plants rely on **wind** to spread their seeds. They may produce very light seeds (ash tree), "parachute" seeds (milkweed), or even seeds with wings (maple). Some plants rely on **water** to spread their seeds. They produce seeds that float (coconuts) or wash away in heavy rains (grasses). Some plants even rely on the **movement** of animals to spread their seeds. They may produce edible **fruit** (berries), or tiny hooks (cocklebur) to grab a ride.*

What We Learned

Answers will vary. Suggested responses are shown at left.

WHAT HAPPENED?

If a plant's seeds all landed in the same place, there wouldn't be enough water, nutrients, or light to go around. Most would die! That's why plants use many different methods to spread their seeds. This gives the embryo (baby plant) in each seed a much better chance of becoming a mature plant.

Some plants rely on wind to spread their seeds. They may produce very light seeds (ash tree), "parachute" seeds (milkweed), or even seeds with wings (maple). Some plants rely on water to spread their seeds. They produce seeds that float (coconuts) or wash away in heavy rains (grasses). Some plants even rely on the movement of animals to spread their seeds. They may produce edible fruit (berries), or tiny hooks (cocklebur) to grab a ride.

WHAT WE LEARNED

1 Describe the items from the seed bags in Step 1. How many kinds were there? How many of each? How were they similar? How were they different?

answers will vary, but should include descriptions like "rough," "dry and hard," "things you can eat," etc.

2 Describe the groups your team made in Step 2. What characteristics did you use to sort the seeds?

answers will vary, but should include logical divisions

24 LIFE

3 What is the baby plant inside a seed called? Name three things that it needs to survive.

a) embryo

b) water, nutrients, light

4 List three different methods plants use to disperse their seeds. Give an example of each.

a) wind: milkweed, maple, etc.

b) water: coconut, some grasses, etc.

c) animal movement: fruit, burrs, etc.

5 A plant produces many more seeds than it needs to replace itself. Based on what you've learned, why is this necessary?

only a small percentage of seeds survive to produce another plant

LIFE 25

Conclusion

Read this section aloud to the class to summarize the concepts learned in this activity.

Food for Thought

Read the Scripture aloud to the class. This parable offers a great introduction to a wonderful method Christ used to help common people understand difficult topics! Discuss this parable and others.

Journal

If time permits, have a general class discussion about students' journal entries. Share and compare observations. Be sure to emphasize that "trial and error" is a valuable part of scientific inquiry!

! CONCLUSION

To ensure survival, plants must spread seeds over great distances. Seed dispersal methods include wind, water, and the movement of animals.

FOOD FOR THOUGHT

Matthew 13:1-23 This parable describes some of the hardships seeds face. Some are eaten up, some sprout in poor soil and don't live long, some are choked out by other plants, and a few fall on good soil where they grow and prosper.

Jesus told parables about common things to help his listeners understand spiritual things. This parable reminds us that hearing God's word is not enough. For God's love to grow and prosper in our hearts, we must let Jesus in to prepare the way. The more time we spend with Jesus, the more open our hearts become to the power of God's presence.

JOURNAL My Science Notes

_____
_____
_____
_____
_____
_____
_____
_____
_____
_____
_____
_____
_____
_____
_____
_____
_____

Extended Teaching

1. Research how modern agriculture enhances food production. Have students compare this to farming methods used in primitive countries. Make a bulletin board comparing the two methods.

2. Invite a representative of the FFA or local agricultural cooperative to visit your class. Discuss the broad range of careers in modern agriculture.

3. Get church members to donate old garden catalogs. Challenge your students to cut out and sort pictures from these catalogs according to seed types. Make a bulletin board showing the results.

4. Invite a forest service representative to visit your classroom. Discuss the ecological role of gymnosperms. Look at ways they contribute to the economy. Discuss the balance between the two.

5. Research world hunger and what students can do to help. Sponsor a food drive in your community to help increase the resources of a neighborhood food pantry or similar facility.

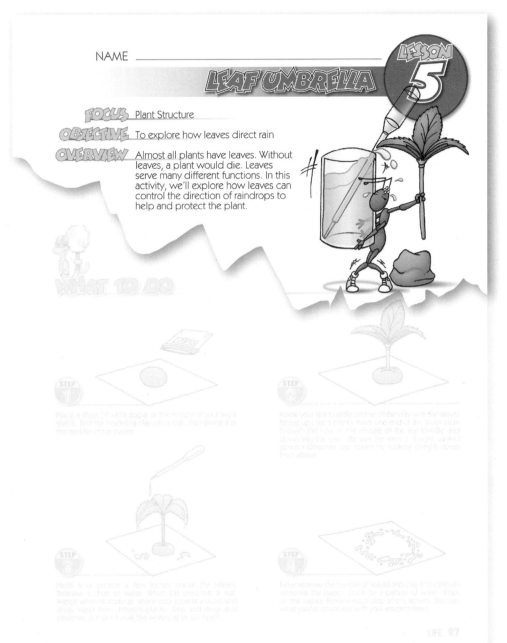

Category

Life Science

Focus

Plant Structure

Objective

To explore how leaves direct rain

National Standards

A1, A2, B1, B2, C1, C3, E3, F2, F3, F4, G1

Materials Needed

leaf bundle (plastic)
green stem (plastic)
pipette
modeling clay
typing paper
water

Safety Concerns

4. Slipping
There is a potential for spills with this activity. Remind students to exercise caution.

Additional Comments

Leaf bundles tend to get mashed in storage. If needed, give each team a plant picture to use as a guideline for arranging leaves in a natural way.

Overview

Read the overview aloud to your students. The goal is to create an atmosphere of curiosity and inquiry. Focus on the physical function and structure of leaves.

WHAT TO DO

Monitor student research teams as they complete each step.

Step 3

Monitor students to make sure they're not overdoing it with the water! They should add only enough to create a noticeable pattern.

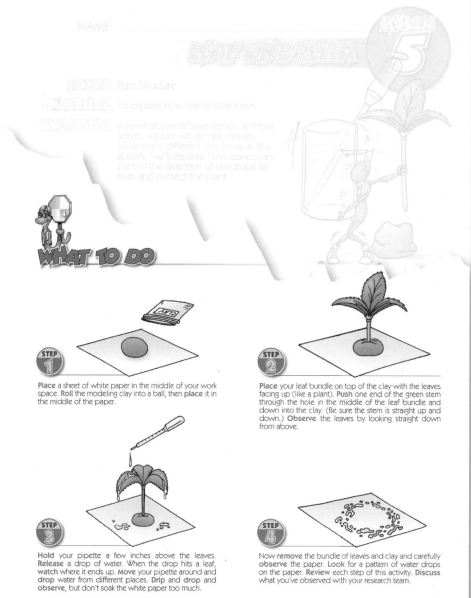

Teacher to Teacher

The structure of a leaf helps it perform many functions. Its wide shape not only creates more area for absorbing light for photosynthesis, but as we saw in this activity, it also acts as a kind of shock absorber. The leaf's shape helps it regulate water — shading plant roots to slow evaporation, or acting as a waterproof barrier to keep excessive rain from leaching away nutrients. In addition, tiny openings on the bottom of a leaf (stomata) let carbon dioxide in and oxygen out. Seemingly simple, a leaf is really a complex plant part that performs many important functions.

WHAT HAPPENED?

Leaves serve many different functions. In this activity, we saw how a plant's leaves help control the direction of raindrops. The leaves spread the falling water evenly to the roots, helping them absorb water more efficiently.

Each raindrop lost some of its kinetic (moving) energy when it hit a leaf. The leaf bent or bounced slightly with each drop, absorbing the energy before the drop hit the ground. This protective action helps keep the soil around the plant from eroding (washing away) during heavy rains.

WHAT WE LEARNED

1 Why was it important to spread the leaves evenly in Step 1? What did the ball of clay represent?

a) to closely model real plants

b) the roots of the plant

2 How is a plant helped by its leaves' ability to control the direction of raindrops? What part of the plant benefits most?

a) it directs rain where it's needed most

b) the roots

28 LIFE

3 Describe how leaves can help keep the soil around a plant from washing away.

leaves act as a kind of shock absorber, breaking the force of the falling rain

4 Describe the pattern left on the paper in Step 4. How does this pattern reflect the work of the leaves?

answers will vary, but should reflect a roughly circular pattern around the plant's base. the leaves help distribute the water evenly around the plant.

5 Based on what you've learned, what kinds of things could happen to a plant that only had leaves on one side?

side with no leaves would lose water to evaporation; would get less water from a light rain; would get too much water in a heavy rain, etc.

What Happened

Review the section with students. Emphasize bold-face words that identify key concepts and introduce new vocabulary.

Leaves serve many different functions. In this activity, we saw how a *plant's* leaves help control the direction of raindrops. The leaves spread the falling water evenly to the *roots*, helping them *absorb* water more efficiently.

Each raindrop lost some of its **kinetic** *(moving)* **energy** *when it hit a leaf. The leaf bent or bounced slightly with each drop, absorbing the energy before the drop hit the ground. This protective action helps keep the* **soil** *around the plant from* **eroding** *(washing away) during heavy rains.*

What We Learned

Answers will vary. Suggested responses are shown at left.

Conclusion

Read this section aloud to the class to summarize the concepts learned in this activity.

Food for Thought

Read the Scripture aloud to the class. Discuss ways God's love protects us. Also, compare leaves working together to help a plant to a group of people working together for God.

Journal

If time permits, have a general class discussion about students' journal entries. Share and compare observations. Be sure to emphasize that "trial and error" is a valuable part of scientific inquiry!

! CONCLUSION

Leaves serve many different functions. Two of these include directing rain to the plant's roots and absorbing the energy of falling water to decrease the chance of erosion.

FOOD FOR THOUGHT

Psalm 61:4 In this activity, we learned how leaves contribute to protecting a plant. When the rain begins to fall, leaves absorb the energy of the falling water. They also divert the water to where it can do the most good.

Just as leaves help protect a plant, so God's love protects his children. This Scripture reminds us that no matter what is happening around us, when we put our trust in God, we can be kept safe from those who would harm us.

JOURNAL   My Science Notes

Extended Teaching

1. Try this activity outdoors with a real plant. Surround it with paper grocery sacks. Use the light spray from a hose or a large watering can. Have students record the results and look for similarities and differences.

2. Collect leaves from various plants and trees, and have students make a leaf bulletin board. Challenge them to find out as much as possible about each plant. Post the results by the appropriate leaf.

3. Invite a gardener to visit your classroom. Discuss the importance of healthy leaves to a plant. Find out what nutrients plants need. Discuss the "tricks" they use to make their flowers or vegetables grow so well.

4. Research reasons plants and trees are so important to people (beauty, food, building materials, chemicals, oxygen, etc.). Have students make bulletin boards showing the results.

5. Bring a high-powered magnifying glass to class. Have teams take turns looking at large leaves to find evidence of stomata. Encourage students to draw pictures or write descriptions of what they observe.

NAME _____

SWELL CREATURE

LESSON 6

FOCUS Dehydration

OBJECTIVE To explore one method of preserving food

OVERVIEW Everyone knows that food spoils easily. How did people keep food from spoiling before refrigerators were invented? In this activity, we'll explore one preservation method.

WHAT TO DO

LIFE 31

Focus

Dehydration

Objective

To explore one method of preserving food

National Standards

A1, A2, B1, B3, C1, C3, D1, E2, E3, F1, F2, F3, F4, G1

Materials Needed

swell creature
ruler
bowl
pie pan or tray
water

Safety Concerns

4. Slipping
There is a potential for spills with this activity. Remind students to exercise caution.

Additional Comments

The "creature" can easily triple in size, so make sure the bowls you use are large enough. For a math connection, this activity provides a great way to introduce the concept of proportions.

Overview

Read the overview aloud to your students. The goal is to create an atmosphere of curiosity and inquiry.

WHAT TO DO

Monitor student research teams as they complete each step.

Step 1

Depending on ability levels, some teams may need assistance with measurements here and in Step 3.

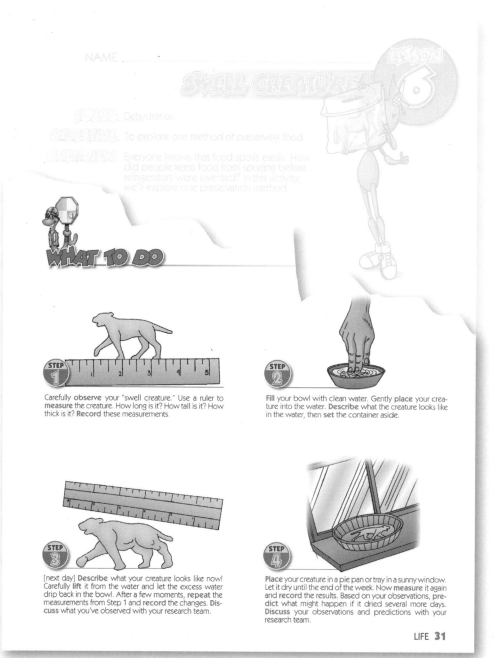

NAME _____

SWELL CREATURE

LESSON 6

Dehydration

To explore one method of preserving food

Everyone knows that food spoils easily. How did people keep food from spoiling before refrigerators were invented? In this activity, we'll explore one preservation method.

WHAT TO DO

STEP 1
Carefully **observe** your "swell creature." Use a ruler to **measure** the creature. How long is it? How tall is it? How thick is it? **Record** these measurements.

STEP 2
Fill your bowl with clean water. Gently **place** your creature into the water. **Describe** what the creature looks like in the water, then **set** the container aside.

STEP 3
[next day] **Describe** what your creature looks like now! Carefully **lift** it from the water and let the excess water drip back in the bowl. After a few moments, **repeat** the measurements from Step 1 and **record** the changes. **Discuss** what you've observed with your research team.

STEP 4
Place your creature in a pie pan or tray in a sunny window. Let it dry until the end of the week. Now **measure** it again and **record** the results. Based on your observations, **predict** what might happen if it dried several more days. **Discuss** your observations and predictions with your research team.

LIFE **31**

Teacher to Teacher

Visit any grocery store and you will find dozens of ways that food preservation impacts our modern life. Refrigeration keeps produce fresh, freezing preserves meats and fruits, chemical preservatives are used in most packaged foods, and the list goes on. It's important to note that all food preservation is an attempt to delay an important natural process — decomposition. Without the decomposition cycle, dead plants and animals would simply pile up and essential nutrients would no longer be available for living creatures! The balance between preservation and decomposition helps keep food supplies plentiful.

What Happened

Review the section with students. Emphasize bold-face words that identify key concepts and introduce new vocabulary.

*Just like food, a large part of your Swell Creature was made of **water**. You could tell because it got much smaller after the water was removed. **Micro-organisms** (tiny living things) like **bacteria** and **mold** need warmth and water to grow. Without adequate supplies of both, food **decomposes** (spoils) much more slowly.*

***Refrigeration** slows spoilage by removing warmth. **Dehydration** slows the process by removing essential water. Since earliest times, people have used dehydration to help preserve food for later use.*

Some forms of food made by dehydration (beef jerky, raisins, dried fruit) are still very popular today!

What We Learned

Answers will vary. Suggested responses are shown at left.

? WHAT HAPPENED?

Just like food, a large part of your Swell Creature was made of water. You could tell because it got much smaller after the water was removed. Micro-organisms (tiny living things) like bacteria and mold need warmth and water to grow. Without adequate supplies of both, food decomposes (spoils) much more slowly.

Refrigeration slows spoilage by removing warmth. Dehydration slows the process by removing essential water. Since earliest times, people have used dehydration to help preserve food for later use.

Some forms of food made by dehydration (beef jerky, raisins, dried fruit) are still very popular today!

? WHAT WE LEARNED

1. Compare the Swell Creature in Step 1 with the Swell Creature in Step 3. How were they similar? How were they different?

a) similar: same general shape, same color

b) different: size, wetness

2. What did you predict in Step 4? How did this prediction reflect what actually happened?

a) answers will vary

b) answers will vary, but should be logical comparisons

32 LIFE

3. Name two things bacteria or mold needs to grow. When micro-organisms thrive, what happens to food?

a) warmth, water

b) it spoils

4. Why does dehydration help preserve food? Give two examples of dehydrated foods.

a) it removes water micro-organisms needed

b) beef jerky, raisins, dried fruit, etc.

5. What are some other methods people use to preserve food?

freezing, refrigeration, canning, etc.

LIFE 33

Conclusion

Read this section aloud to the class to summarize the concepts learned in this activity.

Food for Thought

Read the Scripture aloud to the class. Discuss the "living water" that Jesus offers and how it can change our lives.

Journal

If time permits, have a general class discussion about students' journal entries. Share and compare observations. Be sure to emphasize that "trial and error" is a valuable part of scientific inquiry!

! CONCLUSION

Without preservation, food spoils rapidly. One way to preserve food is to remove most of the water. This process is called dehydration.

FOOD FOR THOUGHT

John 7:38 Your little creature was dry and empty, and it looked really small. But when you placed it in the bowl, it began to absorb a lot of water. It wasn't long before it looked like a new creature!

Sometimes our hearts are dry and empty. We feel very small inside. But this Scripture reminds us that we can be filled with "living water" that comes from Jesus! As we let God's goodness work in our lives, we become new creatures, filled with God's love.

JOURNAL My Science Notes

Extended Teaching

1. Challenge students to go on a "preservation safari" at home. Have them make a list of different items in their kitchen and the way these things are preserved. Have them share/compare findings with team members.

2. Have students discuss why decomposers (bacteria, mold) and scavengers (buzzards, hyenas) are necessary. Have them write a paper telling what the world might be like without them.

3. "Garbology" is the study of wasted food and trash. Using the Internet, have students research how much food is wasted in America each year. Discuss ways to eliminate waste.

4. Have students research diseases that can result from improperly stored or preserved food. (There are many different kinds of "food poisoning.") Create a bulletin board to share their findings.

5. Ask students to write a story telling how their lives would change if there was no refrigeration. Read representative or creative stories to the class.

Category

Life Science

Focus

Nervous System

Objective

To explore human reaction time

National Standards

A1, A2, B1, B2, C1, E3, F1, G1

Materials Needed

popper frog

Safety Concerns

Additional Comments

Not all the frogs will jump at the same time. Remind students to be patient. Also, caution them about turning around so fast in Step 4 that they fall down!

Overview

Read the overview aloud to your students. The goal is to create an atmosphere of curiosity and inquiry.

WHAT TO DO

Monitor student research teams as they complete each step.

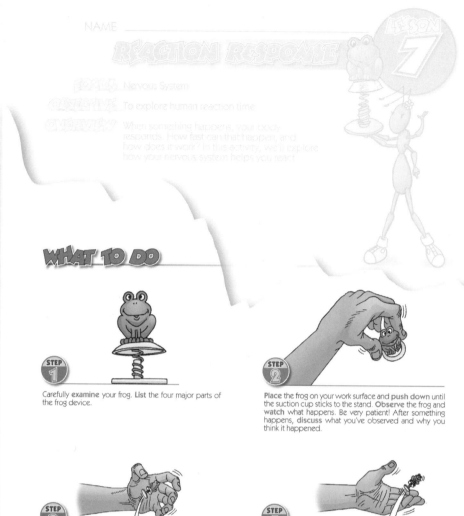

WHAT TO DO

STEP 1
Carefully **examine** your frog. **List** the four major parts of the frog device.

STEP 2
Place the frog on your work surface and **push down** until the suction cup sticks to the stand. **Observe** the frog and **watch** what happens. Be very patient! After something happens, **discuss** what you've observed and why you think it happened.

STEP 3
Retrieve the frog. **Stand** facing the frog with your hands behind your back. **Ask** a team member to "reset" the frog. Now **watch** closely. When the frog jumps, try to grab it before it hits the table. **Repeat** this three times. After everyone on your research team has had a turn, **record** the results.

STEP 4
Reset the frog again. **Stand** with your back to the frog, hands at your sides. **Ask** a team member to watch the frog. When it jumps, they must say, "Now!" Quickly **turn** and try to grab the frog before it hits the table. After everyone has had a turn, **record** the results. **Review** each step in this activity. **Discuss** your observations with your research team.

LIFE **35**

Teacher to Teacher

Energy conversion makes things move. In this activity, we converted kinetic energy (pushing down on the frog) to potential energy (the "loaded" frog). When the spring released, most of this potential energy was converted back into kinetic energy, making the frog jump. Living creatures also convert energy. The food we eat is stored as potential energy. It's converted into kinetic energy when we run, walk, ride a bike, or even just stretch and yawn! The human nervous system helps convert this energy into the ability to perform complex tasks.

WHAT HAPPENED?

Scientists call the process you just observed **stimulus/response**. A stimulus is something that happens (like the frog jumping). A response is something your body does when the stimulus happens (like trying to catch the frog). Although we don't realize it, this can be a very complicated process!

First, your **eyes** had to see the frog jump and **relay** that information to the **brain**. The brain then sent a signal ("Catch that frog!") through your **nerves** to the **muscles** in your arm and hand. Since both the frog and your arm were moving, your brain had to make constant, tiny adjustments to compensate.

As you can see, God designed your marvelous nervous system to perform complex movements rapidly and smoothly.

WHAT WE LEARNED

1 What is a stimulus? What is a response? Give an example of a stimulus/response.

a) something that happens

b) the reaction to something that happens

c) the frog jumped, your hand moved

2 Compare Step 3 with Step 4. How were they similar? How were they different? What additional sense was used in Step 4?

a) similar: same frog, same person

b) different: added another step to the process

c) hearing

3 Describe the difference in reaction times between your team mates. Why might God give different people different kinds of skills?

a) answers will vary

b) answers will vary, but should include the concept of spiritual gifts

4 Give another example of a stimulus/response. List the main body parts and senses involved in reacting to this stimulus.

a) answers will vary (fly bites/hand swats; nose itches/hand scratches; etc.)

b) answers will vary, but should be logical groupings

5 Alcohol slows stimulus/response times. Based on what you've learned, explain why even one drink can make someone a more dangerous driver.

answers will vary, but should include the idea that chemicals slow down the nervous system, increasing response times

What Happened

Review the section with students. Emphasize bold-face words that identify key concepts and introduce new vocabulary.

*Scientists call the process you just observed **stimulus/response**. A stimulus is something that happens (like the frog jumping). A response is something your body does when the stimulus happens (like trying to catch the frog). Although we don't realize it, this can be a very complicated process!*

*First, your **eyes** had to see the frog jump and **relay** that information to the **brain**. The brain then sent a signal ("Catch that frog!") through your **nerves** to the **muscles** in your arm and hand. Since both the frog and your arm were moving, your brain had to make constant, tiny adjustments to compensate.*

As you can see, God designed your marvelous nervous system to perform complex movements rapidly and smoothly.

What We Learned

Answers will vary. Suggested responses are shown at left.

Conclusion

Read this section aloud to the class to summarize the concepts learned in this activity.

Food for Thought

Read the Scripture aloud to the class. Discuss how God's people can work together to serve him. Encourage students to write "thank you" notes to various church personnel.

Journal

If time permits, have a general class discussion about students' journal entries. Share and compare observations. Be sure to emphasize that "trial and error" is a valuable part of scientific inquiry!

! CONCLUSION

A stimulus is something that happens. A response is your reaction. For the stimulus/response process to work properly, several parts of your body must work together.

FOOD FOR THOUGHT

Ephesians 4:16 In this lesson, you discovered that when something happens (a stimulus), your body reacts (a response). This is an important process in many games. To achieve the goal you have in mind, all the parts of your body must work together!

This Scripture tells us that a church functions like that. All the parts must work together for the good of all. We not only need someone to conduct the services, but also to sweep the floor, mow the grounds, and maintain the buildings. Take time this week to thank the people who make your church run so well!

JOURNAL My Science Notes

Extended Teaching

1. Challenge students to make a list of various stimuli. Continue by listing possible responses a body might have to each one. Have them discuss the results with their research team.

2. Place the frog in the refrigerator overnight, then repeat this activity. Now place the frog in the hot sun for several hours. Repeat again. Ask students to determine what effect temperature had on the frog's reaction time.

3. Invite a physical therapist to visit your classroom. Have the therapist demonstrate common body connections and how they move. Discuss voluntary and involuntary reflexes.

4. Have students list common examples of involuntary reflexes. Discuss how these reflexes can help protect us. Have each team write and perform a short skit demonstrating this concept.

5. Using the Internet, an encyclopedia, or a science reading book, have students research Pavlov's classic stimulus/response experiments with dogs. Ask each team to create a poster based on this work.

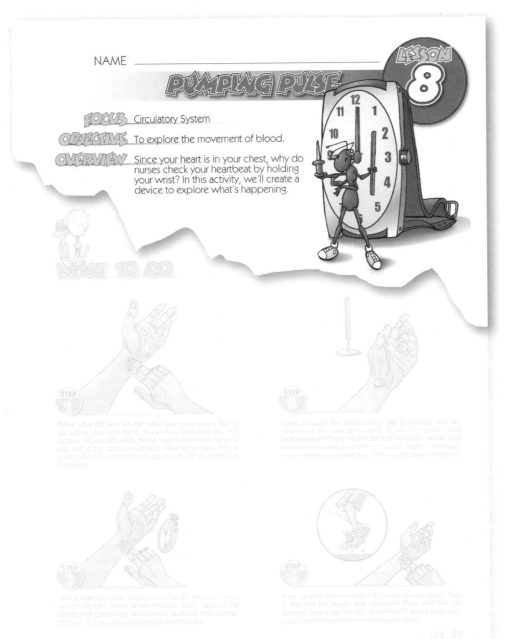

Category
Life Science

Focus
Circulatory System

Objective
To explore the movement of blood

National Standards
A1, A2, B1, B2, C1, E3, F1, G1

Materials Needed
thumb tack
wooden match stick with no head
stopwatch

Safety Concerns
4. Sharp Objects
Remind students to be careful when using the knife.

Additional Comments

Depending on your students, you may wish to make up the tack/match devices ahead of time. Also, cutting the heads off the matches will eliminate the potential for burns. If you don't have access to stopwatches, any clock or watch with an easy-to-see second hand will work.

Overview

Read the overview aloud to your students. The goal is to create an atmosphere of curiosity and inquiry.

WHAT TO DO

Monitor student research teams as they complete each step. Some students have a very difficult time finding their pulse and may need assistance in locating it.

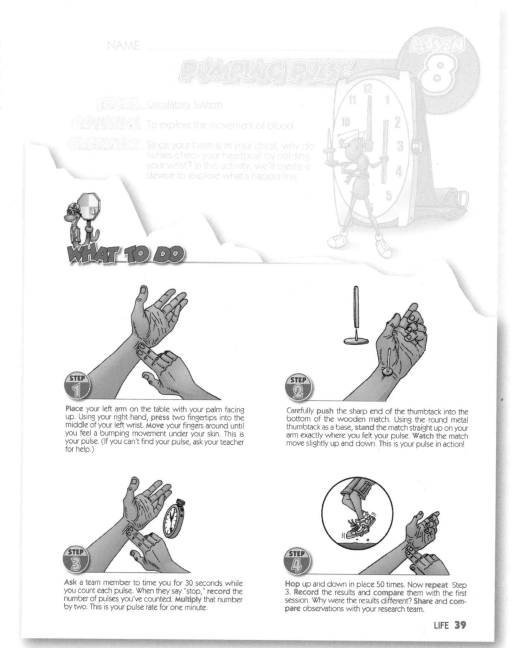

PUMPING PULSE

LESSON 8

TOPIC Circulatory System

OBJECTIVE To explore the movement of blood.

OVERVIEW Since your heart is in your chest, why do nurses check your heartbeat by holding your wrist? In this activity, we'll create a device to explore what's happening.

WHAT TO DO

STEP 1

Place your left arm on the table with your palm facing up. Using your right hand, **press** two fingertips into the middle of your left wrist. **Move** your fingers around until you feel a bumping movement under your skin. This is your pulse. (If you can't find your pulse, ask your teacher for help.)

STEP 2

Carefully **push** the sharp end of the thumbtack into the bottom of the wooden match. Using the round metal thumbtack as a base, **stand** the match straight up on your arm exactly where you felt your pulse. **Watch** the match move slightly up and down. This is your pulse in action!

STEP 3

Ask a team member to time you for 30 seconds while you count each pulse. When they say "stop," **record** the number of pulses you've counted. **Multiply** that number by two. This is your pulse rate for one minute.

STEP 4

Hop up and down in place 50 times. Now **repeat** Step 3. **Record** the results and **compare** them with the first session. Why were the results different? **Share** and **compare** observations with your research team.

LIFE **39**

Teacher to Teacher

Blood pressure is the force of blood against the artery walls. Blood pressure is recorded as two numbers: systolic pressure (as the heart beats) and diastolic pressure (heart relaxed between beats). The measurement is written with the systolic number on top and the diastolic number on the bottom. For example, a blood pressure measurement of 120/80 is expressed verbally as "120 over 80." Although both numbers are important, health professionals monitor the bottom number closely because when it gets higher, it often indicates a number of serious health problems.

? WHAT HAPPENED?

The movement you felt was **blood** being **pushed** through your body by your **heart**. Each time your heart beat, you felt a slight bump. This is called a **pulse**. (Your wrist is simply a handy place for the nurse to check your pulse.)

Your heart is a marvelous **muscle** that pumps 24 hours a day, seven days a week — for your entire life! It can pump around six quarts of blood per minute when you're resting. (That's enough to fill a railroad tank car in less than a day!)

The blood your heart pumps brings oxygen to your entire body. Your heart is constantly adjusting to your body's needs. For instance, when you exercise, your body needs more **oxygen** and **energy**. As you saw in Step 4, your heart compensates for this increased need by pumping faster.

? WHAT WE LEARNED

1 What is a pulse? Describe what your pulse felt like in Step 1.

a) the beat of your heart as it pumps blood through your body

b) answers will vary

2 Compare Step 1 with Step 2. How were they similar? How were they different?

a) similar: same body, same pulse

b) different: Step 1 used touch, Step 2 used sight

3 What does your heart do? Describe how it adjusts to your needs. What would happen if it stopped beating?

a) pumps blood to your body

b) speeds up when more energy is needed

c) you would die

4 Compare Step 3 with Step 4. How were they similar? How were they different? What caused this difference?

a) similar: same body

b) different: pulse higher in Step 4

c) exercise required more energy

5 Based on what you've learned, why is the heart an important muscle?

without it you would immediately die; it pumps the blood that keeps you alive; etc.

What Happened

Review the section with students. Emphasize bold-face words that identify key concepts and introduce new vocabulary.

The movement you felt was **blood** *being* **pushed** *through your body by your* **heart**. *Each time your heart beat, you felt a slight bump. This is called a* **pulse**. *(Your wrist is simply a handy place for the nurse to check your pulse.)*

Your heart is a marvelous **muscle** *that pumps 24 hours a day, seven days a week — for your entire life! It can pump around six quarts of blood per minute when you're resting. (That's enough to fill a railroad tank car in less than a day!)*

The blood your heart pumps brings oxygen to your entire body. Your heart is constantly adjusting to your body's needs. For instance, when you exercise, your body needs more **oxygen** *and* **energy**. *As you saw in Step 4, your heart compensates for this increased need by pumping faster.*

What We Learned

Answers will vary. Suggested responses are shown at left.

Conclusion

Read this section aloud to the class to summarize the concepts learned in this activity.

Food for Thought

Read the Scripture aloud to the class. Discuss how we can better learn to serve others. Talk about where the power for such service comes from.

Journal

If time permits, have a general class discussion about students' journal entries. Share and compare observations. Be sure to emphasize that "trial and error" is a valuable part of scientific inquiry!

! CONCLUSION

Your heart is a muscle that pushes blood through your body. The rate your heart beats is called the pulse. Pulse rates can change depending on your body's needs.

FOOD FOR THOUGHT

Philippians 2:5-8 Using a matchstick to watch your heart beat is a fun way to see evidence of life. Every heartbeat is pushing life-giving blood through your body.

What are you doing with the life God gave you? Does your life revolve around your own wants and needs, or do you think about others' needs and how to help them? This Scripture reminds us that Jesus' entire life was dedicated to serving others. Let Jesus be your example. Like Jesus, make your life a blessing to those around you.

JOURNAL   My Science Notes

_____
_____
_____
_____
_____
_____
_____
_____
_____
_____
_____
_____
_____
_____
_____
_____
_____

42 LIFE

Extended Teaching

1. Invite a nurse to visit your classroom. Have him/her take the pulse and blood pressure of all class members. Make a chart comparing boys with girls, older students with younger, etc.

2. Draw a simple diagram of the heart on the board or an overhead. Have students draw the heart, labeling the main chambers. Now discuss the path that blood takes through the heart, and have them add arrows.

3. Challenge students to research things that can damage the heart (poor diet, tobacco use, substance abuse, etc.). Ask each team to create a poster showing good and bad habits.

4. Invite an EMT to visit your classroom. Have him/her demonstrate CPR or other life-saving First Aid skills. Have students write a paper about the experience.

5. Have students research animal hearts. Ask each team to make a drawing of an animal heart, then share it with the class. Compare similarities and differences with human hearts.

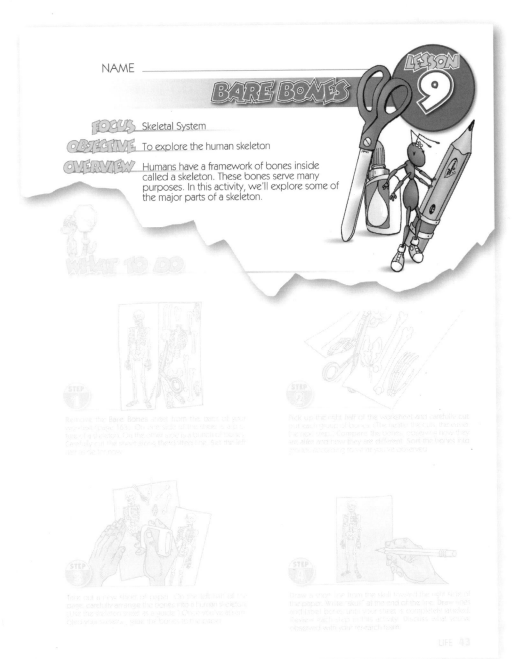

NAME _____

BARE BONES

FOCUS Skeletal System

OBJECTIVE To explore the human skeleton

OVERVIEW Humans have a framework of bones inside called a skeleton. These bones serve many purposes. In this activity, we'll explore some of the major parts of a skeleton.

WHAT TO DO

LIFE 43

Category
Life Science

Focus
Skeletal System

Objective
To explore the human skeleton

National Standards
A1, A2, B1, C1, E3, F1, G1

Materials Needed
Bare Bones worksheet *(student worktext, p. 163)*
scissors
typing paper
glue or glue stick

Safety Concerns
4. Sharp Objects
Remind students to exercise caution when using scissors.

Additional Comments

Help students see the relationship between the structure of an object and its function. Comparing the structure/function of a leg bone to the bones in the hand is a good example. Leg bones must be large and strong to support the body. Hand bones must be small and flexible to allow for grasping and manipulating.

Overview

Read the overview aloud to your students. The goal is to create an atmosphere of curiosity and inquiry.

WHAT TO DO

Monitor student research teams as they complete each step.

Step 2

Watch to make sure students are cutting out GROUPS of bones, not each tiny, individual bone!

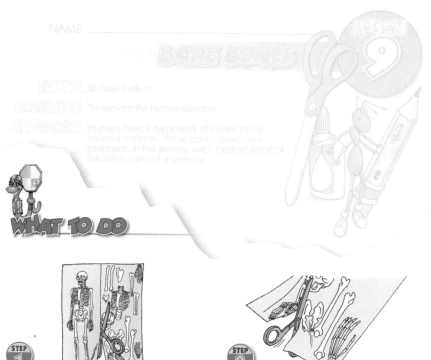

BARE BONES

LESSON 9

TOPIC Skeletal System

OBJECTIVE To explore the human skeleton

OVERVIEW Humans have a framework of bones inside called a skeleton. These bones serve many purposes. In this activity, we'll explore some of the major parts of a skeleton.

WHAT TO DO

STEP 1
Remove the **Bare Bones** sheet from the back of your worktext (page 163). On one side of the sheet is a picture of a skeleton. On the other side is a bunch of bones. Carefully **cut** the sheet along the dotted line. **Set** the left half aside for now.

STEP 2
Pick up the right half of the worksheet and carefully **cut** out each group of bones. (The neater the cuts, the easier the next step.) **Compare** the bones, observing how they are alike and how they are different. **Sort** the bones into groups according to what you've observed.

STEP 3
Take out a new sheet of paper. On the left half of the page, carefully **arrange** the bones into a human skeleton. (Use the skeleton sheet as a guide.) Once you've assembled your skeleton, **glue** the bones to the paper.

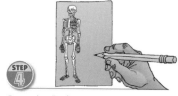

STEP 4
Draw a short line from the skull toward the right side of the paper. **Write** "skull" at the end of the line. Draw lines and **label** bones until your sheet is completely labeled. **Review** each step in this activity. **Discuss** what you've observed with your research team.

LIFE **43**

Teacher to Teacher

Scientists refer to the human skeleton as having two primary parts: the axial skeleton and the appendicular skeleton. The axial skeleton contains 80 bones. It's made of the skull (cranium), spine (vertebrae), sternum (breastbone), and ribs. Think of it as the "tree trunk" of the body. The appendicular skeleton contains 126 bones. It's made of the arms and legs, and bones needed to attach them. These include the pelvis (hip bones), clavicle (collarbone), and scapula (shoulder blades). The appendicular skeleton allows an amazing range of movement — from intricate microsurgery to powerful athletic feats.

WHAT HAPPENED?

Did you know that your **bones** are alive? Ask someone who has broken a bone, and they'll tell you it can hurt! Compare that to clipping your fingernails. That doesn't hurt because fingernails are not alive.

Your **skeleton** is actually 206 individual bones all working together. It's much more than just a frame to hold you up! It works with other body parts (like **tendons**, **ligaments**, and **joints**) to allow you to move. It protects your vital **organs** (heart, lungs, brain, etc.). It protects key parts of your **nervous system** (like the **spinal cord**).

Your bones also contain **nutrients** your body needs, including calcium and phosphorous. Bones even produce special **blood cells** that help fight **disease**.

WHAT WE LEARNED

1 Describe the bones you cut out in Step 2. Were they individual bones or groups of bones? How many bones are there in a human skeleton?

a) answers will vary

b) some individual, some groups

c) 206

2 Describe the skull. What does the skull protect? Why is this important?

a) answers will vary, but should include concepts like round, bony, hard, hollow, etc.

b) the brain

c) the brain is soft and easily damaged

3 Why does it hurt when you break a bone? Why doesn't it hurt to clip your fingernails?

a) because the bone is living tissue

b) because fingernails are dead tissue

4 Describe two things bones do (in addition to holding you up).

answers will vary, but could include "allows you to move," "protects vital organs," "protects spinal cord," etc.

5 A leg bone is large and thick compared to a finger bone. Explain why this might be. How might a bone's size and shape affect its use?

answers will vary, but should focus on the relationship between structure and function

What Happened

Review the section with students. Emphasize bold-face words that identify key concepts and introduce new vocabulary.

Did you know that your **bones** *are alive? Ask someone who has broken a bone, and they'll tell you it can hurt! Compare that to clipping your fingernails. That doesn't hurt because fingernails are not alive.*

Your **skeleton** *is actually 206 individual bones all working together. It's much more than just a frame to hold you up! It works with other body parts (like* **tendons**, **ligaments**, *and* **joints***) to allow you to move. It protects your vital* **organs** (**heart**, **lungs**, **brain**, *etc.). It protects key parts of your* **nervous system** (*like the* **spinal cord***).*

Your bones also contain **nutrients** *your body needs, including calcium and phosphorous. Bones even produce special* **blood cells** *that help fight* **disease***.*

What We Learned

Answers will vary. Suggested responses are shown at left.

Conclusion

Read this section aloud to the class to summarize the concepts learned in this activity.

Food for Thought

Read the Scripture aloud to the class. Talk about God's infinite love for his children, and how the Holy Spirit can help us live happier, healthier lives.

Journal

If time permits, have a general class discussion about students' journal entries. Share and compare observations. Be sure to emphasize that "trial and error" is a valuable part of scientific inquiry!

! CONCLUSION

The human skeleton contains 206 individual bones. It works with other body parts to allow movement. It protects our organs and spinal cord. It even provides nutrients and helps fight disease.

FOOD FOR THOUGHT

Galatians 5:22 You may have started this lesson thinking a skeleton was just a bunch of dead bones. Now you understand the many ways your skeleton works — helping you move, protecting your organs, even fighting disease. You've gained a whole new way of looking at bones!

Just as your skeleton has many functions, God's spirit works in many ways, too. This Scripture talks about exciting changes that happen when the Holy Spirit controls our lives. When you understand God's love, you gain a whole new way of looking at life!

JOURNAL   My Science Notes

_____
_____
_____
_____
_____
_____
_____
_____
_____
_____
_____
_____
_____
_____
_____
_____

Extended Teaching

1. Invite an orthopedic surgeon or chiropractor to visit your classroom. Ask him/her to bring some models of bones. Discuss the human skeleton and how the parts work together.

2. Use a copy machine to enlarge the skeleton parts. Make them as large as possible. Now have students assemble these "life-size" skeletons and label the parts.

3. Have students gently tape their thumb to their palm. Now ask them to write their name, open a door, or similar simple functions. After removing the tape, have them write a story about what it was like to have no thumb!

4. Using the Internet or an encyclopedia, have students research the smallest bones in the body (the ossicles, or "ear bones"). Discuss these bones, then ask each team to make a poster showing their findings.

5. Have students compare the human skeleton to the skeleton of other large mammals. How are they similar? How are they different? Make a bulletin board showing these comparisons.

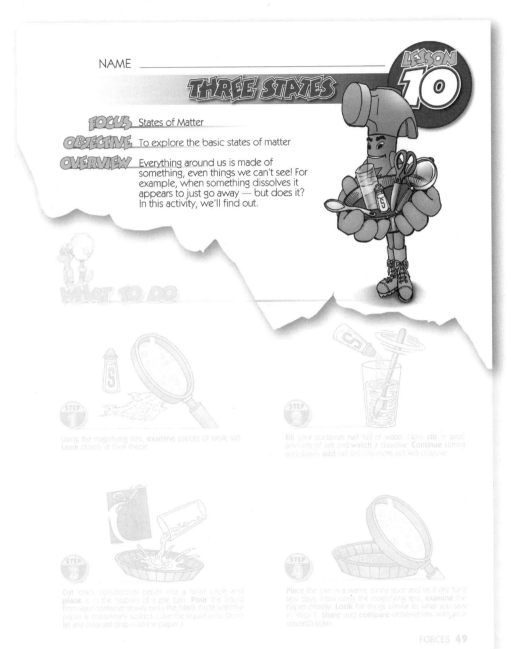

Category

Physical Science
Forces

Focus

States of Matter

Objective

To explore three basic states of matter

National Standards

A1, A2, B1, B2, B3, D1, D3, E3, F4, G1

Materials Needed

paper cup
spoon
magnifying lens
salt
construction paper (black)
pie pan (disposable)
scissors
water

Safety Concerns

4. Slipping
There is a potential for spills with this activity. Remind students to exercise caution.

Additional Comments

Make certain every team has all the needed materials before beginning. Be sure to have plenty of extra salt on hand! Remind students to complete each step before moving to the next. Don't forget to have a sunny place ready to receive the pans.

Overview

Read the overview aloud to the students. Your goal is to create an atmosphere of curiosity and inquiry.

WHAT TO DO

Monitor student research teams as they complete each step.

Step 2

This step requires a lot of salt! Check each team's solution to verify that it has reached the saturation point.

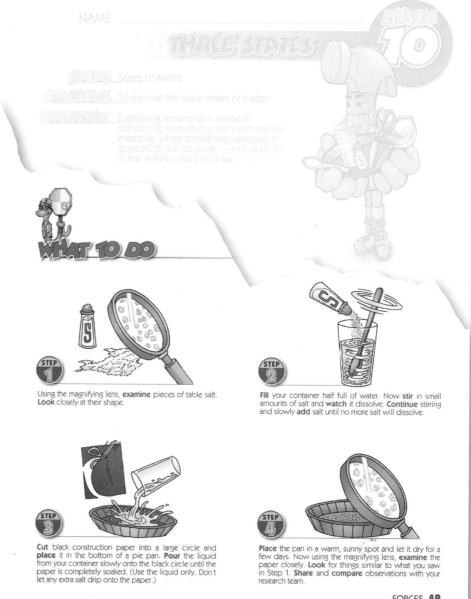

NAME _____

THREE STATES

LESSON 10

FOCUS States of Matter

OBJECTIVE To explore the basic states of matter.

OVERVIEW Everything around us is made of something, even things we can't see! For example, when something dissolves it appears to just go away — but does it? In this activity, we'll find out.

WHAT TO DO

STEP 1
Using the magnifying lens, **examine** pieces of table salt. **Look** closely at their shape.

STEP 2
Fill your container half full of water. Now **stir** in small amounts of salt and **watch** it dissolve. **Continue** stirring and slowly **add** salt until no more salt will dissolve.

STEP 3
Cut black construction paper into a large circle and **place** it in the bottom of a pie pan. **Pour** the liquid from your container slowly onto the black circle until the paper is completely soaked. (Use the liquid only. Don't let any extra salt drip onto the paper.)

STEP 4
Place the pan in a warm, sunny spot and let it dry for a few days. Now using the magnifying lens, **examine** the paper closely. **Look** for things similar to what you saw in Step 1. **Share** and **compare** observations with your research team.

FORCES **49**

Teacher to Teacher

Physical change affects only a substance's *form*. By contrast, chemical change creates a completely different substance. Physical change occurred when students combined salt (solid) and water (liquid) to create a solution. As the solution evaporated (gas), the salt returned to its solid, crystallized state. Thus, the three states of matter demonstrated by this activity are solid, liquid, and gas. (Hannes Alfven won the Nobel prize in 1970 for identifying a *fourth* state of matter called "plasma". But since this state doesn't exist on Earth, it's not a vital concept at this stage in your students' learning.)

What Happened

WHAT HAPPENED?

What are some ways that **matter** was changed in this activity? First, you **dissolved** the **solid** table salt into a **liquid** (water). The salt seemed to disappear, but it really didn't. It was broken down by the water into very tiny parts to form a **solution**.

When you poured the solution onto the paper and let it dry for a few days, the water **evaporated**, changing into a **gas**. The material remaining on the paper is the original salt — now a solid again!

Changes in matter take place around you every day! When you make a powdered drink mix, dry the laundry, or wash your hands, you're creating **physical changes** in the **state of matter**. It's the same material, just a different form.

WHAT WE LEARNED

1 Describe the salt crystals you looked at in Step 1. On a sheet of paper, draw some of the shapes you saw.

a) answers will vary . . . look for words like small, white, hard, sharp, etc.
b) drawings should show angular, sharp-edged shapes

2 In step 2, why did you have to quit adding salt? Why couldn't you add more?

answers will vary, but should include the concept of saturation ("The solution had too much salt," "No more salt would dissolve," etc.)

3 In step 3, what did the liquid look like when you poured it? Could you see any salt on the paper?

a) "It looked like water," "It was clear," or similar answers.

b) this is a checkpoint. if a student answers "yes," then directions were not followed correctly

4 After the paper dried, could you see any salt on the paper? If so, where did the salt come from?

a) yes, although some students may not immediately realize the white material is salt

b) answers will vary, but should include the idea that it was there all the time

5 Give at least two examples of other common physical changes in matter (like a puddle drying up).

answers will vary, including concepts like freezing, thawing, breaking, evaporating, cutting, and so forth (ice freezing, ice cream melting, glass breaking, a drying towel, slicing an apple, etc.) The form must change, but it must remain the same substance!

What Happened

Review the section with students. Emphasize bold-face words that identify key concepts and introduce new vocabulary.

*What are some ways that **matter** was changed in this activity? First, you **dissolved** the **solid** table salt into a liquid (water). The salt seemed to disappear, but it really didn't. It was broken down by the water into very tiny parts to form a **solution**.*

*When you poured the solution onto the paper and let it dry for a few days, the water **evaporated**, changing into a **gas**. The material remaining on the paper is the original salt — now a solid again!*

*Changes in matter take place around you every day! When you make a powdered drink mix, dry the laundry, or wash your hands, you're creating **physical changes** in the **state of matter**. It's the same material, just a different form.*

What We Learned

Answers will vary. Suggested responses are shown at left.

Conclusion

Read this section aloud to the class to summarize the concepts learned in this activity.

Food for Thought

Read the Scripture aloud to the class. This object lesson makes a great introduction for discussing the concept of the Trinity.

Journal

If time permits, have a general class discussion about students' journal entries. Share and compare observations. Be sure to emphasize that "trial and error" is a valuable part of scientific inquiry!

CONCLUSION

Matter changes form. Even though it's the same material, it may appear as a solid, a liquid, or a gas. These kinds of changes happen around us all the time.

FOOD FOR THOUGHT

I John 5:7 In this activity, the pan and the air surrounding it contained all three states of matter — solid, liquid, and gas. All three were matter, but they appeared in different forms!

John tells us that the Father, the Word (Jesus), and the Holy Spirit all work together to provide us with salvation. Even though all three are different, the three are one.

JOURNAL My Science Notes

_____
_____
_____
_____
_____
_____
_____
_____
_____
_____
_____
_____
_____
_____
_____
_____
_____
_____

52 FORCES

Extended Teaching

1. Repeat this activity using Epsom salts. Challenge students to compare the results with the original activity.

2. There are many valuable and interesting crystal forms found on Earth. Using the Internet, have students explore gems, precious stones, and semi-precious stones.

3. Invite a jeweler or gemologist to visit your classroom. Ask them to bring samples of "stones" related to or made from crystals. Compare the appearance of these objects in the ground to the finished product.

4. Challenge students to identify chemical changes in the world around them. Make a bulletin board depicting their findings.

5. Early radios were called "crystal sets." Research the history of these devices. Find an Internet site (or an antique radio buff) and discover how to make a simple crystal set.

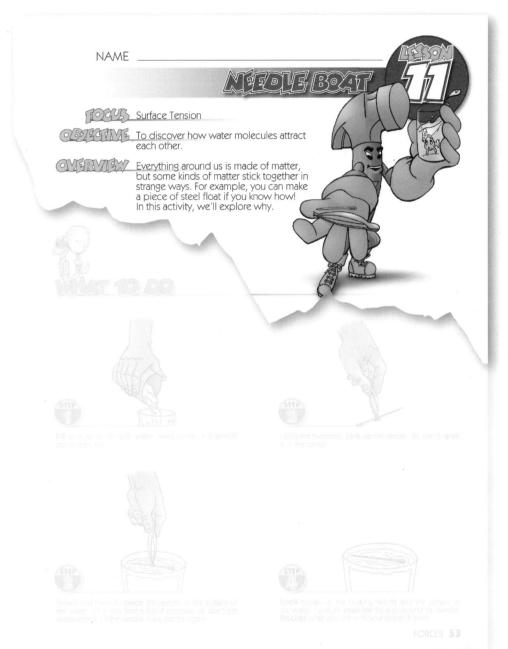

NAME _____

NEEDLE BOAT

FOCUS Surface Tension

OBJECTIVE To discover how water molecules attract each other.

OVERVIEW Everything around us is made of matter, but some kinds of matter stick together in strange ways. For example, you can make a piece of steel float if you know how! In this activity, we'll explore why.

WHAT TO DO

STEP 1
Fill your container with water. Most containers it at almost completely full.

STEP 2
Using the tweezers, pick up the needle. Be sure to grab it in the center.

STEP 3
Slowly and carefully place the needle on the surface of the water. If you have a lot of practice, do don't get discouraged if the needle sinks slowly again.

STEP 4
Look closely at the floating needle and the surface of the water. Carefully examine the area around the needle. Discuss what you see with your research team.

FORCES **53**

Category

Physical Science
Forces

Focus

Surface Tension

Objective

To discover how water molecules attract each other

National Standards

A1, A2, B1, B2, D1, E1, E2, E3, F5, G1

Materials Needed

plastic cup
water
needle
tweezers (pointed)

Safety Concerns

4. Slipping
There is a potential for spills with this activity. Remind students to exercise caution.

Additional Comments

If you have an advanced class, you may wish to tease them a bit. Secretly wet your finger with liquid soap, then touch the water where a needle is floating. The needle will immediately sink! This makes a great lead in to discussing surfactants (see "Teacher to Teacher").

Overview

Read the overview aloud to the students. Your goal is to create an atmosphere of curiosity and inquiry.

WHAT TO DO

Monitor student research teams as they complete each step.

Step 3

Differences in motor skills development may cause some students difficulty. If you see students having problems, join the group and demonstrate. This will shift the focus from the skill to the observation process.

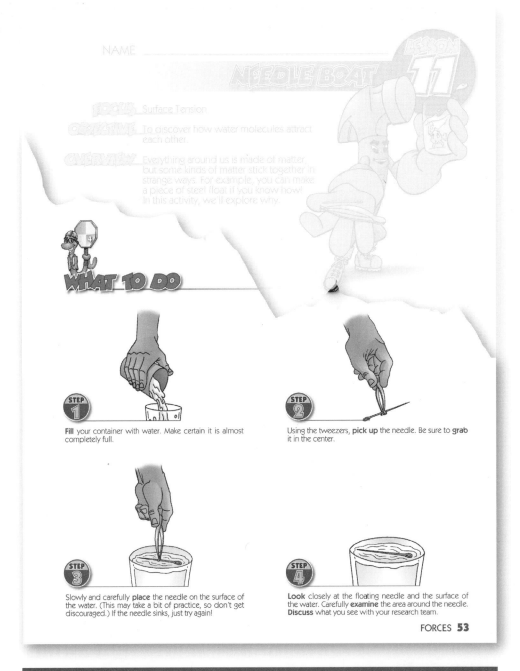

NAME _____

NEEDLE BOAT

LESSON 11

FOCUS Surface Tension

OBJECTIVE To discover how water molecules attract each other.

OVERVIEW Everything around us is made of matter, but some kinds of matter stick together in strange ways. For example, you can make a piece of steel float if you know how! In this activity, we'll explore why.

WHAT TO DO

STEP 1
Fill your container with water. Make certain it is almost completely full.

STEP 2
Using the tweezers, **pick up** the needle. Be sure to **grab** it in the center.

STEP 3
Slowly and carefully **place** the needle on the surface of the water. (This may take a bit of practice, so don't get discouraged.) If the needle sinks, just try again!

STEP 4
Look closely at the floating needle and the surface of the water. Carefully **examine** the area around the needle. **Discuss** what you see with your research team.

FORCES **53**

Teacher to Teacher

Water on a smooth surface beads because surface tension makes molecules stick together. Detergents (also called surfactants) break surface tension. That's why soapy water runs off instead of beading up. But surface tension doesn't tell the whole story. Density plays a major role. Wood floats because it's less dense than water; rocks sink for the opposite reason. But wait! How do you explain the fact that steel ships float? Ships float because they displace more water than they weigh. This is called buoyancy. As long as the water stays out and the cargo isn't too heavy, the ship floats. It wasn't an iceberg that sank the Titanic . . . it was the added weight of the water the iceberg let in!

WHAT HAPPENED?

Water molecules stick together because of their **structure**. We call this tendency **surface tension**. Imagine that the water molecules at the surface are holding hands.

When the needle was placed gently on the water, the little hands were strong enough to hold it up. Their combined **force** was even stronger than **gravity** trying to **pull** the needle down. (The **interaction** between these two forces makes the dent you see in the water around the needle.)

Surface tension is what makes raindrops round. It makes water bead on a window, and it makes the surface bend along the edge of a bucket of water. But remember, surface tension is not a strong force. A needle can't float on its point because there are only a few water molecules to support it!

WHAT WE LEARNED

1 Is the surface of a container of water completely flat? What happens along the edges? Describe the shape of the surface.

a) no

b) it bends

c) descriptions should include the idea of a bent surface

2 Why do you think it was important in Step 2 to grab the needle in the center? Why wouldn't it work to hold it by one end?

answers will vary, but should reflect the concept that the end of the needle wouldn't touch enough molecules to hold it up

3 In Step 3, did the needle float the first time? If not, what did you do differently to succeed?

a) answers will vary

b) success is the result of keeping the needle flat and level to the surface, using just the tip of the tweezers, and placing the needle gently.

4 What do you think the water molecules do that helps the needle float?

answers will vary, but should include the concept of molecular bonding, or "molecules holding hands"

5 Using what you've learned in this lesson, describe why it's easier to dive head-first into a pool than to fall flat on the surface? (Ouch!)

answers will vary, but should be similar to the answer for question #2; it's less painful to break surface tension with a smaller part of your body

What Happened

Review the section with students. Emphasize bold-face words that identify key concepts and introduce new vocabulary.

Water molecules stick together because of *their* **structure**. We call this tendency **surface tension**. Imagine that the water molecules at the surface are holding hands.

When the needle was placed gently on the water, the little hands were strong enough to hold it up. Their combined **force** *was even stronger than* **gravity** *trying to* **pull** *the needle down. (The* **interaction** *between these two forces makes the dent you see in the water around the needle.)*

Surface tension is what makes raindrops round. It makes water bead on a window, and it makes the surface bend along the edge of a bucket of water. But remember, surface tension is not a strong force. A needle can't float on its point because there are only a few water molecules to support it!

What We Learned

Answers will vary. Suggested responses are shown at left.

Conclusion

Read this section aloud to the class to summarize the concepts learned in this activity.

Food for Thought

Read the Scripture aloud to the class. Discuss the importance of cooperation in the classroom, at home, and at church.

Journal

If time permits, have a general class discussion about students' journal entries. Share and compare observations. Be sure to emphasize that "trial and error" is a valuable part of scientific inquiry!

 **CONCLUSION**

Surface tension shows how some kinds of matter (in this case, water molecules) tend to stick together. Understanding this can help us not only float needles, but also float huge ships!

 **FOOD FOR THOUGHT**

Romans 12:4-5 In this Scripture, Paul talks about the importance of working together for the good of all. Just as water molecules must "hold hands" to make the needle float, so we must stand together as God's children.

Even though we are individuals with different skills and abilities, together we can make a difference in our school and in our world!

JOURNAL My Science Notes

_____
_____
_____
_____
_____
_____
_____
_____
_____
_____
_____
_____
_____
_____
_____
_____

56 FORCES

Extended Teaching

1. Run water over a freshly-waxed car hood, then a car hood with no wax. Have students observe the difference, then write a paragraph explaining the process (using what they've learned in this lesson).

2. Research the Exxon Valdez. Find out the difference between single hull and double hull ships. Have each team make a poster showing the differences, and the advantage double hulls have.

3. Have each team make three "ships" from various materials. Use a washtub (preferrably outside!) to take turns testing the ships.

Have students evaluate their ships based on displacement, reaction to waves, and carrying capacity.

4. Research the Titanic disaster. Challenge students to explain why the Titanic sank based on what they've learned in this lesson. Have a class discussion about this.

5. Research cruise ships. Have students find the length, width, and height for one of these ships. Transfer those to the playground. Discuss the enormous amount of water these ships must displace to float!

Category

Physical Science
Forces

Focus

Absorption

Objective

To explore how water is held or absorbed by materials

National Standards

A1, A2, B1, B2, E1, E2, E3, F5, G1

Materials Needed

paper cups (3)
dehydrated gel
water

Safety Concerns

3. Poison Hazard
Students must wash their hands after handling gel. Avoid contact with mouth, eyes and nose.

4. Slipping
There is a potential for spills with this activity. Remind students to exercise caution.

Additional Comments

The old carnival "shell game" provides a great way to introduce this lesson. Tell students you're going to test their powers of observation. Line up three seemingly identical cups on a table. (Secretly pour gel into one of the cups in advance.) Tell students to watch closely, then pour water into the cup with the gel. Now quickly switch the positions of the cups several times. Have students point to the cup with the water. Express surprise at how good they are! Repeat. Again express surprise at the results. Now repeat again, drawing the time out. By now the gel should have absorbed all the water and be swollen and stuck in the cup. When students point to the "water" cup, tip it as though pouring and say, "No water here. Point to another cup." Repeat with the second cup, then the third. Students will be amazed and wonder where the water went. While curiosity is at its peak, begin the student activity.

Overview

Read the overview aloud to the students. Your goal is to create an atmosphere of curiosity and inquiry.

WHAT TO DO

Monitor student research teams as they complete each step.

Step 4

Make sure teams allow sufficient time for the gel to absorb all the water.

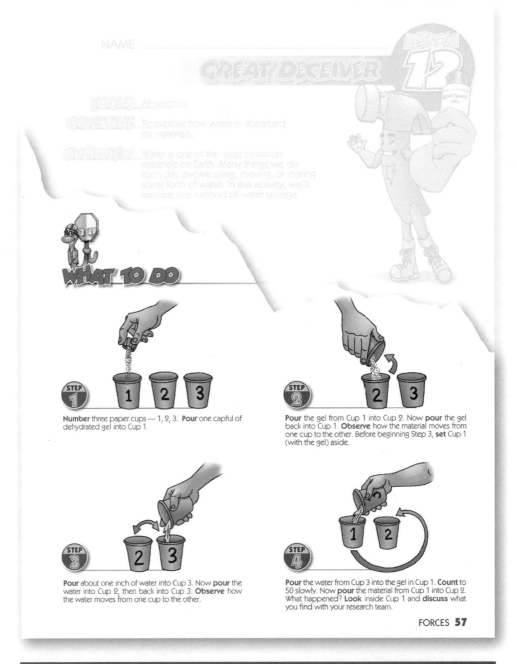

GREAT DECEIVER

LESSON 12

FOCUS Absorption

OBJECTIVE To explore how water is absorbed by materials.

OVERVIEW Water is one of the most common materials on Earth. Many things we do each day involve using, moving, or storing some form of water. In this activity, we'll explore one method of water storage.

WHAT TO DO

STEP 1
Number three paper cups — 1, 2, 3. **Pour** one capful of dehydrated gel into Cup 1.

STEP 2
Pour the gel from Cup 1 into Cup 2. Now **pour** the gel back into Cup 1. **Observe** how the material moves from one cup to the other. Before beginning Step 3, **set** Cup 1 (with the gel) aside.

STEP 3
Pour about one inch of water into Cup 3. Now **pour** the water into Cup 2, then back into Cup 3. **Observe** how the water moves from one cup to the other.

STEP 4
Pour the water from Cup 3 into the gel in Cup 1. **Count** to 50 slowly. Now **pour** the material from Cup 1 into Cup 2. What happened? **Look** inside Cup 1 and **discuss** what you find with your research team.

FORCES **57**

Teacher to Teacher

Materials that contain no water are called anhydrous. Some anhydrous materials (like this gel) are hygroscopic, capable of holding a lot of water. Anhydrous materials can be either solid or liquid. Some anhydrous liquids (like anhydrous ammonia) absorb water so fast they can burn skin. A few absorb so much water they even make their own solutions (like some phosphates). Properties of water loss or gain are even reflected in other materials, too — including the way we store certain foods. For instance, we seal crackers "to keep them dry," but we cover a cake "to keep it moist."

WHAT HAPPENED?

The **dehydrated gel** used in this activity is very **hygroscopic** — a big word that means it can soak up a lot of water! This gel actually can soak up and hold many times its own **weight** in **water**.

The **absorbing** ability of dehydrated gel makes it perfect for many tasks. One of the most common uses is to make disposable diapers!

Dehydrated gel is also helpful in transporting live plants over long distances. The gel prevents water from **evaporating**, making water available to the plant roots for a much longer period of time.

WHAT WE LEARNED

1 Describe the gel in Step 1. What is it similar to? What state of matter is this?

a) answers will vary

b) sand, powder, flour, etc.

c) solid

2 Describe how the gel poured in Step 2. What makes it pour so easily?

a) pours easily

b) answers will vary, but should reflect physical composition (loose, powdery, etc.)

3 Describe how the water poured in Step 3. How did it pour differently from the gel? What state of matter is water?

a) pours easily

b) answers will vary

c) liquid

4 Describe how the gel reacted after Step 4. What do you think happened?

a) it wouldn't pour; it got thick; etc.

b) answers will vary, but should reflect that the material changed forms

5 Give at least three examples of water absorption.

answers will vary; examples include "paper towel absorbing water," "dog's fur absorbing rain," "dirt turning into mud," etc.

What Happened

Review the section with students. Emphasize bold-face words that identify key concepts and introduce new vocabulary.

*The **dehydrated gel** used in this activity is very **hygroscopic** — a big word that means it can soak up a lot of water! This gel actually can soak up and hold many times its own **weight** in **water**.*

*The **absorbing** ability of dehydrated gel makes it perfect for many tasks. One of the most common uses is to make disposable diapers!*

*Dehydrated gel is also helpful in transporting live plants over long distances. The gel prevents water from **evaporating**, making water available to the plant roots for a much longer period of time.*

What We Learned

Answers will vary. Suggested responses are shown at left.

Conclusion

Read this section aloud to the class to summarize the concepts learned in this activity.

Food for Thought

Read the Scripture aloud to the class. Use this as a starting point for discussing deception. Remind students that people who deceive often end up deceiving themselves. Discuss the foolishness of attempting to deceive God.

Journal

If time permits, have a general class discussion about students' journal entries. Share and compare observations. Be sure to emphasize that "trial and error" is a valuable part of scientific inquiry!

! CONCLUSION

Absorption is the attraction and holding of liquid in a material. We use absorption in many ways — like drying our hands, mopping the floor, or even handling huge oil spills.

FOOD FOR THOUGHT

Luke 8:12 Things aren't always what they appear. You were probably fooled by the demonstration the teacher did to introduce this lesson! But once you understood what was happening, you knew the truth.

Some people call the devil the "great deceiver." What they mean is that he's always trying to fool us into believing things that aren't true! The devil doesn't want us to believe that God loves us, or that Jesus died to save us. But if we stay close to Jesus, we won't be deceived by Satan's lies.

JOURNAL My Science Notes

_____
_____
_____
_____
_____
_____
_____
_____
_____
_____
_____
_____
_____
_____
_____
_____

60 FORCES

Extended Teaching

1. Take a field trip to a grocery store. Have students list all the foods they find which are dehydrated (jerky, raisins, drink mix, etc.).

2. Invite a parent with a food dehydrator to bring it to class. Have them demonstrate how it works, and show some of the things they've made using it.

3. Have students research other forms of preserving food. Discuss advantages and disadvantages of each. Make a bulletin board depicting student findings.

4. Bring dehydrated food to class. (A store that sells backpacking supplies is a good source.) Allow students to examine the contents of the packets. Make some samples to eat along with your lunch.

5. Native Americans used dehydration extensively. Research what kinds of foods they dried and how they used them. Have students write a paragraph about what they learn.

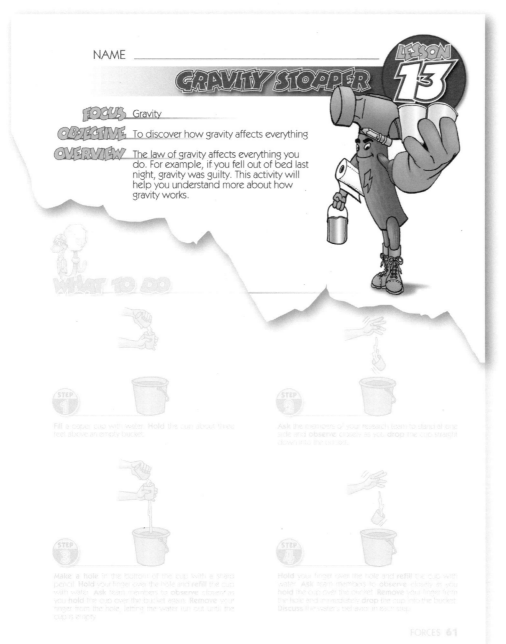

Category

Physical Science
Forces

Focus

Gravity

Objective

To discover how gravity affects everything

National Standards

A1, A2, B1, B2, D1, E3, G1

Materials Needed

paper cups (2)
bucket
paper towels
sharp pencil
water

Safety Concerns

4. Slipping
There is a potential for spilling the water on the floor. Remind students to exercise caution.

Additional Comments

This activity has the potential for being very messy! Be sure to have plenty of paper towels and a mop on hand for clean-up! Even better, save this activity for a nice day and move it outside.

Overview

Read the overview aloud to the students. Your goal is to create an atmosphere of curiosity and inquiry.

WHAT TO DO

Monitor student research teams as they complete each step.

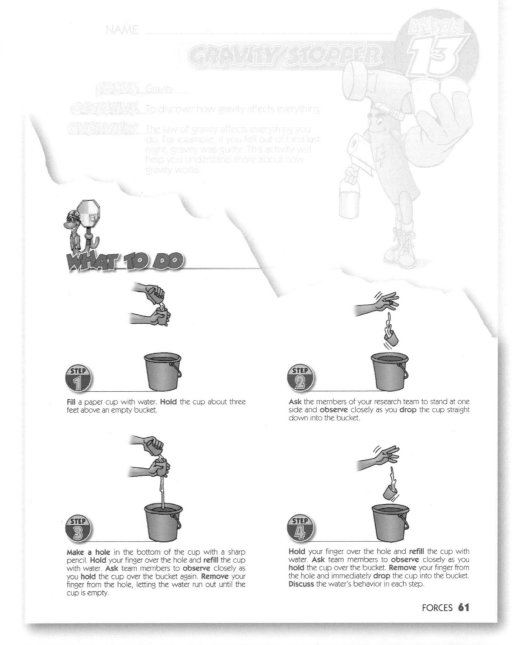

NAME

GRAVITY STOPPER

LESSON 13

FOCUS Gravity

OBJECTIVE To discover how gravity affects everything

OVERVIEW The law of gravity affects everything you do. For example, if you fell out of bed last night, gravity was guilty. This activity will help you understand more about how gravity works.

WHAT TO DO

STEP 1
Fill a paper cup with water. Hold the cup about three feet above an empty bucket.

STEP 2
Ask the members of your research team to stand at one side and observe closely as you drop the cup straight down into the bucket.

STEP 3
Make a hole in the bottom of the cup with a sharp pencil. Hold your finger over the hole and refill the cup with water. Ask team members to observe closely as you hold the cup over the bucket again. Remove your finger from the hole, letting the water run out until the cup is empty.

STEP 4
Hold your finger over the hole and refill the cup with water. Ask team members to observe closely as you hold the cup over the bucket. Remove your finger from the hole and immediately drop the cup into the bucket. Discuss the water's behavior in each step.

FORCES 61

Teacher to Teacher

This activity demonstrated the "equal pull" of gravity. The concept of "equal pull" explains why a bowling ball and a marble fall at essentially the same rate, in spite of a huge difference in weight. Here's another example: A man jumping from a plane is pulled the same regardless of whether his parachute is open or not! However, the open parachute introduces other forces (drag, lift, etc.) that oppose the force of gravity, resulting in a safe landing.

?WHAT HAPPENED?

Once again, the **law of gravity** has been upheld!

Both the cup and the water obeyed the law of gravity. Gravity **pulls** on everything equally. In Step 4, the water quit coming out of the hole because it couldn't fall faster than the cup. They were both being pulled by the same force — gravity!

Gravity is what makes raindrops fall, makes rivers run, and keeps us from floating off the Earth into space. Water, cups, and even people all have to obey the law of gravity.

?WHAT WE LEARNED

1 In Step 1, why didn't the cup fall into the bucket? What force was trying to make the cup drop?

a) answers should reflect the idea of an opposing force, in this case a student holding it

b) gravity

2 In Step 2, what happened when you let go of the cup?

a) it dropped, gravity took over, etc.

3 In Step 3, what force pulled the water out of the cup? What kept the cup from falling?

a) gravity

b) the opposing force of a student holding it

4 In Step 4, what happened to the water when you let go of the cup and removed your finger from the hole at the same time?

a) answers should reflect the fact that the cup and water fell at a similar rate; no water came out of the hole

5 Using what you've learned in this lesson, describe what might happen to us if there were no more gravity.

answers will vary, but should focus on negative gravity phenomenon like, "We'd float off into space," "It wouldn't hurt when we fell down," "I could fly!," etc.

What Happened

Review the section with students. Emphasize bold-face words that identify key concepts and introduce new vocabulary.

*Once again, the **law of gravity** has been upheld!*

*Both the cup and the water obeyed the law of gravity. Gravity **pulls** on everything equally. In Step 4, the water quit coming out of the hole because it couldn't fall faster than the cup. They were both being pulled by the same force — gravity!*

Gravity is what makes raindrops fall, rivers run, and keeps us from floating off the Earth into space. Water, cups, and even people have to obey the law of gravity.

What We Learned

Answers will vary. Suggested responses are shown at left.

Conclusion

Read this section aloud to the class to summarize the concepts learned in this activity.

Food for Thought

Read the Scripture aloud to the class. Talk about the importance of obeying God's laws. Discuss why God gave us a set of rules to live our lives by. (God made us and knows what's best for us!)

Journal

If time permits, have a general class discussion about students' journal entries. Share and compare observations. Be sure to emphasize that "trial and error" is a valuable part of scientific inquiry!

! CONCLUSION

Whether moving, standing still, or falling — everything in our world obeys the law of gravity. No machine or device ever made can move without taking gravity into consideration.

FOOD FOR THOUGHT

Joshua 6:20 One of the best examples of gravity in Scripture is found in the story of Joshua and the battle of Jericho. When the trumpets blew and the people shouted, the walls of the great city came tumbling down!

Just as every object in the universe obeys the law of gravity, all believers should obey the laws of God. Since God made us and knows what is best for us, doesn't it make sense that God's laws are best?

JOURNAL   My Science Notes

Extended Teaching

1. Repeat this activity using different sized containers. Have students compare the results to the original activity.

2. Have students list variables that were constant in this activity (height, amount of water, size of cups, etc.). Challenge them to predict what might happen if one variable was changed. Change this variable and repeat.

3. Research Sir Isaac Newton. Have each team create a poster depicting one thing they learn about this early researcher.

4. Make a bulletin board comparing the gravity on Earth with the gravity on other planets in our solar system.

5. Show a video clip of astronauts in the low gravity environment of space. Have a group discussion about the advantages and disadvantages of such a situation.

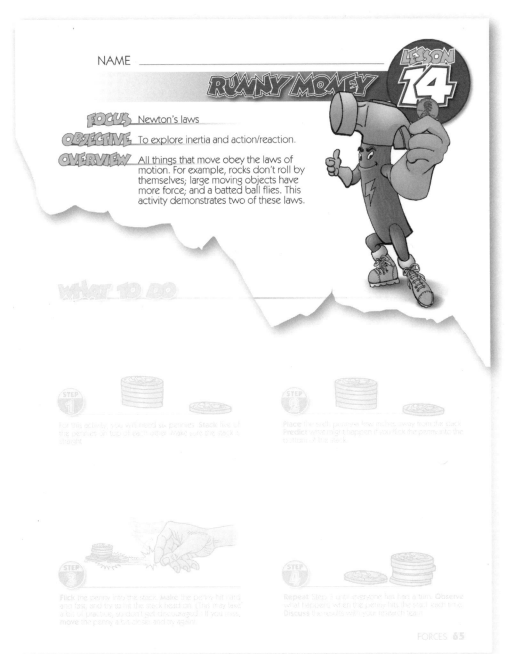

Category

Physical Science
Forces

Focus

Newton's Laws

Objective

To explore inertia and action/reaction

National Standards

A1, A2, B1, B2, E3, F1, G1

Materials Needed

pennies (6)
level surface

Safety Concerns

Additional Comments

Differences in motor skills development may cause some students difficulty. If you see students having problems, join the group and demonstrate. This will shift the focus from the skill to the observation process. You may wish to practice this activity yourself in advance.

Overview

Read the overview aloud to the students. Your goal is to create an atmosphere of curiosity and inquiry.

WHAT TO DO

Monitor student research teams as they complete each step.

RUNNY MONEY

LESSON 14

FOCUS Newton's laws

OBJECTIVE To explore inertia and action/reaction.

OVERVIEW All things that move obey the laws of motion. For example, rocks don't roll by themselves; large moving objects have more force; and a batted ball flies. This activity demonstrates two of these laws.

WHAT TO DO

STEP 1 For this activity, you will need six pennies. **Stack** five of the pennies on top of each other. Make sure the stack is straight.

STEP 2 **Place** the sixth penny a few inches away from the stack. **Predict** what might happen if you flick the penny into the bottom of the stack.

STEP 3 **Flick** the penny into the stack. **Make** the penny hit hard and fast, and try to hit the stack head on. (This may take a bit of practice, so don't get discouraged.) If you miss, **move** the penny a bit closer and try again!

STEP 4 **Repeat** Step 3 until everyone has had a turn. **Observe** what happens when the penny hits the stack each time. **Discuss** the results with your research team.

FORCES **65**

Teacher to Teacher

You're driving home from the store when suddenly someone cuts in front of you. You slam on the brakes and your groceries scatter. You've just had a messy lesson in Newton's laws of motion. First, (obviously) the law of action/reaction. Second, the law of inertia. You stopped because you were seatbelted to the car, but the groceries weren't so lucky. Since they were moving, and no force restrained them, they *kept* moving! Third, the law of acceleration (not in this lesson). You were driving fast, so it took more force to stop than at a slower speed. Your groceries were also moving faster, so they flew with more force. By the way, how's that carton of eggs?

WHAT HAPPENED?

Inertia means that an object that is stopped stays stopped. It also means that an object that is moving stays moving, unless a **force** acts on it. In this case, the stack of pennies stayed put until they were struck by the moving penny.

Action/Reaction means that if a force creates an action, this action will cause something else to happen.

The moving penny (action) stopped when it hit that stack because it **transferred** its force to the bottom penny. The bottom penny moved (reaction), but eventually stopped because of **friction**.

WHAT WE LEARNED

1 In Step 1, once you made the stack, what kept it from moving around? What law is this?

a) answers should reflect that fact that something doesn't move unless a force acts on it

b) the law of inertia

2 In Step 2, what did you predict would happen when the penny hit the stack? Why?

answers will vary, but should reflect logical assumptions (even if the assumption was wrong)

3 Why do you think it was important to hit the stack "head on" in Step 3?

answers should reflect that a "heads-on" hit transfers the most force; other angles lead to deflection

4 What was the "action" in Step 4? What was the "reaction"? How was inertia involved?

a) flicking the penny

b) the bottom penny taking off

c) stack motionless until hit; penny moved until another force stopped it

5 Using what you've learned in this lesson, describe why it's important to always wear a seatbelt.

answers should reflect the "moving inertia" concept discussed above; for instance, "A seatbelt makes me part of the car, so when the car stops, so do I!"

What Happened

Review the section with students. Emphasize bold-face words that identify key concepts and introduce new vocabulary.

Inertia *means that an object that is stopped stays stops. It also means that an object that is moving stays moving, unless a* ***force*** *acts on it. In this case, the stack of pennies stayed put until they were struck by the moving penny.*

Action/Reaction *means that if a force creates an action, this action will cause something else to happen.*

The moving penny (action) stopped when it hit the stack because it ***transferred*** *its force to the bottom penny. The bottom penny moved (reaction), but eventually stopped because of* ***friction***.

What We Learned

Answers will vary. Suggested responses are shown at left.

Conclusion

Read this section aloud to the class to summarize the concepts learned in this activity.

Food for Thought

Read the Scripture aloud to the class. Discuss appropriate ways to deal with problems. Even at this young age, children are often sad and depressed. Talk about how Jesus, our families, and our friends can help.

Journal

If time permits, have a general class discussion about students' journal entries. Share and compare observations. Be sure to emphasize that "trial and error" is a valuable part of scientific inquiry!

CONCLUSION

All objects obey the laws of motion. Inertia and Action/Reaction are two of Newton's three laws of motion.

FOOD FOR THOUGHT

Matthew 11:28-29 Sometimes we have a lot in common with that bottom penny. Our problems seem to keep stacking up on top of us until we can't move. They get heavier and heavier, holding us down so we feel we can never escape.

Then Jesus comes along and applies a powerful force to our lives! Just as the moving penny replaces the trapped penny, Jesus takes our place and sets us free. Since Jesus has taken such a powerful action, what should your reaction be?

JOURNAL My Science Notes

_____
_____
_____
_____
_____
_____
_____
_____
_____
_____
_____
_____
_____
_____
_____

68 FORCES

Extended Teaching

1. Running in school hallways can lead to accidents. Challenge students to use Newton's laws to explain why.

2. Have students point out examples of inertia around the classroom. Usually they will focus on non-moving objects. Expand the discussion to include "moving" inertia.

3. Challenge each team to make a poster encouraging seatbelt use. Post these safety posters around the school.

4. Set up a row of dominos for the classic "domino effect." Before starting the chain reaction, ask students to explain how inertia is at play. After all the dominos have fallen, discuss how inertia was also working as the dominos fell.

5. Repeat this activity in the gym using a row of balls. Have students write a paragraph comparing this with the original activity.

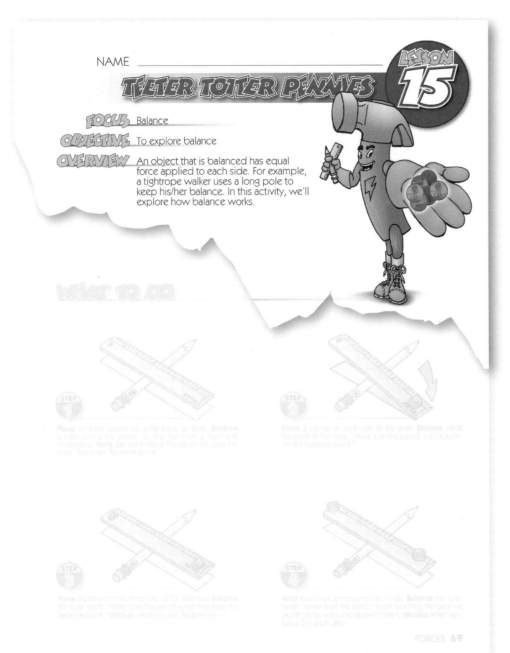

Category

Physical Science
Forces

Focus

Balance

Objective

To explore balance

National Standards

A1, A2, B1, B2, E3, G1

Materials Needed

pennies (6)
ruler
round pencil

Safety Concerns

Additional Comments

This activity is safe and easy to do. If you're concerned about losing the pennies, you can substitute similar-sized metal washers instead. If your school has a teeter-tooter, you may wish to go to the playground to follow up on what students have learned.

Overview

Read the overview aloud to the students. Your goal is to create an atmosphere of curiosity and inquiry.

Monitor student research teams as they complete each step.

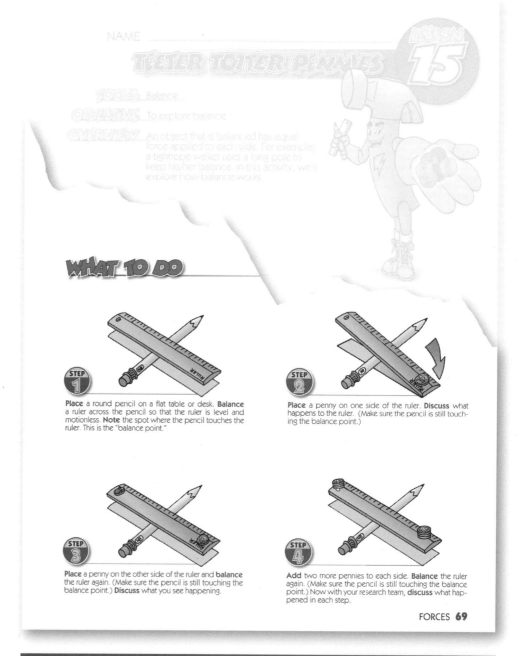

NAME

TEETER TOTTER PENNIES

LESSON 15

TOPIC Balance

OBJECTIVE To explore balance.

OVERVIEW An object that is balanced has equal force applied to each side. For example, a tightrope walker uses a long pole to keep his/her balance. In this activity, we'll explore how balance works.

WHAT TO DO

STEP 1
Place a round pencil on a flat table or desk. **Balance** a ruler across the pencil so that the ruler is level and motionless. **Note** the spot where the pencil touches the ruler. This is the "balance point."

STEP 2
Place a penny on one side of the ruler. **Discuss** what happens to the ruler. (Make sure the pencil is still touching the balance point.)

STEP 3
Place a penny on the other side of the ruler and **balance** the ruler again. (Make sure the pencil is still touching the balance point.) **Discuss** what you see happening.

STEP 4
Add two more pennies to each side. **Balance** the ruler again. (Make sure the pencil is still touching the balance point.) Now with your research team, **discuss** what happened in each step.

FORCES **69**

Teacher to Teacher

A lever is a simple machine that helps increase torque. Levers help us lift, balance, and move things into place. Your body constantly uses its natural levers (arms, legs, fingers, even toes) to accomplish tasks. And in sports, the one who supplies the most torque usually wins! For example, torque in baseball is increased by using longer bats, longer arms, or harder swings — making the ball fly farther. It's no accident that sports which rely on torque are filled with tall athletes. This is because the longer the object we swing, the greater the torque!

❓WHAT HAPPENED?

You had to apply equal **force** (weight) to each side of the ruler to make it **balance**. The balance point is also called a **fulcrum**. When the ruler is balanced on the fulcrum, it acts as a **lever**.

We use levers and fulcrums in different ways for different tasks. Tightrope walkers need equal force on both sides of their long poles (a form of lever), or they will fall!

However, if you're opening a paint can with a screwdriver (lever) you don't want balanced force, or the lid won't open! More force is required on one side of the fulcrum (in this case, the rim of the can) for the process to work.

❓WHAT WE LEARNED

1 In Step 1, how much of the ruler was on each side of the pencil when the ruler was balanced?

half was on each side

2 In Step 2, why did the ruler tilt to one side? Predict what you might do to balance it again.

a) the weight of the penny made it tilt

b) balance the weight; take away the penny; add another penny; etc.

3 Compare the location of the second penny added in Step 3 to the first penny added in Step 2. How do they relate to the balance point?

they are the same distance away from the middle, only on opposite sides of the balance point

4 How did adding more pennies in Step 4 affect the balance of the ruler? What did you have to keep in mind?

a) as long as they were added at the same time, the ruler stayed balanced

b) to hold the ruler until the pennies were in place

5 Using what you've learned in this lesson, describe where four equal-size kids would need to sit to make a teeter-totter operate best.

two students on one side, two on the other, equal distance from balance point

What Happened

Review the section with students. Emphasize bold-face words that identify key concepts and introduce new vocabulary.

*You had to apply equal **force** (weight) to each side of the ruler to make it **balance**. The balance point is also called a **fulcrum**. When the ruler is balanced on the fulcrum, it acts as a **lever**.*

We use levers and fulcrums in different ways for different tasks. Tightrope walkers need equal force on both sides of their long poles (a form of lever), or they will fall!

However, if you're opening a paint can with a screwdriver (lever) you don't want balanced force, or the lid won't open! More force is required on one side of the fulcrum (in this case, the rim of the can) for the process to work.

What We Learned

Answers will vary. Suggested responses are shown at left.

Conclusion

Read this section aloud to the class to summarize the concepts learned in this activity.

Food for Thought

Read the Scripture aloud to the class. Discuss the importance of "balance" in life. Talk about how we can create a place and time for peaceful moments with God.

Journal

If time permits, have a general class discussion about students' journal entries. Share and compare observations. Be sure to emphasize that "trial and error" is a valuable part of scientific inquiry!

! CONCLUSION

Balance is a result of equal force applied to both sides of a lever. Using levers and fulcrums, we use balance in many ways to make our work easier.

FOOD FOR THOUGHT

Matthew 14:23 Scripture tells us that Jesus always made special time to be alone with God. This is what helped him keep his life in balance no matter what happened.

But sometimes we get so busy with school and sports and music and hobbies and all sorts of other things, that we forget about God. Leaving God out of our lives will eventually make us unbalanced. This leads to all sorts of problems! Fortunately, God never forgets about us. Ask your teacher to help you discover ways to spend more time with God. Begin now to find balance for the rest of your life!

JOURNAL My Science Notes

Extended Teaching

1. Repeat this activity, using different numbers of pennies or different placement. Challenge students to find variations that will still keep the ruler balanced.

2. Have students research other simple machines. Challenge each team to create a poster showing a simple machine and explaining some of its uses.

3. Have students write a paragraph explaining why a taller person can usually kick a ball much farther than a shorter person.

4. Have students list other forms of levers they can find at school, home, or around town. Have a group discussion comparing these lists.

5. Invite a baseball or softball coach to visit your classroom. Have him/her explain the correct way to hold a bat. Discuss how hand placement affects torque. Encourage students to practice what they've learned.

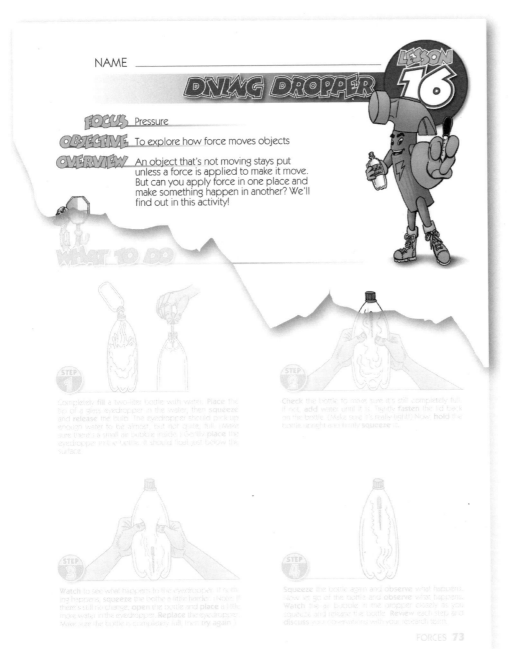

Category

Physical Science
Forces

Focus

Pressure

Objective

To explore how force moves objects

National Standards

A1, A2, B1, B2, D1, E1, E2, E3, F5, G1

Materials Needed

eyedropper
soft drink bottle (2 liter)
water

Safety Concerns

4. Slipping
There is a potential for spills with this activity. Remind students to exercise caution.

Additional Comments

A couple of things can keep this activity from working, but both problems are easily fixed. If the bottle isn't completely full, the air bubble under the lid will contract instead of the bubble in the eyedropper. To correct this problem, remove the lid and fill the bottle with water. Another problem is the amount of water in the eyedropper. The eyedropper should just barely float. Otherwise the bubble is too big and the pressure will have little result. To correct this problem, simply draw a little more water into the eyedropper.

Overview

Read the overview aloud to the students. Your goal is to create an atmosphere of curiosity and inquiry.

WHAT TO DO

Monitor student research teams as they complete each step.

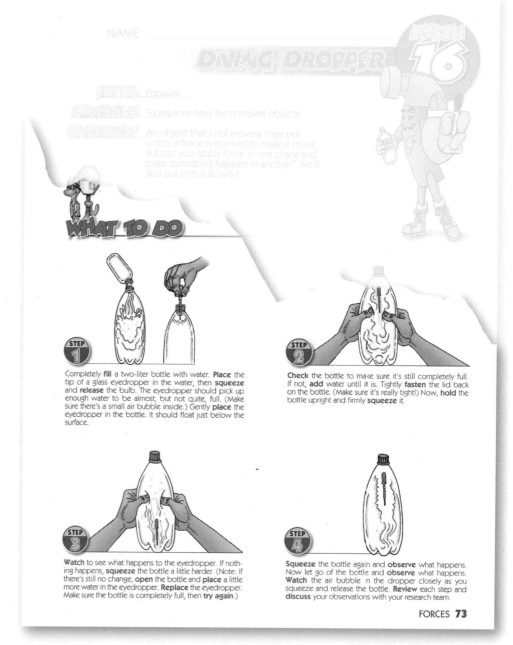

NAME

DIVING DROPPER

LESSON 16

TOPIC: Pressure

OBJECTIVE: To explore how force moves objects

OVERVIEW: An object that's not moving stays put unless a force is applied to make it move. But can you apply force in one place and make something happen in another? We'll find out in this activity!

WHAT TO DO

STEP 1
Completely **fill** a two-liter bottle with water. **Place** the tip of a glass eyedropper in the water, then **squeeze** and **release** the bulb. The eyedropper should pick up enough water to be almost, but not quite, full. (Make sure there's a small air bubble inside.) Gently **place** the eyedropper in the bottle. It should float just below the surface.

STEP 2
Check the bottle to make sure it's still completely full. If not, **add** water until it is. Tightly **fasten** the lid back on the bottle. (Make sure it's really tight!) Now, **hold** the bottle upright and firmly **squeeze** it.

STEP 3
Watch to see what happens to the eyedropper. If nothing happens, **squeeze** the bottle a little harder. (Note: If there's still no change, **open** the bottle and **place** a little more water in the eyedropper. **Replace** the eyedropper. Make sure the bottle is completely full, then **try again**.)

STEP 4
Squeeze the bottle again and **observe** what happens. Now let go of the bottle and **observe** what happens. **Watch** the air bubble in the dropper closely as you squeeze and release the bottle. **Review** each step and **discuss** your observations with your research team.

FORCES **73**

Teacher to Teacher

The science of fluids and their movement is called hydraulics. Our modern world depends on hydraulics. For example, an automobile's steering, brakes, transmission, shocks, cooling system, and oil pressure can all be hydraulic in action. Also, most of the electricity we use in our homes and schools is either generated by fluids (hydro-electric dams) or otherwise dependent on them (cooling systems for nuclear plants). Even our bodies rely on hydraulic systems. They must have plenty of fluids, and these fluids must circulate correctly for optimum health. Problems with the systems that regulate and control our fluids can be serious, even leading to death!

What Happened

Review the section with students. Emphasize bold-face words that identify key concepts and introduce new vocabulary.

Gravity is always trying to pull things down. In order to keep the eyedropper floating, another force had to oppose (fight) gravity. In this case, the trapped air bubble provided buoyancy (floating) to oppose gravity and keep the eyedropper floating.

But when you squeezed the bottle, you added another force! Since liquids (like water) can't compress, but gases (like air) can, change could only occur in the eyedropper. When you squeezed the bottle, it compressed the bubble, letting more water in the eyedropper. This made the eyedropper heavier, so it sank! Releasing the force made the bubble expand, pushing out water so the eyedropper could float again.

Applying force in one place caused something to happen in another. Scientists call this the "transfer of forces."

What We Learned

Answers will vary. Suggested responses are shown at left.

WHAT HAPPENED?

Gravity is always trying to **pull** things down. In order to keep the eyedropper floating, another **force** had to **oppose** (fight) gravity. In this case, the trapped air bubble provided **buoyancy** (floating) to oppose gravity and keep the eyedropper floating.

But when you squeezed the bottle, you added another force! Since **liquids** (like water) can't **compress**, but **gases** (like air) can, change could only occur in the eyedropper. When you squeezed the bottle it compressed the bubble, letting more water in the eyedropper. This made the eyedropper heavier, so it sank! Releasing the force made the bubble **expand**, pushing out water so that the eyedropper could float again.

Applying force in one place caused something to happen in another. Scientists call this the "**transfer of forces.**"

WHAT WE LEARNED

1 In Step 1, what force was trying to pull your eyedropper down? Why didn't the eyedropper sink?

a) gravity

b) answers should reflect an opposing force; "it was floating," "the air bubble held it up," etc.

2 Why was it important to make sure the lid was screwed on tightly in Step 2?

without a tight lid, the water would come out of the bottle when pressure was applied

3 What happened when you squeezed the bottle in Step 3? Where did the force that made the dropper sink come from?

a) answers will vary

b) the student squeezing the bottle

4 In Step 4, what happened when you stopped squeezing the bottle (stopped applying force)? Why?

a) the eyedropper came back up

b) answers should reflect that the force is gone, and equilibrium regained

5 Using what you learned in this activity, explain how submarines dive and surface. Would a sub need more or less water in its tanks to dive? What would it need to do to surface?

Answers should reflect the fact that submarines must get heavier to dive, so they have to take on water. The reverse is true for surfacing

Conclusion

Read this section aloud to the class to summarize the concepts learned in this activity.

Food for Thought

Read the Scripture aloud to the class. Discuss how we can allow God's power to influence our lives. Continue the discussion of quiet, prayerful places from Lesson 15.

Journal

If time permits, have a general class discussion about students' journal entries. Share and compare observations. Be sure to emphasize that "trial and error" is a valuable part of scientific inquiry!

 **CONCLUSION**

Forces move things. Planes fly, cars drive, submarines dive . . . all thanks to different forces making them move. Force can also be transferred from one place to another.

 **FOOD FOR THOUGHT**

Mark 9:23; 10:27 Sometimes we face things that seem impossible — like schoolwork, a big project, or a situation at home. But just as we put our force into the bottle to help the eyedropper dive, God can put his force inside us to help us accomplish what seems impossible!

How can this happen? Spend time each day getting to know God better, and soon you'll learn to trust Him with all your needs. Get connected with God, the source of all power, and dive into life!

JOURNAL My Science Notes

Extended Teaching

1. Have students make a list of various fluids they find at home. Have them describe each fluid and explain how it is used. Compare safe and unsafe fluids.

2. Take a field trip to an automotive garage. Discuss the kinds of fluids an automobile needs and what purpose they serve. Talk about what happens when a fluid leaks.

3. Take a field trip to a hydroelectric dam. Find out how it works. Have teams make posters describing and illustrating their findings.

4. Place a map of the United States on the bulletin board. Have students research where several large hydroelectric dams are located. Mark these on the map.

5. Blood is an important fluid! Invite a nurse to visit your class to talk about blood pressure. Take blood pressure readings of volunteers before and after exercise. Discuss what we can do to maintain good blood pressure.

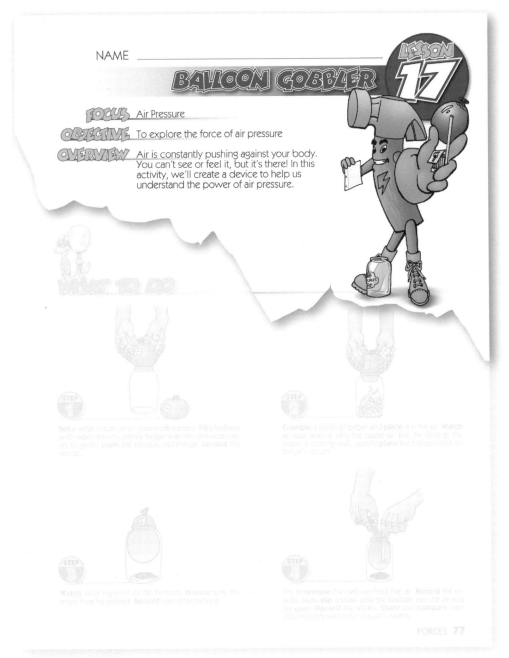

Category

Physical Science
Forces

Focus

Air Pressure

Objective

To explore the force of air pressure

National Standards

A1, A2, B1, B2, B3, D1, D3, E3, G1

Materials Needed

balloon
soda straw
glass jar (1 gallon, wide-mouth)
lighter
paper

Safety Concerns

2. Open Flame
Remind students to exercise caution around the open flame and with the hot jar.

4. Breakage
Remind students to exercise caution when handling the glass jar.

Additional Comments

Keep a few extra water balloons handy in case of accidents. Depending on the maturity of your students, you may wish to do this activity as a teacher demonstration only. Although this activity is relatively safe, it's a good idea to keep a fire extinguisher handy in case of emergencies.

Overview

Read the overview aloud to your students. The goal is to create an atmosphere of curiosity and inquiry.

WHAT TO DO

Monitor student research teams as they complete each step.

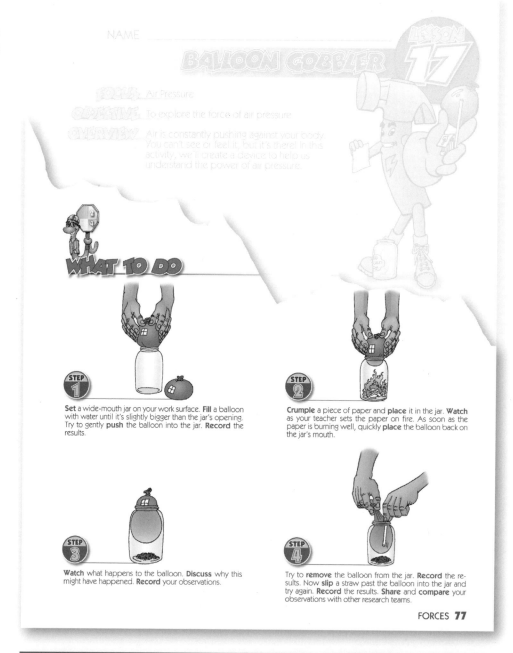

NAME

BALLOON GOBBLER

LESSON 17

FOCUS: Air Pressure

OBJECTIVE: To explore the force of air pressure

OVERVIEW: Air is constantly pushing against your body. You can't see or feel it, but it's there! In this activity, we'll create a device to help us understand the power of air pressure.

WHAT TO DO

STEP 1
Set a wide-mouth jar on your work surface. **Fill** a balloon with water until it's slightly bigger than the jar's opening. Try to gently **push** the balloon into the jar. **Record** the results.

STEP 2
Crumple a piece of paper and **place** it in the jar. **Watch** as your teacher sets the paper on fire. As soon as the paper is burning well, quickly **place** the balloon back on the jar's mouth.

STEP 3
Watch what happens to the balloon. **Discuss** why this might have happened. **Record** your observations.

STEP 4
Try to **remove** the balloon from the jar. **Record** the results. Now **slip** a straw past the balloon into the jar and try again. **Record** the results. **Share** and **compare** your observations with other research teams.

FORCES **77**

Teacher to Teacher

Air pressure differences don't just push/pull balloons into a jar. They also control our weather! Think of a high pressure area as a mountain of air, and a low pressure area as a valley. Heavy, moisture-laden clouds slide down the side of the mountain into the valley where they begin to pile up. High air pressure is usually associated with clear weather; low air pressure usually means cloudy or wet weather. Meteorology is the science that uses air pressure difference (and other data) to predict day-to-day changes and make weather forecasts.

WHAT HAPPENED?

Air is made of tiny invisible particles called **molecules**. In Step 1, the balloon wouldn't go in because the jar was full of air molecules. **Burning** the paper in Step 2 caused the air to expand, pushing a lot of molecules past the balloon and out of the jar. (You probably saw them shaking the balloon.)

The fire used all the **oxygen** in the jar and went out. As the remaining air began to cool, the molecules began to **contract** (squeeze together). This made the **air pressure** inside the jar lower than the air pressure outside. The combination of low pressure inside **pulling**, and high pressure outside **pushing**, forced the balloon into the jar.

But the lower air pressure in the jar trapped the balloon! You couldn't pull it back out until you slipped the straw past it, allowing pressure in the jar to **equalize** again.

WHAT WE LEARNED

1 Why wouldn't the balloon go into the jar in Step 1? What was holding it out?

answers will vary, but should include the idea that the air in the jar was holding it out

2 How did the burning paper affect the air pressure in the jar? Describe the balloon's behavior as the fire burned.

a) the burning paper caused the air to expand

b) it jumped, it wobbled, it bounced, etc.

3 Describe what happened to the balloon in Step 3. Why did this occur?

a) it began to be pulled/pushed into the jar

b) the cooling air in the jar created lower air pressure

4 Explain how the straw helped you remove the balloon from the jar in Step 4.

the straw let air into the jar, equalizing the pressure inside and outside the jar

5 When you pour liquid from a full bottle, it doesn't pour smoothly. When the bottle is nearly empty, the flow becomes smooth. Based on what you learned, explain why this happens.

nearly empty bottle lets air in as liquid flows out, equalizing pressure; nearly full bottle doesn't

What Happened

Review the section with students. Emphasize bold-face words that identify key concepts and introduce new vocabulary.

Air is made of tiny invisible particles called **molecules.** *In Step 1, the balloon wouldn't go in because the jar was full of air molecules.* **Burning** *the paper in Step 2 caused the air to expand, pushing a lot of molecules past the balloon and out of the jar. (You probably saw them shaking the balloon.)*

The fire used all the **oxygen** *in the jar and went out. As the remaining air began to cool, the molecules began to* **contract** *(squeeze together). This made the* **air pressure** *inside the jar lower than the air pressure outside. The combination of low pressure inside* **pulling,** *and high pressure outside* **pushing,** *forced the balloon into the jar.*

But the lower air pressure in the jar trapped the balloon! You couldn't pull it back out until you slipped the straw past it, allowing pressure in the jar to **equalize** *again.*

What We Learned

Answers will vary. Suggested responses are shown at left.

Conclusion

Read this section aloud to the class to summarize the concepts learned in this activity.

Food for Thought

Read the Scripture aloud to the class. Discuss ways we can learn to trust God more fully and open our hearts to his life-changing power.

Journal

If time permits, have a general class discussion about students' journal entries. Share and compare observations. Be sure to emphasize that "trial and error" is a valuable part of scientific inquiry!

 **CONCLUSION**

Air is made of tiny particles called molecules. Air molecules take up space, and are constantly pushing or pulling on everything. Scientists call the push/pull action of air molecules "air pressure."

 **FOOD FOR THOUGHT**

Matthew 19:25-26 When you first tried to push the balloon into the jar, it seemed impossible. How could such a big balloon fit through that small opening? But you trusted your teacher to show you a way, and the balloon popped through without your pushing at all!

In this Scripture, the disciples are worried. Looking at their own efforts, they can't see how it's possible for anyone to be saved. But Jesus reminds them that the answer is to trust God. The impossible doesn't happen because of what we try to do, but from relying totally on God's power!

JOURNAL My Science Notes

Extended Teaching

1. Challenge each team to list places air pressure is really important! (bicycle tires, air tools, weather, balloons, lungs, etc.) Share these lists with the class.

2. Take a field trip to a garage or construction site. Discuss tools that use air pressure to work. Have a crew member demonstrate their use.

3. Using the Internet, search for sites that will let students view satellite and radar images. Based on what they've learned, challenge them to point out high and low pressure systems. (Hint: look for clouds!)

4. Have students research air pressure on high mountains. How do climbers compensate for this? What are the potential dangers of long exposure to low air pressure?

5. Purchase an inexpensive barometer and mount it in your classroom. Have students record the pressure each day and compare it to the weather outside. After a few weeks, make comparisions and draw conclusions.

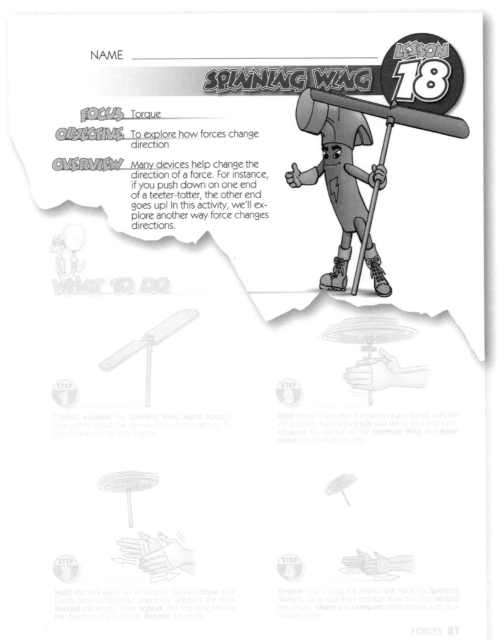

NAME _____

SPINNING WING

LESSON 18

FOCUS Torque

OBJECTIVE To explore how forces change direction

OVERVIEW Many devices help change the direction of a force. For instance, if you push down on one end of a teeter-totter, the other end goes up! In this activity, we'll explore another way force changes directions.

WHAT TO DO

STEP 1 Carefully examine the Spinning Wing. Make notes in your journal about the various parts of the device. Pay special attention to their shapes.

STEP 2 Hold the stick between the palms of your hands with the wing on top. Now slowly rub your hands back and forth. Observe the motion of the Spinning Wing and make notes about what you see.

STEP 3 Hold the stick again as in Step 2. Quickly move your hands once in opposite directions, releasing the stick. Record the results. Now repeat, but this time reverse the direction of your hands. Record the results.

STEP 4 Repeat Step 3 using the motion that made the Spinning Wing fly. Give each team member three tries, then record the results. Share and compare observations with your research team.

FORCES **81**

Category

Physical Science
Forces

Focus

Torque

Objective

To explore how forces change direction

National Standards

A1, A2, B1, B2, E1, E2, E3, F5, G1

Materials Needed

spinning wing

Safety Concerns

4. Other
To avoid bruises or cuts, keep noses, hair, fingers, etc., away from the spinning surface. Encourage students to start by spinning the wing slowly until they develop some skill.

Additional Comments

This activity requires plenty of room, so use the gym — or the playground when winds are calm. Spinning Wings are fragile, so encourage careful use. Caution students to watch where they're going when chasing their Spinning Wing.

Overview

Read the overview aloud to the students. Your goal is to create an atmosphere of curiosity and inquiry.

WHAT TO DO

Monitor student research teams as they complete each step.

Step 3

A counter-clockwise spin makes the wing go up; a clockwise spin makes it go down.

Step 4

Differences in motor skills development may cause some students difficulty. If you see students having problems, join the group and demonstrate. This will shift the focus from the skill to the observation process.

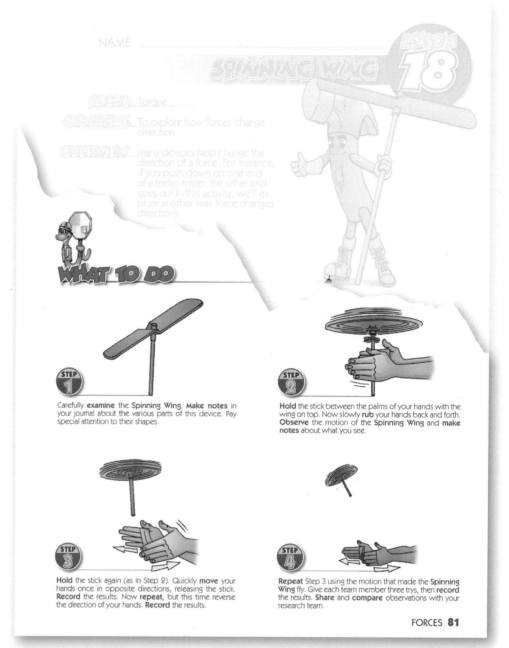

NAME

SPINNING WING

LESSON 18

FOCUS Torque

OBJECTIVE To explore how forces change direction

OVERVIEW Many devices help change the direction of a force. For instance, if you push down on one end of a teeter-totter, the other end goes up! In this activity, we'll explore another way force changes directions.

WHAT TO DO

STEP 1 Carefully **examine** the Spinning Wing. **Make notes** in your journal about the various parts of this device. Pay special attention to their shapes.

STEP 2 **Hold** the stick between the palms of your hands with the wing on top. Now slowly **rub** your hands back and forth. **Observe** the motion of the Spinning Wing and **make notes** about what you see.

STEP 3 **Hold** the stick again (as in Step 2). Quickly **move** your hands once in opposite directions, releasing the stick. **Record** the results. Now **repeat**, but this time reverse the direction of your hands. **Record** the results.

STEP 4 **Repeat** Step 3 using the motion that made the Spinning Wing fly. Give each team member three trys, then **record** the results. **Share** and **compare** observations with your research team.

FORCES **81**

Teacher to Teacher

The scientific study of how objects move is called mechanics. Torque and changing the direction of force are key concepts in mechanics. Many machines use these processes to perform useful work. For example, the up/down movement of your car's pistons is converted to a circular motion by the crankshaft, and with the help of the transmission, provides torque to the wheels. Non-mechanical examples of torque include pedaling a bicycle, batting a ball, and prying open a paint can.

?WHAT HAPPENED?

The shape of the wing is what makes the **Spinning Wing** fly. When you made the wing spin, its shape caused the air to go over the top faster than under the bottom. Faster air has lower **air pressure**, so the wing was **pulled** upward. Scientists call this upward force **lift**.

So how was the direction of **force** changed? Your hands moved back and forth, but the stick changed the direction to round and round, then the wing changed the direction to up!

The twisting force you used is called **torque**. The more torque you provided, the longer your **Spinning Wing** flew. Torque is an important force in many modern devices.

?WHAT WE LEARNED

1 Describe your observations from Step 1. How were the two sides of the wing different? Where did the stick fasten to the wing? Why do you think this was important?

a) answers will vary

b) their tilt was opposite

c) in the center

d) for balance

2 How were the two parts of Step 3 similar? How were they different? Which way did your right hand need to move (toward your body or away) in order to make the Spinning Wing fly?

a) both required the same hand motion

b) the wing spun in a different direction

c) away

3 What force caused the Spinning Wing to spin? What force caused it to move upward? What force was trying to pull it down?

a) torque

b) lift

c) gravity

4 Where did the energy to make the Spinning Wing fly come from? When you moved your hands faster (providing more torque), what did the Spinning Wing do?

a) force was provided by the student

b) flew longer, higher, faster, etc.

5 Based on what you've learned, describe at least two other devices that use torque (twisting force).

answers will vary; examples include boats (propellers), cars (drive train), bicycles (pedaling), batting a ball, using a pencil sharpener, jumping rope, etc.

What Happened

Review the section with students. Emphasize bold-face words that identify key concepts and introduce new vocabulary.

*The shape of the wing is what makes the Spinning Wing fly. When you made the wing spin, its shape caused the air to go over the top faster than under the bottom. Faster air has lower **air pressure**, so the wing was **pulled** upward. Scientists call this upward force **lift**.*

*So how was the direction of **force** changed? Your hands moved back and forth, but the stick changed the direction to round and round, then the wing changed the direction to up!*

*The twisting force you used is called **torque**. The more torque you provided, the longer your Spinning Wing flew. Torque is an important force in many modern devices.*

What We Learned

Answers will vary. Suggested responses are shown at left.

Conclusion

Read this section aloud to the class to summarize the concepts learned in this activity.

Food for Thought

Read the Scripture aloud to the class. Discuss what it means to "change the direction of your life." Talk about ways we can become more open to God's will for our lives.

Journal

If time permits, have a general class discussion about students' journal entries. Share and compare observations. Be sure to emphasize that "trial and error" is a valuable part of scientific inquiry!

 CONCLUSION

All movement requires some kind of force. Twisting force is called torque. Many devices are designed to cause force to change directions.

 FOOD FOR THOUGHT

II Corinthians 5:17 In this activity, you discovered how a force can change directions. You moved your hands one way, but the **Spinning Wing** moved in another.

This Scripture talks about a change of direction that's caused by the force of God's love. The apostle Paul says that when your heart is filled with God's love, it changes the direction of your life so much that you're like a brand-new person!

JOURNAL **My Science Notes**

Extended Teaching

1. Invite a pilot to visit your classroom. Discuss the roles of torque, lift, and gravity on an airplane. Have students write a paragraph about one thing they learned.

2. Have students research wing shapes and designs through history. The NASA website (www.nasa.gov) is a great place to start! Have teams report their findings to the class.

3. Challenge teams to list devices that change the direction of force. Share these lists with the class. Talk about how each device works.

4. Take a "torque safari"! Tour your school, making a list of devices or places where torque is used. Challenge teams to make a poster depicting one item found on the hunt, including a description of how it works.

5. Assign each team a famous person connected with flying (Leonardo Da Vinci, Amelia Earhart, Wilber or Orville Wright, Eddie Rickenbacker, Wiley Post, Chuck Yeager, Igor Sigorsky, etc.). Have them make a bulletin board about this person.

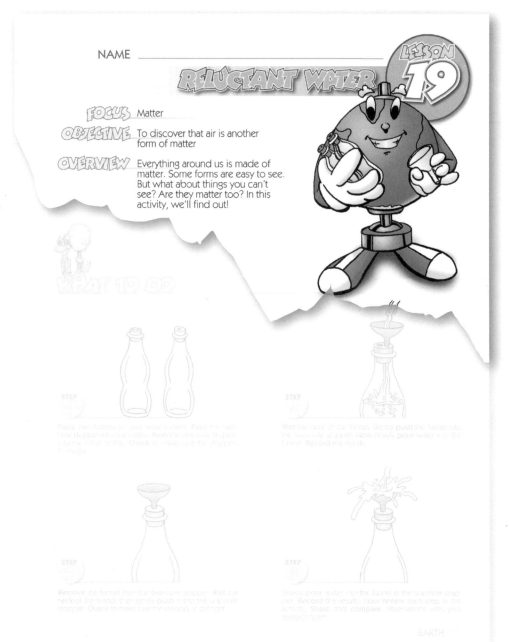

NAME

FOCUS Matter

OBJECTIVE To discover that air is another form of matter

OVERVIEW Everything around us is made of matter. Some forms are easy to see. But what about things you can't see? Are they matter too? In this activity, we'll find out!

Category

Earth Science

Focus

Matter

Objective

To discover that air is a form of matter

National Standards

A1, A2, B1, B2, D1, D3, E3, G1

Materials Needed

one-hole stopper (#3)
two-hole stopper (#3)
plastic funnel
water
soft drink bottles - 2

Safety Concerns

4. Slipping
There is a potential for spills with this activity. Remind students to exercise caution.

Additional Comments

Soft drink bottles (20 oz.) work well for this activity. The bottles tend to be top-heavy with a funnel full of water, so caution students to hold them steady. Depending on the motor-skills development of your students, this activity can be a little messy. Keep paper towels and a mop handy in case clean-up is needed.

Overview

Read the overview aloud to your students. The goal is to create an atmosphere of curiosity and inquiry.

WHAT TO DO

Monitor student research teams as they complete each step.

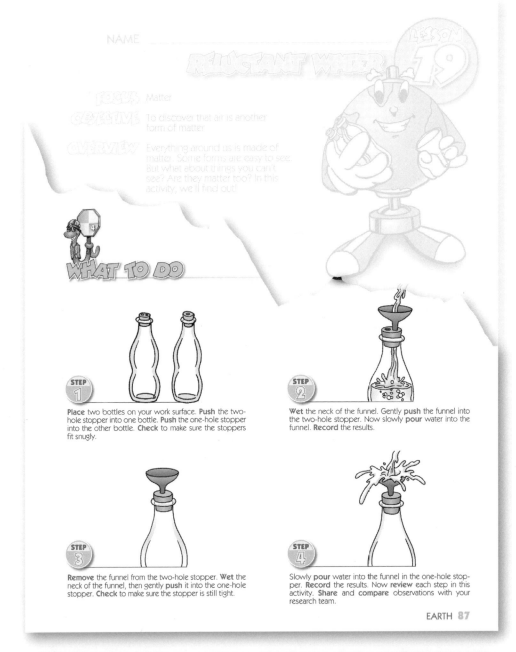

Matter

To discover that air is another form of matter

Everything around us is made of matter. Some forms are easy to see. But what about things you can't see? Are they matter too? In this activity, we'll find out!

WHAT TO DO

STEP 1
Place two bottles on your work surface. **Push** the two-hole stopper into one bottle. **Push** the one-hole stopper into the other bottle. **Check** to make sure the stoppers fit snugly.

STEP 2
Wet the neck of the funnel. Gently **push** the funnel into the two-hole stopper. Now slowly **pour** water into the funnel. **Record** the results.

STEP 3
Remove the funnel from the two-hole stopper. **Wet** the neck of the funnel, then gently **push** it into the one-hole stopper. **Check** to make sure the stopper is still tight.

STEP 4
Slowly **pour** water into the funnel in the one-hole stopper. **Record** the results. Now review each step in this activity. **Share** and **compare** observations with your research team.

EARTH **87**

Teacher to Teacher

Since air is a gas, the idea that it's a form of matter is sometimes hard to grasp (both literally and figuratively). Yet matter is defined as anything that has mass and volume, so air easily qualifies. This activity was a good way to prove the concept, but many other examples surround us — the "whoosh" of a passing truck, the strong winds of a thunderstorm, the "pop" in your ears when you close the door on a new car, etc.

What Happened

Review the section with students. Emphasize bold-face words that identify key concepts and introduce new vocabulary.

*Are there **forms** of **matter** that you can't see? Yes! Even though you couldn't see anything in the bottle, it was full of the gaseous matter we call **air.***

*Trying to add **water** to the bottles showed the presence of this invisible matter. In Step 2, the water flowed smoothly into one hole while the air came out the other. But in Step 4, there was no way for the air to get out. The water had a hard time getting in because invisible matter (air) was in the way!*

*Earth's **atmosphere** (air) is constantly **pushing** and **pulling** everything on the planet. This constant movement of matter even shoves around large air masses full of energy, creating what we call weather!*

What We Learned

Answers will vary. Suggested responses are shown at left.

WHAT HAPPENED?

Are there **forms** of **matter** that you can't see? Yes! Even though you couldn't see anything in the bottle, it was full of the gaseous matter we call **air.**

Trying to add **water** to the bottles showed the presence of this invisible matter. In Step 2, the water flowed smoothly into one hole while the air came out the other. But in Step 4, there was no way for the air to get out. The water had a hard time getting in because invisible matter (air) was in the way!

Earth's **atmosphere** (air) is constantly **pushing** and **pulling** everything on the planet. This constant movement of matter even shoves around large air masses full of energy, creating what we call weather!

WHAT WE LEARNED

1 In Step 1, why was it important for the stoppers to fit snuggly? What form of matter was in the bottles?

a) so air could only come out the holes

b) air

2 Describe what happened in Step 2. What happened to the water? How did the air leave the bottle?

a) the water flowed into the bottle easily

b) through the open hole in the stopper

3 Describe what happened in Step 4. What happened to the water? Why couldn't the air leave the bottle?

a) it was difficult to get the water into the bottle

b) there was only an "in" hole, not an "out" hole

4 Based on what you've learned, explain how you know that matter can be invisible.

answers will vary, but should reflect the results of this activity

5 Give two examples of air moving something.

answers will vary; examples include windmills, kites, swaying trees, etc.

Conclusion

Read this section aloud to the class to summarize the concepts learned in this activity.

Food for Thought

Read the Scripture aloud to the class. Talk about why people might be reluctant to let God into their lives. Discuss ways we can reach out to others.

Journal

If time permits, have a general class discussion about students' journal entries. Share and compare observations. Be sure to emphasize that "trial and error" is a valuable part of scientific inquiry!

 **CONCLUSION**

Everything around us is made of matter — even some things we can't see! Air is a form of matter. Air takes up space and can move. It also can move other things.

 **FOOD FOR THOUGHT**

Matthew 13:15, 16 In this activity we discovered what happens when two forms of matter try to fit into the same space. The bottles couldn't be full of air and full of water at the same time. There's no room for both inside.

This Scripture reminds us that we have something in common with those bottles. When we're "full of ourselves," there's not much room for God inside. But when we open our hearts, God's love can come rushing in. When God fills our hearts with love, there's no room for selfish things any more!

JOURNAL My Science Notes

Extended Teaching

1. Fill a gallon jug with water, then turn it upside-down. Have students watch the "glug" effect, then determine the moment when the water flows freely. Challenge them to explain what's happening.

2. Have students research the "jet stream." What causes it? How powerful is it? What effect does it have on weather, air travel, etc. Have students write a paragraph or two to describe their findings.

3. Invite a "sailor" to visit your classroom. Discuss how air masses and weather impact a sailboat's operation. Talk about parts of the sailboat and how they utilize the wind.

4. Have students research the "trade winds." What are they? Why were they called this? What effect did they have on early exploration and trade? Have students write a paragraph or two to describe their findings.

5. Take a field trip to visit a TV meteorologist (or have him/her visit your classroom). Ask him/her to show/explain how they measure different things about air in order to predict weather changes.

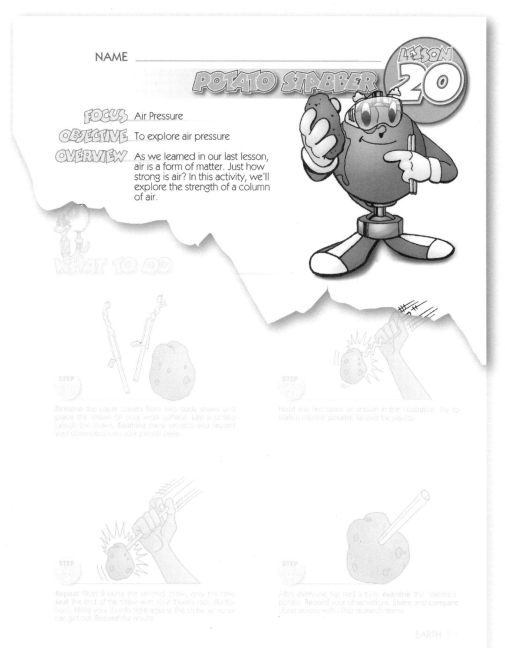

Category
Earth Science

Focus
Air Pressure

Objective
To explore air pressure

National Standards
A1, A2, B1, B2, D1, D3, E1, E2, E3, F5, G1

Materials Needed
straws (2)
fresh potato

Safety Concerns

1. Goggles
There is a potential for flying juice from the potato. Goggles are a reasonable precaution. Caution students not to "stab" their hand!

Additional Comments

The fresher the potato, the better! Sometimes it takes a little practice to stab the straw into the potato. Depending on the motor-skills development of your students, you may wish to do this activity as a teacher demonstration.

Overview

Read the overview aloud to the students. Your goal is to create an atmosphere of curiosity and inquiry.

WHAT TO DO

Monitor student research teams as they complete each step.

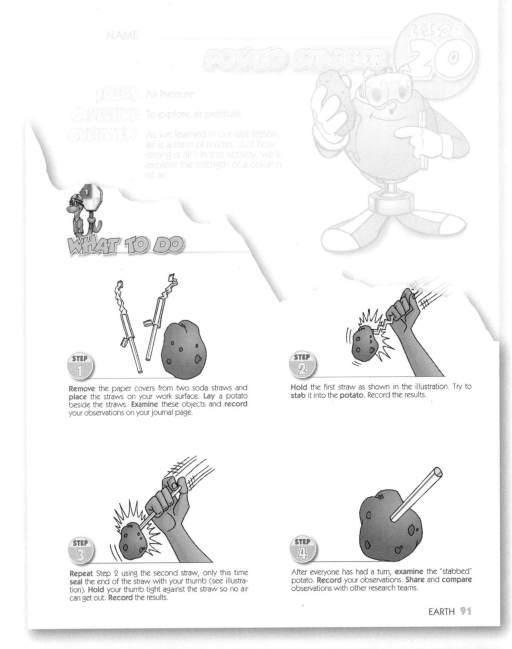

POTATO STABBER

LESSON 20

FOCUS Air Pressure

OBJECTIVE To explore air pressure

OVERVIEW As we learned in our last lesson, air is a form of matter. Just how strong is air? In this activity, we'll explore the strength of a column of air.

WHAT TO DO

STEP 1
Remove the paper covers from two soda straws and **place** the straws on your work surface. **Lay** a potato beside the straws. **Examine** these objects and **record** your observations on your journal page.

STEP 2
Hold the first straw as shown in the illustration. Try to **stab** it into the **potato**. Record the results.

STEP 3
Repeat Step 2 using the second straw, only this time **seal** the end of the straw with your thumb (see illustration). **Hold** your thumb tight against the straw so no air can get out. **Record** the results.

STEP 4
After everyone has had a turn, **examine** the "stabbed" potato. **Record** your observations. **Share** and **compare** observations with other research teams.

EARTH 91

Teacher to Teacher

We usually think of air as almost "not there." But the mass and volume of air can generate tremendous forces: hurricanes, thunderstorms, blizzards, etc. High and low pressure systems create our weather. Air flowing over an airplane's wing creates the lift that allows flight. Pneumatic tools (air wrenches, nailers, staplers, etc.) rely on compressed air to perform many useful tasks. Your car tires are held up by air pressure. And without air pressure, your lungs would cease to function and you'd suffocate!

In Step 2, the straw wasn't strong enough to pierce the potato. When the straw hit the potato, the **air** inside the straw escaped and the straw crumpled. But in Step 3, your finger trapped a column of air inside the straw. When the straw hit the potato, the trapped air **compressed** and its **pressure** helped support the straw. The result was a pierced potato!

Examples of **air pressure** are all around us. The air pressure in tires holds up your car. Air pressure keeps your basketball from going flat. Air pressure is used to run many commercial tools. Air pressure in the **atmosphere** (the air you breathe) even affects the **weather,** creating highs or lows, sunny days or storms.

1. Is air a form of matter? Does it take up space? Explain how you know this.

a) yes

b) yes

c) answers will vary, but should reflect concepts from this activity or Lesson 19

2. Describe what happened when the straw hit the potato in Step 2. What caused this to happen?

a) it crumpled, it broke, it smashed, etc.

b) it had no support, it was weak, etc.

3. Describe what happened when the straw hit the potato in Step 3. What caused this to happen?

a) it stabbed the potato

b) answers will vary, but should reflect the fact that air trapped inside strengthened it

4. Compare Step 2 with Step 3. How were they similar? How were they different?

a) similar: same motion, same potato, same kind of straw

b) different: thumb trapped air inside the straw

5. Give at least three examples of air pressure and tell how they affect us.

answers will vary; examples include air in tires, balls, inflatable water toys, air tools, weather, etc.

What Happened

Review the section with students. Emphasize bold-face words that identify key concepts and introduce new vocabulary.

In Step 2, the straw wasn't strong enough to pierce the potato. When the straw hit the potato, the **air** *inside the straw escaped and the straw crumpled. But in Step 3, your finger trapped a column of air inside the straw. When the straw hit the potato, the trapped air* **compressed** *and its* **pressure** *helped support the straw. The result was a pierced potato!*

Examples of **air pressure** *are all around us. The air pressure in tires holds up your car. Air pressure keeps your basketball from going flat. Air pressure is used to run many commercial tools. Air pressure in the* **atmosphere** *(the air you breathe) even affects the* **weather,** *creating highs or lows, sunny days or storms.*

What We Learned

Answers will vary. Suggested responses are shown at left.

Conclusion

Read this section aloud to the class to summarize the concepts learned in this activity.

Food for Thought

Read the Scripture aloud to the class. Give examples of how God strengthened different people in Scripture. Discuss how learning to trust God gives us strength.

Journal

If time permits, have a general class discussion about students' journal entries. Share and compare observations. Be sure to emphasize that "trial and error" is a valuable part of scientific inquiry!

 **CONCLUSION**

Air has pressure. Air under pressure can do many things. Air pressure even affects the weather.

 **FOOD FOR THOUGHT**

Isaiah 40:21 That weak little straw just didn't have the strength to pierce a tough potato. But when your finger trapped the air, it provided the strength needed to do what seemed impossible!

This Scripture reminds us that our strength comes from God. Your life may seem full of impossible tasks as you try to keep up with school work, the needs of your friends, and responsibilities at home. Just remember to spend time learning to trust God, waiting for him to guide you — and he will give you all the strength you need!

JOURNAL My Science Notes

Extended Teaching

1. Challenge teams to research different examples of air pressure. Have each team make a poster depicting their findings.

2. Visit a garage or construction site. Have someone demonstrate the use of air tools. Discuss both the advantages and dangers of such tools. Have students write a paragraph about something they learn.

3. Have students research thunderstorms. Make a bulletin board with pictures of wind damage. Talk about ways for staying safe during violent weather.

4. Research the Bernoulli Principle. (Students love the sound of this phrase!) Discuss how it creates lift and allows flight. Have teams make posters showing air flow over a wing, and describing how it works.

5. Research ways people have used wind power in the past and are still using it today. Find out about modern technology for grabbing wind power! Have students write a paragraph describing one thing they learn.

NAME _____

LESSON 21

WATERPROOF COTTON

FOCUS   States of Matter

OBJECTIVE   To explore the three states of matter

OVERVIEW   Everything on Earth is made of matter. This matter comes in three forms: solid, liquid, and gas. In this activity, we'll explore these forms with some surprising results!

WHAT TO DO

STEP 1
Hold a cotton ball above a cup of water. Predict what will happen to the cotton ball if you hold it above water. Record this prediction in your journal page.

STEP 2
Push the cotton ball down into the cup. Hold it under the water for a few seconds. Now lift it up and hold it up to the light. Record the results.

STEP 3
Watch as your teacher places cotton balls in a glass. Predict what will happen to the cotton balls when the glass is pushed under the water. Record the data you see on your journal page.

STEP 4
Watch carefully as your teacher pushes the glass under the water. Record your observations. Compare the results with Step 3. Share and compare observations with your research team.

EARTH

Category
Earth Science

Focus
States of Matter

Objective
To explore the three states of matter

National Standards
A1, A2, B1, B2, D1, D3, E1, E2, E3, F5, G1

Materials Needed
cotton balls
plastic cup
aquarium
water
paper towels

Safety Concerns
4. **Slipping**
There is a potential for spills with this activity. Remind students to exercise caution.

Additional Comments

Step 1 and Step 2 are team activities; Step 3 and Step 4 are teacher demonstration. If you don't have access to an aquarium, a large, clear bowl can be substituted as long as the cup can be pushed completely under water. For best results, keep the cup level and push it down slowly. Cotton balls must be wedged securely in the bottom before beginning!

Overview

Read the overview aloud to the students. Your goal is to create an atmosphere of curiosity and inquiry.

WHAT TO DO

Monitor student research teams as they complete each step.

Step 3
The cotton balls must be packed securely in the bottom so they can't move!

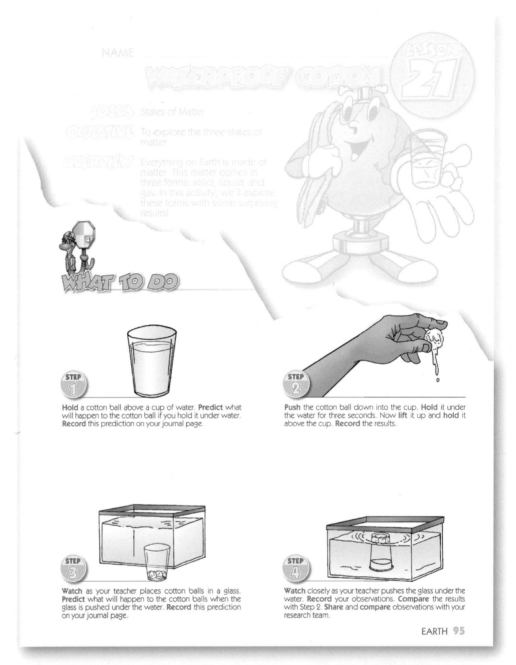

WATERPROOF COTTON

LESSON 21

TOPIC States of Matter

OBJECTIVE To explore the three states of matter

OVERVIEW Everything on Earth is made of matter. This matter comes in three forms: solid, liquid, and gas. In this activity, we'll explore these forms with some surprising results!

WHAT TO DO

STEP 1 **Hold** a cotton ball above a cup of water. **Predict** what will happen to the cotton ball if you hold it under water. **Record** this prediction on your journal page.

STEP 2 **Push** the cotton ball down into the cup. **Hold** it under the water for three seconds. Now **lift** it up and **hold** it above the cup. **Record** the results.

STEP 3 **Watch** as your teacher places cotton balls in a glass. **Predict** what will happen to the cotton balls when the glass is pushed under the water. **Record** this prediction on your journal page.

STEP 4 **Watch** closely as your teacher pushes the glass under the water. **Record** your observations. **Compare** the results with Step 2. **Share** and **compare** observations with your research team.

EARTH 95

Teacher to Teacher

On Earth, the three states of matter are constantly interacting. Large interactions include weather shifts, ocean currents, and plate tectonics. A good example of smaller interactions is eating your lunch: you bite your sandwich (solid), take a sip of your drink (liquid), and continue breathing (gas). The recycling of matter allows both living and non-living things to borrow and use various forms of energy. (By the way, the most common form of matter in the universe doesn't exist on Earth! This fourth state of matter is called plasma.)

⟨?⟩ WHAT HAPPENED?

Most science books define **matter** as something that has **volume** (it takes up space) and **mass** (it has substance). There are three **states** (kinds) of matter: **solid, liquid,** and **gas.** In this activity, the cotton is a solid, the water is a liquid, and the air is a gas.

Many people don't understand how air and other gases can be matter. You can't see air and you usually don't think of air as having substance.

In Step 4 of this activity, your teacher trapped air inside a cup. When the cup was **pushed** under water, the volume and mass of the air pushed back on the water, keeping it out. Instead of water soaking the cotton ball (as in Step 2), the gas/matter/air in the cup kept the water out and the cotton ball dry!

⟨?⟩ WHAT WE LEARNED

1 What are the two main characteristics of matter? What does "volume" mean? What does "mass" mean?

a) volume and mass

b) it takes up space

c) it has substance

2 What are the three states of matter? Give an example of each.

a) solid, liquid, gas

b) answers will vary but should be logical

3 What did you predict in Step 1?
How did this prediction reflect what actually happened?

a) most students will predict that the cotton will get wet

b) the cotton got wet

4 What did you predict in Step 3?
How did this prediction reflect what actually happened?

a) most students will predict that the cotton will get wet

b) the cotton did not get wet

5 Based on what you've learned, explain why the cotton balls didn't get wet in Step 4.

answers will vary, but should include the idea that the mass of the air kept the water out of the cup

What Happened

Review the section with students. Emphasize bold-face words that identify key concepts and introduce new vocabulary.

Most science books define **matter** *as something that has* **volume** *(it takes up space) and* **mass** *(it has substance). There are three* **states** *(kinds) of matter:* **solid, liquid,** *and* **gas.** *In this activity, the cotton is a solid, the water is a liquid, and the air is a gas.*

Many people don't understand how air and other gases can be matter. You can't see air and you usually don't think of air as having substance.

In Step 4 of this activity, your teacher trapped air inside a cup. When the cup was **pushed** *under water, the volume and mass of the air pushed back on the water, keeping it out. Instead of water soaking the cotton ball (as in Step 2), the gas/matter/air in the cup kept the water out and the cotton ball dry!*

What We Learned

Answers will vary. Suggested responses are shown at left.

Conclusion

Read this section aloud to the class to summarize the concepts learned in this activity.

Food for Thought

Read the Scripture aloud to the class. Talk about other examples of God's protection. Discuss how trusting God can lead to things we never thought possible.

Journal

If time permits, have a general class discussion about students' journal entries. Share and compare observations. Be sure to emphasize that "trial and error" is a valuable part of scientific inquiry!

 **CONCLUSION**

Everything on Earth is made of matter. There are three states of matter: solid, liquid, and gas. Each of these states has unique characteristics that affect all of us and the world we live in.

 **FOOD FOR THOUGHT**

Exodus 14:16 Things don't always happen the way we think they will. In Step 3, you probably thought the cotton balls would get soaked, even with the protection of the cup. But that's not what happened at all!

Imagine the people of Israel facing the sea with Pharaoh's army closing in. They probably thought their only choice was to be killed or to drown! But God's mighty power parted the waters, and his people walked to safety on dry land. Whenever things get rough and you think you can't go any further, remember that amazing things are possible through God.

JOURNAL My Science Notes

Extended Teaching

1. Have students research the "diving bell". Challenge each team to create a poster showing similarities and differences between a diving bell and this activity.

2. Create a bulletin board for each of the three states of matter. Label them: Solid, Liquid, Gas. Have students cut out and post pictures on the correct board.

3. Invite a pilot or flight attendant to visit your classroom. Discuss how airplane cabins are pressurized and why this is important. Have them explain what happens in the event pressure is lost.

4. Have students research the history of submarines. Have each team make a poster of a submarine and list ways the three states of matter interact in this environment.

5. Have each team create a three-part poster showing the three states of matter. Challenge them to be creative, using drawings, pictures, and descriptions.

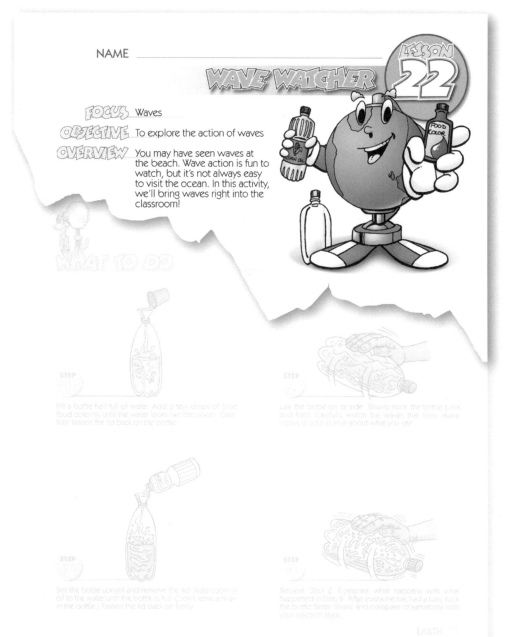

Category

Earth Science

Focus

Waves

Objective

To explore the action of waves

National Standards

A1, A2, B1, B2, D1, D3, E3, F3, G1

Materials Needed

soft drink bottle (2 liter)
water
blue food coloring
cooking oil

Safety Concerns

4. Slipping
There is a potential for spills with this activity. Remind students to exercise caution. The oil can make things *very* slippery!

Additional Comments

This activity is sometimes called the "poor man's lava lamp." Depending on the maturity of your students, you may wish to be the only one to handle the oil. Be very aware of the potential for spills and slipping hazards with this activity.

Overview

Read the overview aloud to your students. The goal is to create an atmosphere of curiosity and inquiry.

WHAT TO DO

Monitor student research teams as they complete each step.

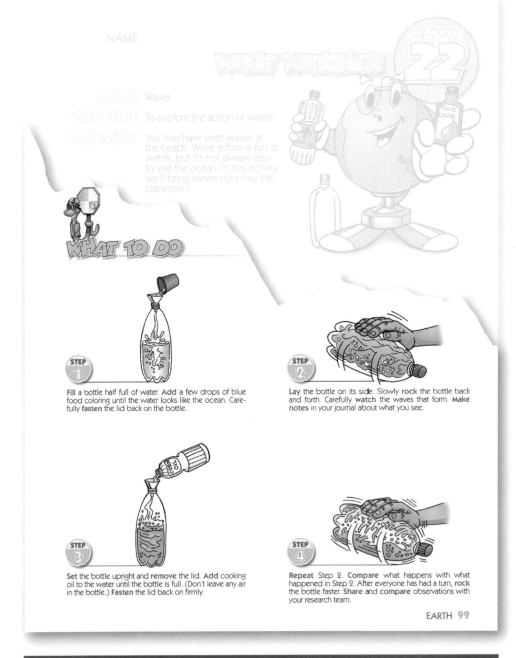

WAVE WATCHER

LESSON 22

FOCUS Waves

OBJECTIVE To explore the action of waves

OVERVIEW You may have seen waves at the beach. Wave action is fun to watch, but it's not always easy to visit the ocean. In this activity, we'll bring waves right into the classroom!

WHAT TO DO

STEP 1 Fill a bottle half full of water. Add a few drops of blue food coloring until the water looks like the ocean. Carefully fasten the lid back on the bottle.

STEP 2 Lay the bottle on its side. Slowly rock the bottle back and forth. Carefully watch the waves that form. Make notes in your journal about what you see.

STEP 3 Set the bottle upright and remove the lid. Add cooking oil to the water until the bottle is full. (Don't leave any air in the bottle.) Fasten the lid back on firmly.

STEP 4 Repeat Step 2. Compare what happens with what happened in Step 2. After everyone has had a turn, rock the bottle faster. Share and compare observations with your research team.

EARTH 99

Teacher to Teacher

All waves (light, sound, heat, electrical, x-ray, etc.) have one thing in common: Energy! Simply put, waves move energy from one place to another. Ocean waves get their energy from the wind, sunlight (temperature differences and currents), gravity (tides), and occasionally from earthquakes. Given the right conditions, an earthquake can produce a huge, dangerous wave called a tsunami (sometimes incorrectly called a "tidal wave" since it has nothing to do with tides!).

?WHAT HAPPENED?

Your muscles provided the energy that created waves in the bottle. Wind (and other forces) provides the energy that creates waves in the ocean. Waves contain powerful amounts of energy. Waves pound shorelines, eroding the land. Waves rearrange beaches by moving sand. Waves carry nutrients needed for life around the planet.

To make your Wave Watcher, you used two liquids — oil and water. Even though the volume of each liquid is about the same, they formed two distinct layers. The oil moved to the top because it is less dense (lighter) than water. The water has greater density than the oil, so the water sank to the bottom.

?WHAT WE LEARNED

1 What was the energy source for the waves in Step 2 and Step 4? What causes waves in the ocean?

a) the students' muscles

b) wind and other forces

2 What ingredients did you use to make your Wave Watcher? How were they similar? How were they different?

a) water, oil

b) both are fluids, used the same volume

c) oil less dense (lighter) than water

3 Compare the wave action in Step 2 with Step 4. How were they similar? How were they different?

answers will vary, but should reflect that action in Step 2 was smoother, and choppy in Step 4

4 Which has the greater density — water or oil? How do you know this?

a) water

b) the water sank, the oil floated

5 Based on what you've learned, if you spilled cooking oil in a swimming pool would it float or sink? Why?

a) float

b) because the cooking oil is lighter (less dense) than the pool water

What Happened

Your muscles provided the **energy** *that created waves in the bottle.* **Wind** *(and other* **forces***) provides the energy that creates waves in the ocean.* **Waves** *contain powerful amounts of energy. Waves pound shorelines,* **eroding** *the land. Waves rearrange beaches by moving sand. Waves carry* **nutrients** *needed for life around the planet.*

To make your Wave Watcher, you used two **liquids** *— oil and water. Even though the* **volume** *of each liquid is about the same, they formed two distinct* **layers***. The oil moved to the top because it is less dense (lighter) than water. The water has greater* **density** *than the oil, so the water sank to the bottom.*

What We Learned

Answers will vary. Suggested responses are shown at left.

Conclusion

Read this section aloud to the class to summarize the concepts learned in this activity.

Food for Thought

Read the Scripture aloud to the class. Talk about some of the "forces" constantly trying to turn our attention away from God. Discuss why spending time with God is the best way to "fight" these forces.

Journal

If time permits, have a general class discussion about students' journal entries. Share and compare observations. Be sure to emphasize that "trial and error" is a valuable part of scientific inquiry!

 **CONCLUSION**

Waves are caused by wind and other forces. Waves help transfer energy around the Earth. Wave action can cause erosion. Wave energy can also move nutrients over vast distances.

 **FOOD FOR THOUGHT**

James 1:5-8 The waves in your bottle didn't have much choice. You could make them move smoothly back and forth, or toss them around in confusion! They were instantly affected by whatever was happening around them.

This Scripture reminds us that our lives don't have to be jumbled and confused like endlessly tossed waves. When you learn to trust in God and listen to his voice, his love can fill your heart with peace — no matter what your surroundings!

JOURNAL My Science Notes

102 EARTH

Extended Teaching

1. Have students research various kinds of waves. Challenge each team to create a poster showing one type of wave and explaining how it transfers energy.

2. Invite a broadcast engineer or ham radio buff to visit your classroom. Discuss radio waves. Talk about the difference between AM and FM waves. Have students write a paragraph about one thing they learn.

3. Make a bulletin board with sections for waves. Label them with titles like Light, Sound, Water, Electric, etc. Have stu-dents post pictures and drawings in the correct sections.

4. Using the Internet, have students find activities that relate to sound waves. (example: http://pbskids.org/zoom/sci/glassxylophonepartii.html) Have each team report on one of these activities. Choose one activity to try as a class.

5. Have students research famous tsunamis. Post a world map on the bulletin board and have them locate and label locations where these huge waves have struck.

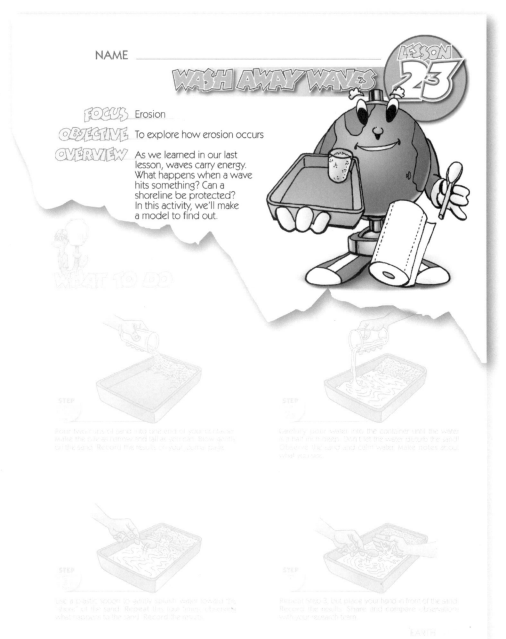

Additional Comments

The best container for this activity is waterproof, rectangular, and clear. This allows students to get better side views of the process. However, a cake pan makes a reasonable substitute, and even a cardboard box lined with plastic will do in a pinch. This activity has the potential to be messy, so keep a supply of paper towels handy.

Overview

Read the overview aloud to your students. The goal is to create an atmosphere of curiosity and inquiry.

Category

Earth Science

Focus

Erosion

Objective

To explore how erosion occurs

National Standards

A1, A2, B1, B2, D1, D3, E1, E2, E3, F3, F5, G1

Materials Needed

sand
paper cup
plastic spoon
container
water

Safety Concerns

4. Slipping
There is a potential for spills with this activity. Remind students to exercise caution.

WHAT TO DO

Monitor student research teams as they complete each step.

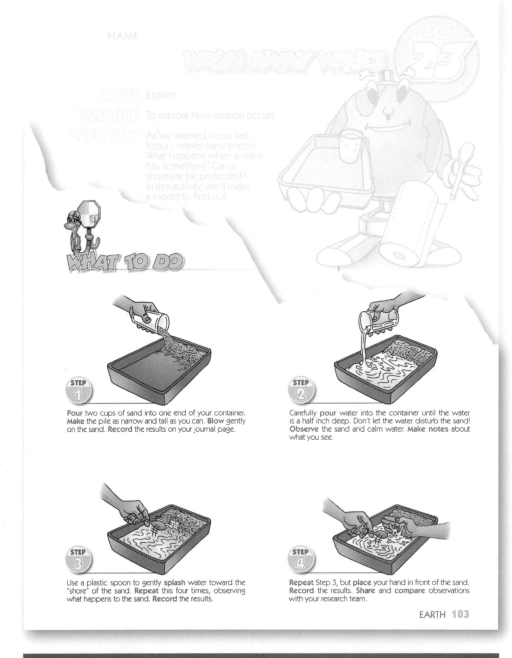

WHAT TO DO

STEP 1

Pour two cups of sand into one end of your container. Make the pile as narrow and tall as you can. Blow gently on the sand. Record the results on your journal page.

STEP 2

Carefully pour water into the container until the water is a half inch deep. Don't let the water disturb the sand! Observe the sand and calm water. Make notes about what you see.

STEP 3

Use a plastic spoon to gently splash water toward the "shore" of the sand. Repeat this four times, observing what happens to the sand. Record the results.

STEP 4

Repeat Step 3, but place your hand in front of the sand. Record the results. Share and compare observations with your research team.

EARTH 103

Teacher to Teacher

As we saw, one way to prevent erosion is with a barrier. But real world solutions aren't always that simple. The Law of Conservation of Energy states that energy cannot be destroyed. Although a new barrier may protect one section of beach, the energy that bounces off may reappear somewhere else! For example, Bayocean, Oregon (once called "The Atlantic City of the East") was completely destroyed by erosion in the early 1900's, due to a major change in ocean currents. Some have speculated that this disaster was the direct result of a huge breakwater built just up the coast.

What Happened

It takes **energy** to make anything move. You provided the energy to move the spoon, which moved the water toward the sand. When the moving water hit the sand, the sand began to move as well. Scientists call this shifting of materials by moving water **erosion**. Erosion can happen along a beach, the shore of a lake, a river bank, or even in the middle of a farmer's field after a heavy rain!

Erosion is a serious problem in some areas. To control erosion along the edges of huge lakes or ocean shorelines, engineers design special **barriers** to **absorb** or **divert** some of the moving water's energy. You **modeled** this in Step 4 when you used your hand as a barrier.

And as you saw in Step 1, wind erosion can also be a potential problem!

WHAT WE LEARNED

1 Describe the model you created in Step 1 and Step 2. What were the parts? What did each part represent?

a) answers will vary

b) sand = beach or river bank;
water = ocean, river, rain, etc.

2 Compare the "shore" in Step 2 with the same shore after Step 3. How were they similar? How were they different?

a) similar: same material

b) different: shape changed

3 Describe what happened in Step 3. When materials are shifted by moving water, what is it called?

a) answers will vary

b) erosion

4 Where did the energy come from in Step 3 and Step 4? What caused the shore to erode in Step 3? What kept it from eroding in Step 4?

a) the student's muscles

b) water hitting the unprotected shore

c) the hand used as a barrier

5 Based on what you've learned, name at least one thing that determines the amount of erosion.

the type of material, the force of the water or wind, the amount of protection, etc.

What Happened

Review the section with students. Emphasize bold-face words that identify key concepts and introduce new vocabulary.

It takes **energy** *to make anything move. You provided the energy to move the spoon, which moved the water toward the sand. When the moving water hit the sand, the sand began to move as well. Scientists call this shifting of materials by moving water* **erosion.** *Erosion can happen along a beach, the shore of a lake, a river bank, or even in the middle of a farmer's field after a heavy rain!*

Erosion is a serious problem in some areas. To control erosion along the edges of huge lakes or ocean shorelines, engineers design special **barriers** *to* **absorb** *or* **divert** *some of the moving water's energy. You* **modeled** *this in Step 4, when you used your hand as a barrier.*

And as you saw in Step 1, wind erosion can also be a potential problem!

What We Learned

Answers will vary. Suggested responses are shown at left.

Conclusion

Read this section aloud to the class to summarize the concepts learned in this activity.

Food for Thought

Read the Scripture aloud to the class. Talk about how "building on the rock" can keep our faith from eroding. Discuss ways to create special moments to commune with God.

Journal

If time permits, have a general class discussion about students' journal entries. Share and compare observations. Be sure to emphasize that "trial and error" is a valuable part of scientific inquiry!

 **CONCLUSION**

Erosion occurs due to the energy in moving water. Unless this energy is absorbed or diverted by a barrier, erosion can damage a shoreline.

 **FOOD FOR THOUGHT**

Matthew 17:20-21 Erosion happens rapidly on soft, sandy surfaces. It takes a little longer when the ground is tougher. But given enough time, erosion can even wear away solid rock!

This Scripture reminds us that our lives are only secure when they're built on the "rock" of a relationship with God. Take time every day to talk to God. Look for ways to learn more about his love and power. Then when problems surround you, like angry waves crashing in, you'll be safe and secure in God's care.

JOURNAL My Science Notes

Extended Teaching

1. Invite an Agricultural Extension Agent to visit your classroom. Find out how land is protected from erosion by planting trees, grasses and shrubs. Have students write a paragraph about one thing they learn.

2. Take a field trip to places in your neighborhood, or along local roads and rivers, to see structures built to control erosion. Challenge each team to make a poster describing one of these structures and how it works.

3. Have students research windbreaks. Ask teams to discover and list ways that windbreaks are help-ful. Have them report one of their findings to the class.

4. Start a collection of rocks that show signs of erosion (by water or wind). Have students compare these rocks to rocks dug from the ground. (Eroded rocks have smooth edges; freshly dug rocks usually don't.)

5. Find out about the Army Corps of Engineers. What is their role in controlling erosion and floods? Have each team create a poster depicting their findings.

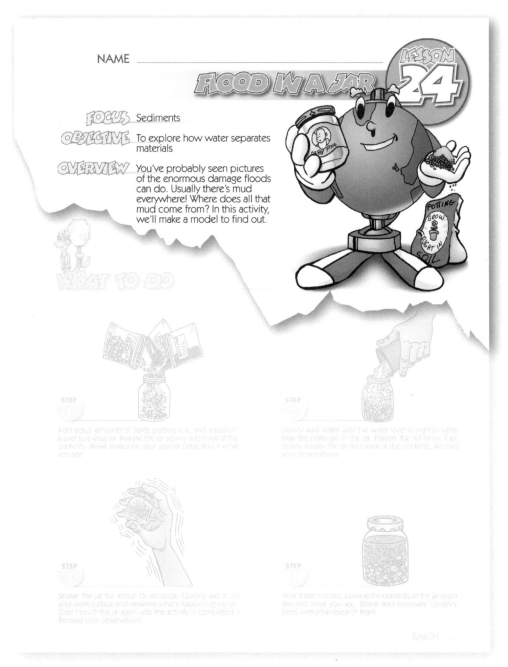

NAME _____

FLOOD IN A JAR

FOCUS Sediments

OBJECTIVE To explore how water separates materials

OVERVIEW You've probably seen pictures of the enormous damage floods can do. Usually there's mud everywhere! Where does all that mud come from? In this activity, we'll make a model to find out.

WHAT TO DO

STEP 1
Add equal amounts of sand, potting soil, and aquarium gravel to a glass jar. Rotate the jar slowly and look at the contents. Make notes on your journal page about what you see.

STEP 2
Slowly add water until the water level is slightly higher than the materials in the jar. Fasten the lid firmly, then slowly rotate the jar and look at the contents. Record your observations.

STEP 3
Shake the jar for about 15 seconds. Quickly set it on your work surface and observe what's happening inside. (Don't touch the jar again until the activity is completed.) Record your observations.

STEP 4
Wait three minutes. Look at the contents of the jar again. Record what you see. Share and compare observations with your research team.

EARTH

Category
Earth Science

Focus
Sediments

Objective
To explore how water separates materials

National Standards
A1, A2, B1, B2, D1, D3, E3, G1

Materials Needed
aquarium gravel
sand
potting soil
small glass jar
water

Safety Concerns

4. Slipping
There is a potential for spills with this activity. Remind students to exercise caution.

4. Breakage
If you use glass baby jars, watch out for breakage. Remind students to exercise caution.

Additional Comments

Be sure the jars seal tightly or this activity can get messy! Also, remind students to keep a tight grip on the jars during the shaking process. You can make up your own mixture using materials other than those listed if you wish. This activity has the potential to be messy, so keep a supply of paper towels handy.

Overview

Read the overview aloud to your students. The goal is to create an atmosphere of curiosity and inquiry.

WHAT TO DO

Monitor student research teams as they complete each step.

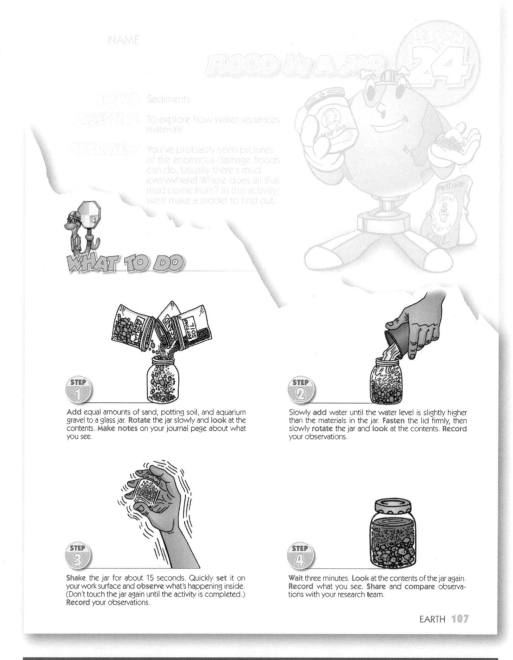

Teacher to Teacher

The terms "suspension" and "solution" are often confused. Sugar water is a good example of a solution. When mixed with a solvent (like water), sugar particles get smaller and smaller (dissolve) until they disappear. When you stop stirring, nothing falls to the bottom. By contrast, a suspension (like the water and sand) only holds materials as long as it's moving. As the water slows, the material begins to sink with the heavier items falling first.

When time and pressure turns these fallen materials (sediment) into rock, the resulting layers are called strata. Often strata formed by floods clearly show the sorting effect described above. The rapid burial process and small particle size also make this kind of strata great for preserving fossils!

When flood waters hit, there's usually a huge amount of material being carried along in the water. The **force** of the water holds and carries these materials until the water slows down. Scientists call this a **suspension**. You demonstrated a suspension when you shook the jar. As long as you kept shaking, the heavy pieces (like gravel) were just mixed in with all the rest.

But when you stopped shaking, gravity began to pull things down. As water slows, it loses energy. Since it takes more energy to keep large materials suspended, they fall first. And since it takes less energy to keep light materials suspended, they fall last and end up on top. This process sorts the materials into layers, and these layers are known as **sediments** (materials that are deposited by wind or water action).

?WHAT WE LEARNED

1 What ingredients did you add to the jar in Step 1?
What happened to these ingredients as you rotated the jar?

a) sand, potting soil, aquarium gravel

b) they became blended or mixed

2 What ingredient did you add in Step 2?
What affect did this have on the materials already in the jar?

a) water

b) it made them wet, muddy, etc.

3 Describe what happened in Step 3.
What did the force of the moving water do to the heavy pieces?

a) answer should be a description of
the shaking process

b) kept them suspended, moving around, etc.

4 Describe the contents of the jar after Step 4. Describe the top layer.
How is it different from the other layers?

a) same materials, but in layers

b) muddy, fine, solid looking, etc.

c) much smaller particles

5 A flood hits your school, sweeping away a stack of test papers, a pile of marbles, and a large iron doorstop. It dumps the debris in a nearby field. Based on what you've learned, where would you look for each item?

test papers on top, marbles near the middle,
doorstop at the lowest spot

What Happened

Review the section with students. Emphasize bold-face words that identify key concepts and introduce new vocabulary.

*When flood waters hit, there's usually a huge amount of material being carried along in the water. The **force** of the water holds and carries these materials until the water slows down. Scientists call this a **suspension**. You demonstrated a suspension when you shook the jar. As long as you kept shaking, the heavy pieces (like gravel) were just mixed in with all the rest.*

*But when you stopped shaking, **gravity** began to **pull** things down. As water slows, it loses **energy**. Since it takes more energy to keep large materials suspended, they fall first. And since it takes less energy to keep light materials suspended, they fall last and end up on top. This process **sorts** the materials into **layers**, and these layers are known as **sediments** (materials that are deposited by wind or water action).*

What We Learned

Answers will vary. Suggested responses are shown at left.

Conclusion

Read this section aloud to the class to summarize the concepts learned in this activity.

Food for Thought

Read the Scripture aloud to the class. Talk about God's amazing power. Discuss ways we can allow God's power to enter our hearts and lives.

Journal

If time permits, have a general class discussion about notes and drawings various students added to their journal pages. Discuss correct and incorrect predictions, and remind students that this "trial and error" process is part of the scientific process.

CONCLUSION

Moving water has energy that can carry materials long distances in a mixture called a suspension. As moving water slows, the heaviest materials settle out first. The lightest materials can form sediments.

FOOD FOR THOUGHT

Psalm 29:10 Your model demonstrated how the power of moving water can suspend heavy objects. You may have seen pictures of floods sweeping away bridges, huge trees, even homes and businesses! Moving water has tremendous power!

Although a raging flood may seem like one of the most powerful forces on Earth, this Scripture reminds us that even during the largest flood ever known, God was still in control. What tremendous power! Isn't it amazing to think that this powerful God knows you individually and that his love for you will last forever?

JOURNAL My Science Notes

110 EARTH

Extended Teaching

1. Invite a representative of the Army Corp of Engineers to visit your classroom. Talk about floods and the importance of dams in flood control. Have students write a paragraph about one thing they learn.

2. Research dam construction. Do dams ever do more harm than good? (See China's "three gorges" dam.) Have a class discussion about man's responsibilty when modifying the environment.

3. Invite a "rock hound" to visit your classroom. Ask him/her to bring samples of sedimentary rocks. See if students can point out the various strata. Challenge each team to create a poster about sedimentary rocks.

4. Take a field trip to a nearby river or stream, or a road construction site cutting through a hill. Examine the bank for signs of stratification. See if students can spot the different layers.

5. Look up historical floods, both natural and man-made (like Johnstown). Find out what changes have been made to prevent such floods in the future. Have students write a paragraph about something they've learned.

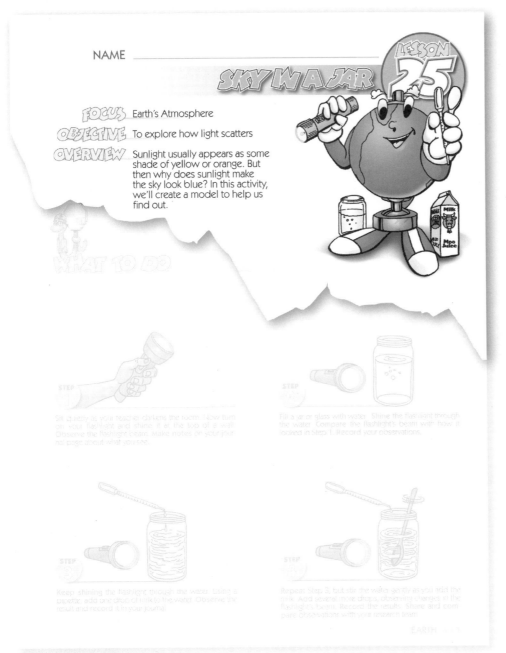

NAME _____

FOCUS Earth's Atmosphere

OBJECTIVE To explore how light scatters

OVERVIEW Sunlight usually appears as some shade of yellow or orange. But then why does sunlight make the sky look blue? In this activity, we'll create a model to help us find out.

WHAT TO DO

STEP 1
Sit quietly as your teacher darkens the room. Now turn on your flashlight and shine it at the top of a wall. Observe the flashlight beam. Make notes on your journal page about what you see.

STEP 2
Fill a jar or glass with water. Shine the flashlight through the water. Compare the flashlight's beam with how it looked in Step 1. Record your observations.

STEP 3
Keep shining the flashlight through the water. Using a pipette, add one drop of milk to the water. Observe the result and record it in your journal.

STEP 4
Repeat Step 3, but stir the water gently as you light the milk. Add several more drops, observing changes in the flashlight's beam. Record the results. Share and compare observations with your research team.

Category
Earth Science

Focus
Earth's Atmosphere

Objective
To explore how light scatters

National Standards
A1, A2, B1, B2, D1, D2, D3, E3, G1

Materials Needed
pipette
plastic spoon
clear glass jar
flashlight
water
milk

Safety Concerns

4. Slipping
There is a potential for spills with this activity. Remind students to exercise caution.

4. Breakage
Glass jars can break! Remind students to exercise caution.

Additional Comments

Although a plastic jar would be safer to use, plastic reacts differently to light than glass. Make sure students remain seated while the room is dark. Keep paper towels and a mop handy in case clean-up is needed.

Overview

Read the overview aloud to your students. The goal is to create an atmosphere of curiosity and inquiry.

WHAT TO DO

Monitor student research teams as they complete each step.

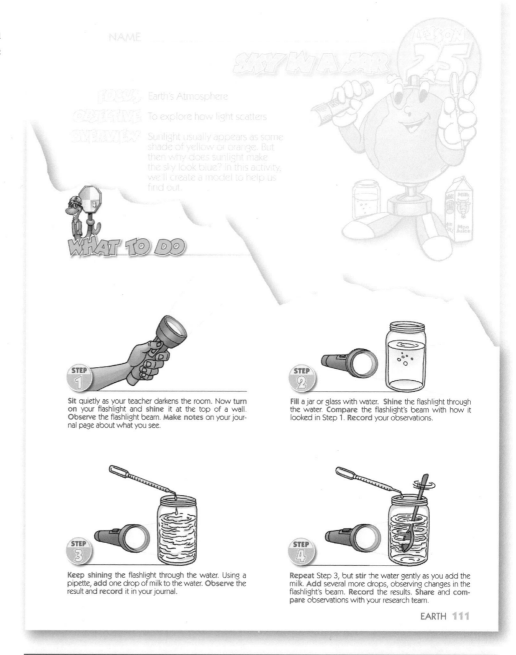

SKY IN A JAR

LESSON 25

FOCUS Earth's Atmosphere

OBJECTIVE To explore how light scatters

OVERVIEW Sunlight usually appears as some shade of yellow or orange. But then why does sunlight make the sky look blue? In this activity, we'll create a model to help us find out.

WHAT TO DO

STEP 1
Sit quietly as your teacher darkens the room. Now turn on your flashlight and shine it at the top of a wall. Observe the flashlight beam. Make notes on your journal page about what you see.

STEP 2
Fill a jar or glass with water. Shine the flashlight through the water. Compare the flashlight's beam with how it looked in Step 1. Record your observations.

STEP 3
Keep shining the flashlight through the water. Using a pipette, add one drop of milk to the water. Observe the result and record it in your journal.

STEP 4
Repeat Step 3, but stir the water gently as you add the milk. Add several more drops, observing changes in the flashlight's beam. Record the results. Share and compare observations with your research team.

EARTH 111

Teacher to Teacher

The scattered light from bright sunlight shining through dry, clean air usually results in the blue color of a clear day. But at sunrise and sunset, another phenomenon called "refraction" occurs. The steep angle of the sun to the horizon causes sunlight to bend (refract) so the dry air produces mostly shades of red.

There's even an old saying about this: "Red sky at night, sailor's delight." Since most of our weather systems travel west to east, very dry in the west results in a very red sunset. Dry air usually means clear skies (hence the sailor's delight).

?WHAT HAPPENED?

In Step 2, you shined **light** through air, then glass, then water, and out the other side. The light went through without much trouble since all of these materials are **transparent**. Then you began to add milk to the water. The protein and fat **molecules** in the milk are much larger than water molecules. When you shined the light again, the beam hit these large particles and began bouncing off, creating the changes you saw.

Scientists call this effect **scattering**. Our model helped us see it on a small scale. Did you notice that the light scattered by your model was a light bluish gray? This is because blue light scatters easily due to its wavelength. On a much larger scale, light from the sun shines though space, then hits the air molecules in Earth's atmosphere. The sunlight scatters, and we get a blue sky!

?WHAT WE LEARNED

1 What did the flashlight beam represent in this model? What did the molecules in the milk represent?

a) sunlight

b) molecules in the Earth's atmosphere

2 Why was there no significant light change in Step 2? What did the materials involved have in common?

a) there was nothing to stop the light

b) they were all transparent

3 Describe why the light began to change in Step 3. What do scientists call this effect?

a) light bounced off the milk molecules

b) scattering

4 Compare the light in Step 1 with the light in Step 4. How were they similar? How were they different?

a) similar: both light, both shining through jar

b) different: light in Step 4 was bluish-gray

5 Based on what you've learned, explain why the sky looks blue even though sunlight appears to be yellow or orange.

light hits the molecules in Earth's atmosphere and bounces off, and blue light scatters the easiest

What Happened

Review the section with students. Emphasize bold-face words that identify key concepts and introduce new vocabulary.

*In Step 2, you shined **light** through air, then glass, then water, and out the other side. The light went through without much trouble since all of these materials are **transparent**. Then you began to add milk to the water. The protein and fat **molecules** in the milk are much larger than water molecules. When you shined the light again, the beam hit these large particles and began bouncing off, creating the changes you saw.*

*Scientists call this effect **scattering**. Our model helped us see it on a small scale. Did you notice that the light scattered by your model was a light bluish gray? This is because blue light scatters easily due to its wavelength. On a much larger scale, light from the sun shines though space, then hits the air molecules in Earth's atmosphere. The sunlight scatters, and we get a blue sky!*

What We Learned

Answers will vary. Suggested responses are shown at left.

Conclusion

Read this section aloud to the class to summarize the concepts learned in this activity.

Food for Thought

Read the Scripture aloud to the class. Talk about how Jesus is the ultimate model for our lives. Discuss ways we can spend time with God.

Journal

If time permits, have a general class discussion about notes and drawings various students added to their journal pages. Discuss correct and incorrect predictions, and remind students that this "trial and error" process is part of the scientific process.

 **CONCLUSION**

Sunlight scatters when it strikes air molecules in Earth's atmosphere. Since blue light scatters the easiest, it causes Earth's sky to look blue.

 **FOOD FOR THOUGHT**

I Corinthians 10:31 - 11:1 This model helped us see how light can be scattered. Using a model is certainly much easier than taking a trip into space! A model is often a great tool for helping us understand difficult ideas in an easy way.

Jesus is the ultimate model for our lives. Paul reminds us that rather than doing what we like best, we should focus on doing what is best for others. We should always follow the example Jesus set for us. The more time we spend with God, the better we will understand how important this is, and the easier it will become.

JOURNAL My Science Notes

Extended Teaching

1. Have students collect pictures of sunsets from old magazines. Make a bulletin board of beautiful and unusual sunsets. (If available, photographs taken by students are also a nice touch!)

2. Fill a tall, clear glass with water. Slowly lower a pencil into the water as students watch. Discuss why the pencil appears bent or broken (refracted light).

3. Repeat this activity using skim milk, 2% milk, and chocolate milk. Carefully track changes as you add each drop.

Challenge students to find similarities and differences between the experiments.

4. Repeat this activity shining a laser pen through the water. (Observe only from the side to protect eyes!) Challenge students to compare the results with the original activity.

5. Visit NASA's website and find out about the atmosphere on other planets. Have each team make a poster about the atmospheric conditions on one of the planets studied.

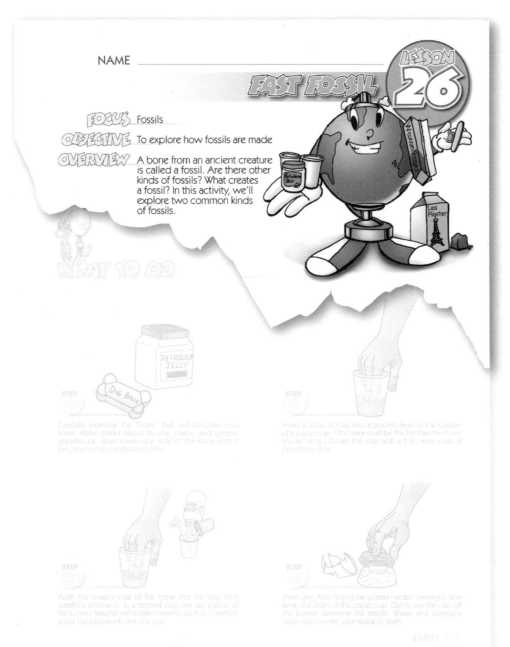

Category

Earth Science

Focus

Fossils

Objective

To explore how fossils are made

National Standards

A1, A2, B1, B2, D1, D3, E3, G1

Materials Needed

dog bone
paper cups - 2
plaster of Paris
craft stick
clay
petroleum jelly
water

Safety Concerns

4. Slipping
There is a potential for spills with this activity. Remind students to exercise caution.

Additional Comments

Monitor to make certain students are coating the "bone" evenly with petroleum jelly. No big globs! If you wish to substitute another object, it must be smooth (no large indentations or small parts). Possible substitutions include smooth sea shells, animal crackers, and large, clean chicken bones.

Overview

Read the overview aloud to the students. Your goal is to create an atmosphere of curiosity and inquiry.

WHAT TO DO

Monitor student research teams as they complete each step.

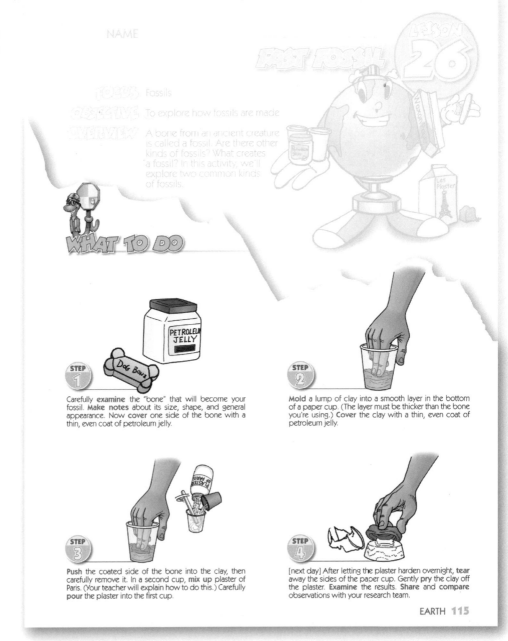

Fossils

To explore how fossils are made

A bone from an ancient creature is called a fossil. Are there other kinds of fossils? What creates a fossil? In this activity, we'll explore two common kinds of fossils.

WHAT TO DO

STEP 1
Carefully **examine** the "bone" that will become your fossil. **Make notes** about its size, shape, and general appearance. Now **cover** one side of the bone with a thin, even coat of petroleum jelly.

STEP 2
Mold a lump of clay into a smooth layer in the bottom of a paper cup. (The layer must be thicker than the bone you're using.) **Cover** the clay with a thin, even coat of petroleum jelly.

STEP 3
Push the coated side of the bone into the clay, then carefully remove it. In a second cup, **mix up** plaster of Paris. (Your teacher will explain how to do this.) Carefully **pour** the plaster into the first cup.

STEP 4
[next day] After letting the plaster harden overnight, **tear** away the sides of the paper cup. Gently pry the clay off the plaster. **Examine** the results. **Share** and **compare** observations with your research team.

EARTH **115**

Teacher to Teacher

A common misconception is that all fossils are large dinosaur bones. Actually, most fossils are microscopic. Known as "microfossils," they include pollen and tiny sea creatures. These tiny fossils are important because they offer clues about ancient environments. Petroleum Geologists are thrilled to find certain microfossils in drilling samples since they usually indicate the presence of oil and natural gas deposits.

?WHAT HAPPENED?

Normally when living things die, their remains decompose (rot away) quickly. But under special conditions, the object or imprint is preserved, sometimes even turning to stone. Scientists define a fossil as any preserved part of an ancient living thing, or evidence that it once existed. For instance, a footprint is a kind of fossil even though every part of the creature that made it is long gone!

In this activity, you made models of two types of fossils: a mold fossil and a cast fossil. The dent you made in the clay (using the bone) created a mold. An imprint like this is called a mold fossil. The plaster you poured in the mold hardened to form a cast. A cast fossil looks a lot like the original object. Notice that neither of these fossils is the object itself, just a sign that it once existed.

?WHAT WE LEARNED

1 What was the purpose of the petroleum jelly in Step 1 and Step 2? What might have happened without it?

a) to keep the materials from sticking together

b) sticking could ruin the mold

2 How were mold fossils made? Give an example of a mold fossil.

a) something is pressed into the earth leaving a dent

b) the shape of a sea shell in stone, a footprint, etc.

3 How were cast fossils made? Which looks more like the original, a cast fossil or mold fossil? Why?

a) material fills the mold, taking its shape

b) the cast fossil since it's not reversed

4 Which was more detailed, the original object or the cast fossil model you made? What does this tell you about the study of fossils?

a) the original

b) it's easier to discover general shapes than it is to find tiny details

5 Based on what you've learned, name two things you could know about an object from a fossil. Name two things you could not know about an object from a fossil.

a) its general shape, its size, its location, etc.

b) skin color, hair color, how fat it was, etc.

What Happened

Review the section with students. Emphasize bold-face words that identify key concepts and introduce new vocabulary.

*Normally when living things **die,** their remains decompose (rot away) quickly. But under special conditions, the object or imprint is **preserved,** sometimes even turning to stone. Scientists define a **fossil** as any preserved part of an ancient living thing, or evidence that it once existed. For instance, a footprint is a kind of fossil even though every part of the creature that made it is long gone!*

*In this activity, you made **models** of two types of fossils: a **mold fossil** and a **cast fossil.** The dent you made in the clay (using the bone) created a mold. An imprint like this is called a mold fossil. The plaster you poured in the mold hardened to form a cast. A cast fossil looks a lot like the original object. Notice that neither of these fossils is the object itself, just a sign that it once existed.*

What We Learned

Answers will vary. Suggested responses are shown at left.

Conclusion

Read this section aloud to the class to summarize the concepts learned in this activity.

Food for Thought

Read the Scripture aloud to the class. Talk about how Scripture gives us a clear picture of God's character. Discuss ways we can learn to fully trust God.

Journal

If time permits, have a general class discussion about students' journal entries. Share and compare observations. Be sure to emphasize that "trial and error" is a valuable part of scientific inquiry!

 CONCLUSION

A fossil is any preserved part of an ancient living thing, or evidence that it once existed. Although there are many missing details, fossils offer clues about ancient plants and animals.

 FOOD FOR THOUGHT

John 14:9 In this activity, you learned how different types of fossils are made, and how they offer clues about ancient plants and animals. But at best, fossils only give us a fuzzy picture of the past. It's like putting a puzzle together with some of the pieces missing!

Fortunately, God is not like that! Through stories, lessons, and parables, the Scriptures give us a clear picture of God's character. Jesus' life was the ultimate reflection of God's great love. God is willing to help you know him better and better if you'll only learn to trust in him.

JOURNAL My Science Notes

Extended Teaching

1. Repeat this activity using other objects (see note under "Additional Comments"). Have students write a paragraph comparing the results with the original activity.

2. Take a field trip to a local museum. Ask the curator to explain how fossils are collected, measured, cleaned, preserved, and displayed. Have a class discussion about why this process is important.

3. Research coal. Discover the origins of coal. Find out how it's made, what it is used for, and why it's important. Discuss environmental issues related to burning coal.

4. Invite a paleontologist or geologist to visit your classroom. Ask them to bring samples and talk about their field work. Have students write a paragraph about one thing they learn.

5. Research fossils on the Internet or in books and encyclopedias. Have students make sketches and notes. Challenge each team to create a poster about a particular kind of fossil.

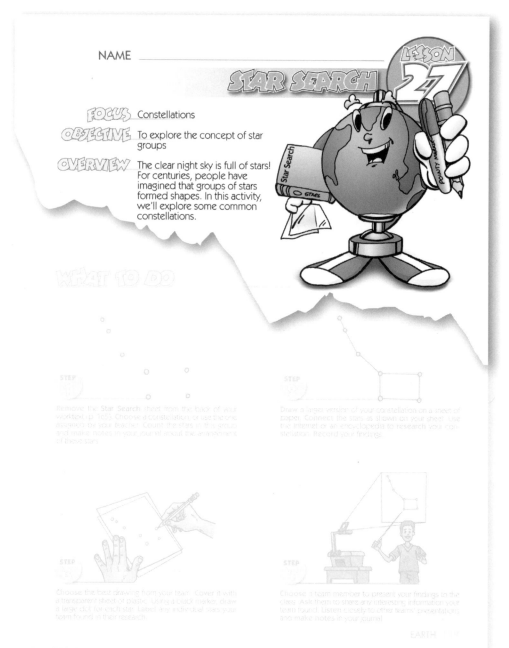

Additional Comments

The worksheet provides several examples of common constellations. If you choose to assign different constellations, be sure to use only constellations from the northern hemisphere. This way students can locate "their" constellation at night. Also, students may need a little help to properly focus the overhead projector.

Overview

Read the overview aloud to your students. The goal is to create an atmosphere of curiosity and inquiry.

WHAT TO DO

Monitor student research teams as they complete each step.

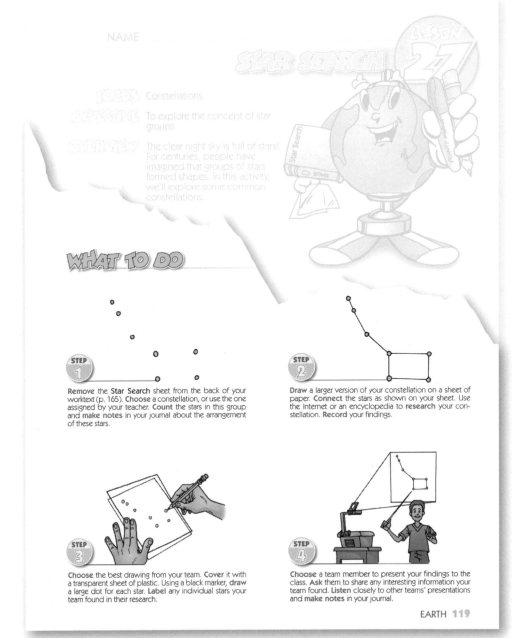

Teacher to Teacher

Students often confuse the terms "astronomy" and "astrology." The first is the scientific study of matter in outer space. Using astronomical instruments, scientists can discover and record information about stars, planets, moons, asteroids, and other objects in space. By contrast, astrology is a pseudo-science that claims celestial bodies influence the course of human affairs. Real science is always measurable and repeatable. Pseudo-science is based on superstition or even worse!

WHAT HAPPENED?

Constellations are groupings of stars that are based on imaginary shapes people created to help them remember the night sky. This was very important to ancient people who used stars to navigate the oceans or to determine directions after dark on a long journey!

There are 88 constellations that can be seen from the Earth's surface. Many of the names and arrangements go back to ancient times.

But since **sky patterns** shift over time, the constellations you see are not quite the same as the ones that ancients saw. In fact, if you were far out in space, the arrangements wouldn't look the same at all! Still, constellations are a fun way to memorize star positions and to enjoy the night sky.

WHAT WE LEARNED

1 Which constellation did your research team study? How many stars did it include? Describe their arrangement.

a) answers will vary

b) answers will vary

c) answer should include a logical description

2 What did you discover about your constellation in Step 2? Did any stars in your constellation have names? If so, what were they?

a) anwers will vary

b) answers will vary

3 Name the constellations studied by other research teams. Describe at least one thing about each.

a) answers will vary

b) answers should include logical data

4 Why did ancient people give star groupings names? What practical purpose did it serve?

a) to help them remember the constellations

b) stars were vital for navigation

5 Based on what you've learned, would the constellations look the same from a million miles out in space? Why or why not?

a) no

b) you would be looking from a different angle

What Happened

Review the section with students. Emphasize bold-face words that identify key concepts and introduce new vocabulary.

Constellations are groupings of *stars* that are based on imaginary shapes people created to help them remember the night sky. This was very important to ancient people who used stars to navigate the oceans or to determine directions after dark on a long journey!

There are 88 constellations that can be seen from the Earth's surface. Many of the names and arrangements go back to ancient times.

But since **sky patterns** *shift over time, the constellations you see are not quite the same as the ones that ancients saw. In fact, if you were far out in space, the arrangements wouldn't look the same at all! Still, constellations are a fun way to memorize star positions and to enjoy the night sky.*

What We Learned

Answers will vary. Suggested responses are shown at left.

Conclusion

Read this section aloud to the class to summarize the concepts learned in this activity.

Food for Thought

Read the Scripture aloud to the class. Talk about the "wondrous light" that comes from God. Discuss ways we can let God's love shine though us.

Journal

If time permits, have a general class discussion about notes and drawings various students added to their journal pages. Discuss correct and incorrect predictions, and remind students that this "trial and error" process is part of the scientific process.

CONCLUSION

Constellations are star groups based on imaginary shapes that ancient people created to help them remember the night sky. The shape of a constellation changes with time and distance.

FOOD FOR THOUGHT

Matthew 2:1-2 This activity has given you a glimpse into the wonders of the night sky. Did you know that there are over 9,000 stars visible without using a telescope? Millions more can be seen with the powerful tools scientists have developed. And the deeper into space they look, the more stars they find!

As ancient astronomers studied the night sky, they saw something surprising — a new star! That wondrous light led them to the King of the universe, the tiny child Jesus. Why not follow their example and let Jesus into your heart? Be a "star" and let the love of God shine though you!

JOURNAL My Science Notes

Extended Teaching

1. Research other constellations. Challenge each team to create a poster about a constellation, including information about its position in the night sky.

2. Invite an astronomer (amateur or professional) to visit your classroom. Ask them to bring a telescope, demonstrate its use, and talk about stars. Have students write a paragraph about one thing they learn.

3. Native Americans have great legends about constellations. Research what constellations they recognized, and the special stories they told about each one. Discuss the role stories play in various cultures.

4. Telescopes are important astronomy tools! Use the Internet to learn more about reflecting telescopes, refracting telescopes, and radio telescopes. Have students make simple drawings of how these telescopes work.

5. Have each team research a famous astronomer using the Internet, books, or encyclopedias. Challenge each team to create a bulletin board sharing what they learned about their astronomer by.

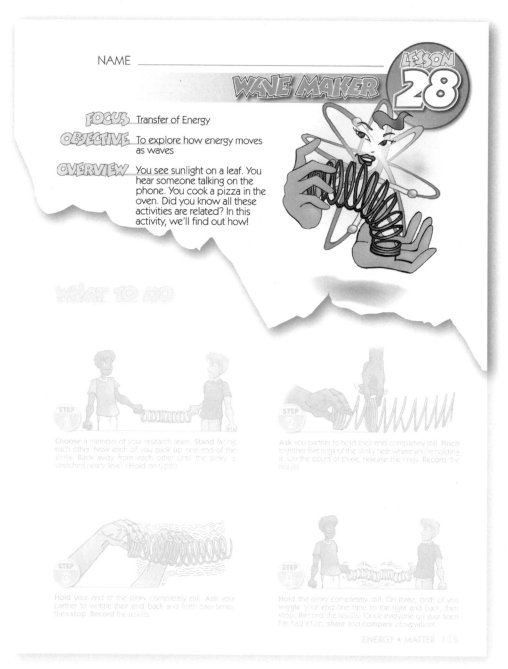

Category

Physical Science
Energy/Matter

Focus

Transfer of Energy

Objective

To explore how energy moves as waves

National Standards

A1, A2, B1, B2, B3, E1, E2, E3, F5, G1

Materials Needed

slinky

Safety Concerns

Additional Comments

A slinky can be damaged by stretching it too far. If students let go while the slinky is stretched, tangles can result. Remind students to hold the ends until they are close together. An interesting option is to do this activity over an overhead projector. This allows the entire class to clearly see the waves.

Overview

Read the overview aloud to your students. The goal is to create an atmosphere of curiosity and inquiry.

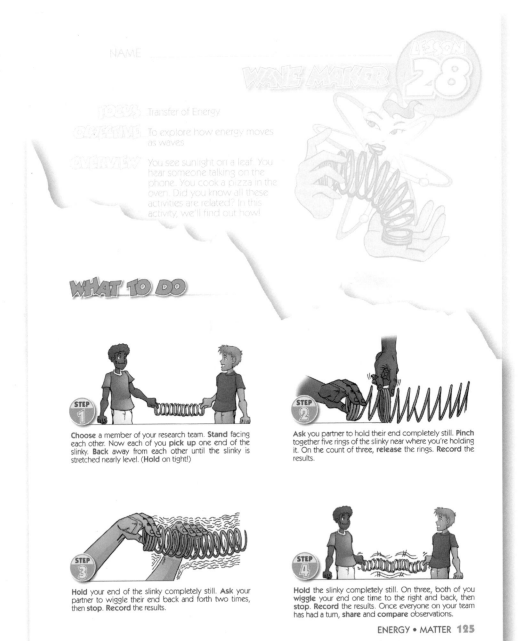

WAVE MAKER

LESSON 28

NAME _____

FOCUS: Transfer of Energy

OBJECTIVE: To explore how energy moves as waves

OVERVIEW: You see sunlight on a leaf. You hear someone talking on the phone. You cook a pizza in the oven. Did you know all these activities are related? In this activity, we'll find out how!

WHAT TO DO

STEP 1
Choose a member of your research team. **Stand** facing each other. Now each of you **pick up** one end of the slinky. **Back** away from each other until the slinky is stretched nearly level. (**Hold** on tight!)

STEP 2
Ask you partner to hold their end completely still. **Pinch** together five rings of the slinky near where you're holding it. On the count of three, **release** the rings. **Record** the results.

STEP 3
Hold your end of the slinky completely still. **Ask** your partner to wiggle their end back and forth two times, then **stop**. **Record** the results.

STEP 4
Hold the slinky completely still. On three, both of you **wiggle** your end one time to the right and back, then **stop**. **Record** the results. Once everyone on your team has had a turn, **share** and **compare** observations.

ENERGY • MATTER **125**

Teacher to Teacher

In 1943, naval engineer, Richard James, was trying to develop a meter to monitor the horsepower on battleships. He was working with tension springs when one of them fell to the floor. James noticed how the spring kept on moving and an idea for a new toy was born. Introduced during the 1945 Christmas season, the slinky became an instant hit! Today, the Internet has dozens of sites dedicated to this interesting toy, many with related physics experiments.

WHAT HAPPENED?

It takes **energy** to make anything move. Your muscles provided the energy for this activity. When you wiggled your end of the slinky, the energy produced a **wave**. The wave traveled down the slinky to your partner, then it bounced back. Scientists call this **reflection**. (Drop a pebble in a bucket of water and you can see reflection when the wave bounces back from the sides.)

Many forms of energy travel in waves. You see the sunlight on a leaf — that **light** is traveling in waves. You hear someone talking on the phone — the **sound** is traveling in waves. You cook a pizza in the oven — the **heat** is traveling in waves.

Although we rarely think about it, many of our daily activities involve energy traveling in waves.

WHAT WE LEARNED

1 In Step 1, what is connecting the two people? Why isn't the slinky moving?

a) the slinky

b) the two students holding it are not moving

2 Describe what happened in Step 2. What was transferred from one end of the slinky to the other? What form did it take as it traveled?

a) answers will vary

b) energy

c) a wave

3 Compare Step 2 with Step 3. How were they similar? How were they different?

a) both held by two people, both showed waves

b) the wave patterns were different

4 Name at least three forms of energy that travel in waves. Give an example of each.

light, sunlight; heat, sound, someone talking on the phone; heat, cooking a pizza; etc.

5 What might happen to the wave if a third person held the slinky in the middle? Compare this to the erosion barrier in Lesson 23?

a) wave would only go to where they held it

b) third person's hand forms a barrier

What Happened

Review the section with students. Emphasize bold-face words that identify key concepts and introduce new vocabulary.

*It takes **energy** to make anything move. Your muscles provided the energy for this activity. When you wiggled your end of the slinky, the energy produced a **wave**. The wave traveled down the slinky to your partner, then it bounced back. Scientists call this **reflection**. (Drop a pebble in a bucket of water and you can see reflection when the wave bounces back from the sides.)*

*Many forms of energy travel in waves. You see the sunlight on a leaf — that **light** is traveling in waves. You hear someone talking on the phone — the **sound** is traveling in waves. You cook a pizza in the oven — the **heat** is traveling in waves.*

Although we rarely think about it, many of our daily activities involve energy traveling in waves.

What We Learned

Answers will vary. Suggested responses are shown at left.

Conclusion

Read this section aloud to the class to summarize the concepts learned in this activity.

Food for Thought

Read the Scripture aloud to the class. Talk about how God answers prayers. Discuss how prayer relates to trusting God (like talking to a friend).

Journal

If time permits, have a general class discussion about notes and drawings various students added to their journal pages. Discuss correct and incorrect predictions, and remind students that this "trial and error" process is part of the scientific process.

 CONCLUSION

It takes energy to make anything move. Some forms of energy travel in waves (light, heat, sound, etc.). Waves can move in different ways.

 FOOD FOR THOUGHT

1 Thessalonians 5:16-18 In this activity, you moved the slinky to create a wave, which traveled down the slinky to your partner, then bounced back.

Prayer can also be like that. When you pray, your prayer travels to God, then an answer bounces back. God always answers prayers, even though the answer is sometimes "no" or "wait a while." God always wants what is best for you. Keep on praying, learn to trust him, and be thankful for the blessings he provides.

JOURNAL My Science Notes

Extended Teaching

1. Take a field trip to a recording studio or radio station. Ask the engineer to explain how materials on the walls absorb sound so recording can be better controlled. Have students write a paragraph about one thing they learn.

2. Have teams line cardboard boxes with various materials (foam rubber, aluminum foil, etc.), then shout into the box to see how these materials absorb sound. Make a list of the most and least efficient materials.

3. Find a place where students can make echoes (large, empty hall; valley with cliffs; etc.). Have students practice making echoes. Have a class discussion about how sound waves create echoes by "bouncing back."

4. Play some music. Have students listen for 10 seconds, then cover their ears for 10 seconds. Talk about the difference in sound. Option: bring ear protectors (earmuff style, or moldable inserts) for students to try.

5. Invite a landscape specialist to visit your classroom. Ask him/her to talk about landscaping for sound control. Discuss how this works, then challenge teams to create a poster illustrating this concept.

Category

Physical Science
Energy/Matter

Focus

Sound Waves

Objective

To explore how sound waves are amplified

National Standards

A1, A2, B1, B3, D2, E1, E2, E3, F4, G1

Materials Needed

slinky
pencil
milk jug (1 gallon)
scissors
tape

Safety Concerns

4. Sharp Objects
Remind students to exercise caution when using scissors.

Additional Comments

Milk jugs need to be thoroughly washed in detergent and hot water before starting the activity. If you're concerned about students using scissors, cut the jugs for them in advance. Monitor to make sure every team member gets a turn.

Overview

Read the overview aloud to your students. The goal is to create an atmosphere of curiosity and inquiry.

WHAT TO DO

Monitor student research teams as they complete each step.

NAME

MILK JUG MEGAPHONE

FOCUS Sound Waves

OBJECTIVE To explore how sound waves are amplified

OVERVIEW In Lesson 28, we discovered that energy travels in waves. Sound is a good example. In this activity, we'll explore how weak sound waves can be made stronger.

WHAT TO DO

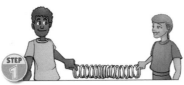

Choose a member of your research team. **Stand** facing each other. Now each of you **pick up** one end of the slinky. **Back** away from each other until the slinky is stretched nearly level. (**Hold** on tight!)

Carefully **hold** the slinky up to your ear. **Ask** your partner to softly tap the other end of the slinky with a pencil. **Record** the results. **Trade** places and **repeat** this step.

Repeat Step 2, but this time **tap** the pencil harder. **Record** the results. Now **cut** the bottom off a milk jug. **Cut** through the handle, then **slip** two end rings of the slinky onto the handle. **Tape** to secure.

Aim the open end of the jug at your ear. **Repeat** the taps from Step 2 and Step 3. **Record** the results. **Trade** places and **repeat** this step. Once everyone on your team has had a turn, **share** and **compare** observations.

ENERGY • MATTER **129**

Teacher to Teacher

An amplifier is a device that increases sound energy. This activity demonstrated a mechanical amplifier. (A megaphone is a similar device.) Electronic amplifiers take the mechanical energy of a voice, add electrical energy to increase the size (amplitude) of the wave, then transmit this to a speaker which projects the increased energy as sound. The same kind of amplification happens with a hearing aide, only on a miniature scale.

WHAT HAPPENED?

Sound is a form of **energy** that travels in **waves**. When you tapped the pencil on the slinky, it made a sound. But the sound was very weak. By attaching the milk jug to the other end of the slinky, you created a device to make the sound louder. Scientists call this **amplification**. Amplification can help us hear or see weak waves.

Imagine trying to talk to someone across a football field. A megaphone might help, but what if they were hundreds of miles away? A telephone provides a way to **transfer** the sound of your voice over great distances. Most communication devices (radio, television, telephones, etc.) rely on this ability to **amplify** energy waves.

WHAT WE LEARNED

1 What is sound a form of? How does it travel?

a) energy

b) waves

2 Describe what happened in Step 2 and Step 3. How difficult was it to hear the pencil tapping?

a) answers will vary

b) it was relatively hard to hear

3 Compare Step 2 with Step 4. How were they similar? How were they different?

a) similar: same taps as Steps 2 and 3

b) different: much louder in Step 4

4 What was the purpose of the milk jug in Step 4? What is the process of making weak waves stronger called?

a) to increase the sound, make it easier to hear, etc.

b) amplification

5 Based on what you've learned, list at least three devices that use amplification and explain their purpose.

television, radio, telephone, stereo, public address system, etc.

What Happened

Review the section with students. Emphasize bold-face words that identify key concepts and introduce new vocabulary.

*Sound is a form of **energy** that travels in **waves**. When you tapped the pencil on the slinky, it made a sound. But the sound was very weak. By attaching the milk jug to the other end of the slinky, you created a device to make the sound louder. Scientists call this **amplification**. Amplification can help us hear or see weak waves.*

*Imagine trying to talk to someone across a football field. A megaphone might help, but what if they were hundreds of miles away? A telephone provides a way to **transfer** the sound of your voice over great distances. Most communication devices (radio, television, telephones, etc.) rely on this ability to **amplify** energy waves.*

What We Learned

Answers will vary. Suggested responses are shown at left.

Conclusion

Read this section aloud to the class to summarize the concepts learned in this activity.

Food for Thought

Read the Scripture aloud to the class. Talk about the power of God's love. Discuss how spending quality time with God can help that power flow into our lives.

Journal

If time permits, have a general class discussion about notes and drawings various students added to their journal pages. Discuss correct and incorrect predictions, and remind students that this "trial and error" process is part of the scientific process.

CONCLUSION

Sound travels in waves. Weak waves can be amplified. Amplified waves can transfer energy over great distances and make weak waves easier to hear or see.

FOOD FOR THOUGHT

Romans 8:38-39 The pencil taps were solid, but they weren't very loud. The milk jug amplified that sound so it was easier to hear. Now imagine placing a microphone inside the milk jug, and hooking it up to a loudspeaker. A simple pencil tap might sound like an explosion!

Most of us have family and friends who love us. That's a good feeling, isn't it? But that love is only a "weak wave" compared to God's love. This Scripture tells us that nothing can separate us from God's love — not angels or devils or fear or even death itself! Spend time with God each day, and experience the awesome power of his love.

JOURNAL My Science Notes

Extended Teaching

1. Invite a hearing specialist to visit your classroom. Ask them to bring several styles of hearing aids and talk about their use. Have students write a paragraph about one thing they learn.

2. Bring a stringed instrument (violin, guitar, etc.) to class. Demonstrate how high and low sounds are made. Let students practice this concept by plucking long and short rubber bands.

3. Visit the local police station. Ask the safety officer talk about the dangers of speeding and demonstrate the use of radar. Discuss how radar waves are similar to sound waves and other forms of energy.

4. Visit a local pond. Take turns tossing small rocks into the water. Watch the resulting waves closely. Challenge students to create a poster showing the action of such waves.

5. Have students research sound sources that can damage hearing. (Headphones are high on that list!) Have a class discussion about their findings and talk about ways to protect your hearing.

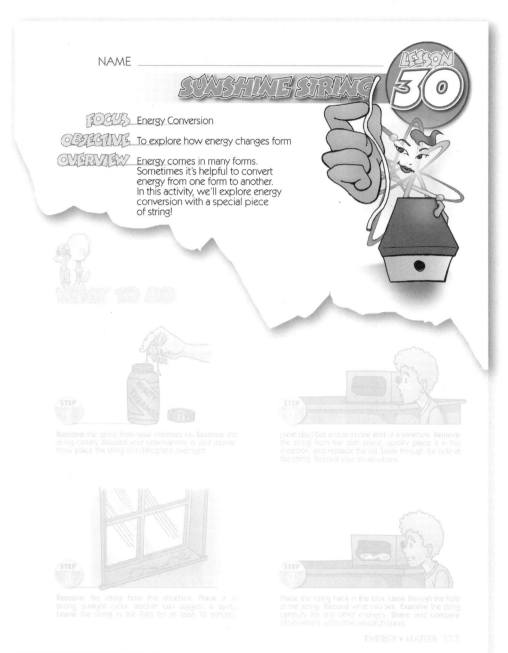

Safety Concerns

4. Sharp Objects
Remind students to exercise caution when using scissors.

Additional Comments

Step 2 and Step 4 illustrations show a viewing port in the side of the box. This is for illustrative purposes only! Monitor to make certain students only cut a small view port in the end of the box. Step 3 requires direct exposure to bright sunlight. The illustration shows a windowsill, but taking the string outdoors works even better.

Overview

Read the overview aloud to your students. The goal is to create an atmosphere of curiosity and inquiry.

WHAT TO DO

Monitor student research teams as they complete each step.

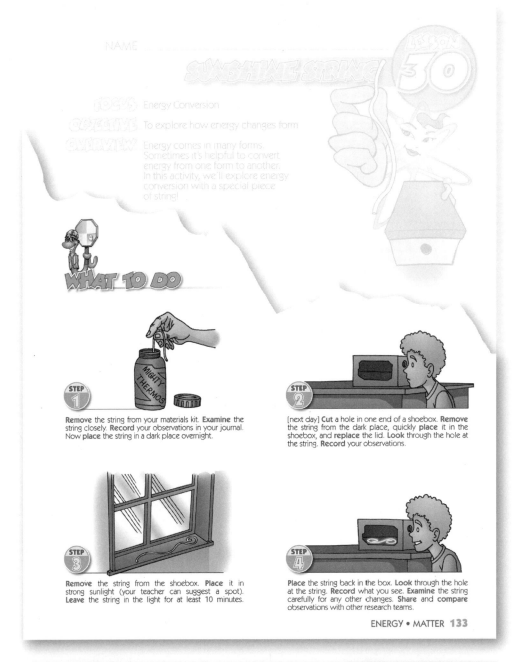

Energy Conversion

To explore how energy changes form

Energy comes in many forms. Sometimes it's helpful to convert energy from one form to another. In this activity, we'll explore energy conversion with a special piece of string!

WHAT TO DO

STEP 1
Remove the string from your materials kit. **Examine** the string closely. **Record** your observations in your journal. Now **place** the string in a dark place overnight.

STEP 2
[next day] **Cut** a hole in one end of a shoebox. **Remove** the string from the dark place, quickly **place** it in the shoebox, and **replace** the lid. **Look** through the hole at the string. **Record** your observations.

STEP 3
Remove the string from the shoebox. **Place** it in strong sunlight (your teacher can suggest a spot). **Leave** the string in the light for at least 10 minutes.

STEP 4
Place the string back in the box. **Look** through the hole at the string. **Record** what you see. **Examine** the string carefully for any other changes. **Share** and **compare** observations with other research teams.

ENERGY • MATTER **133**

Teacher to Teacher

Three key aspects of energy are absorption, conversion, and release. Absorption is primarily done by plants through photosynthesis, providing the foundation for the energy cycle. Fossil fuels (coal, oil, and natural gas) are examples of plants converted into another form of energy. When energy is released, it can power every kind of machine, as well as every living creature. Solving the problems faced by America's energy-dependent culture requires a clear understanding of these three aspects of energy.

❓ WHAT HAPPENED?

This string contains a special material that **absorbs** and **releases** light **energy**. Think of it as a kind of sponge that soaks up **light**, then gives it back. Scientists call such materials **phosphorescent** (fos' fo res' ent). Your phosphorescent string stored the sunlight in Step 3, then released the stored light in Step 4.

Changing the **form** of **energy** is very important in our modern world. The light, heat, air conditioning, and electricity in your school all involve energy changing forms. Without this ability to **change** and **store** energy our way of life would be vastly different!

❓ WHAT WE LEARNED

1 Why was it important to start this activity by placing the string in the dark?

this allowed us to check the string's response with no exposure to light

2 Describe Step 2. What did the string look like in the box?

a) put string from dark place into box

b) could barely see it, dark, like ordinary string; etc.

3 Why was it important to place the string in direct sunlight? What did this allow the string to do?

a) to check its response to light

b) absorb energy from the light

4 Compare Step 2 with Step 4. How were they similar? How were they different?

a) similar: same string, same box

b) different: string in box glowed in Step 4

5 Why is the ability to change or store energy important in our modern world?

light, heat, air conditioning, transportation, etc., all rely on energy changing forms

What Happened

Review the section with students. Emphasize bold-face words that identify key concepts and introduce new vocabulary.

*This string contains a special material that **absorbs** and **releases** light **energy.** Think of it as a kind of sponge that soaks up **light,** then gives it back. Scientists call such materials **phosphorescent** (fos' fo res' ent). Your phosphorescent string stored the sunlight in Step 3, then released the stored light in Step 4.*

*Changing the **form** of **energy** is very important in our modern world. The light, heat, air conditioning, and electricity in your school all involve energy changing forms. Without this ability to **change** and **store** energy, our way of life would be vastly different!*

What We Learned

Answers will vary. Suggested responses are shown at left.

Conclusion

Read this section aloud to the class to summarize the concepts learned in this activity.

Food for Thought

Read the Scripture aloud to the class. Talk about how a heart filled with God's love makes us "overflow with love and light." Discuss ways to share this with others.

Journal

If time permits, have a general class discussion about notes and drawings various students added to their journal pages. Discuss correct and incorrect predictions, and remind students that this "trial and error" process is part of the scientific process.

 CONCLUSION

Energy can change forms. A change in forms often involves storing energy for later use. Materials that store and release light energy are called phosphorescent.

 FOOD FOR THOUGHT

Exodus 34:28, 29 When your Sunshine String was left alone in the dark, it became rather dull and uninteresting. But when it was exposed to the sun, it developed a pleasing glow!

This Scripture talks about a special time Moses spent with God. When he returned to the people, his face glowed brightly because he had seen God face-to-face. Without God's love in our hearts, we're often dull and uninteresting inside. But when our hearts are filled with God's love, we overflow with love and light!

JOURNAL **My Science Notes**

Extended Teaching

1. Repeat this activity, only start by refrigerating the string overnight. Have students compare this with the original activity. Ask them to write a paragraph stating their conclusions.

2. Invite a power company representative to visit your classroom. Discuss ways to minimize energy use at home and school. Have students write a paragraph about one thing they learn.

3. Have teams invent ways to use Sunshine String. Challenge each team to create a poster advertisement marketing one idea to the class.

Discuss "new products" students have seen that are either good or bad.

4. Have teams list ways energy changes from one form to another. (Example: a flashlight converts chemical energy from batteries into light energy.) Have a class discussion about their findings.

5. Invite a geologist or rock collector to visit your classroom. Ask him/her to bring samples of phosphorescent minerals. Dim the lights and examine these samples. Have students write a paragraph about one thing they learn.

NAME _____

BUG'S EYE VIEW

FOCUS Images

OBJECTIVE To explore how a lens affects an image

OVERVIEW Different creatures have different types of eyes with different lenses. Ever wonder what the world looks like through a bug's eye? In this activity, we'll use a special lens to find out!

LESSON 31

Category

Physical Science
Energy/Matter

Focus

Images

Objective

To explore how a lens affects an image

National Standards

A1, A2, B1, B2, B3, E1, E2, E3, F5, G1

Materials Needed

kaleidoscope lens
ball

Safety Concerns

Additional Comments

To avoid tripping hazards, make sure students stand in one place while using the kaleidoscope lens. Remind partners to toss the ball gently!

Overview

Read the overview aloud to your students. The goal is to create an atmosphere of curiosity and inquiry.

WHAT TO DO

Monitor student research teams as they complete each step.

Step 4

Have students trade places, and repeat the activity until everyone has had a turn.

WHAT TO DO

STEP 1
Choose a member of your research team. **Stand** facing each other about five feet apart. Gently **toss** a ball to your partner so they can catch it. **Ask** them to toss it back. **Record** the results in your journal.

STEP 2
Repeat Step 1, but this time make the tossing and catching a little tougher by closing one eye. **Record** the results in your journal.

STEP 3
Standing in the same position, **close** one eye. Now with your open eye, **look** at your partner through the "bug's eye." **Record** the results. Let your partner try the bug's eye. **Discuss** your observations.

STEP 4
Repeat Step 1, but use only the bug's eye to see. **Record** the results. Make sure all members of your research team get a turn. **Share** and **compare** observations.

ENERGY • MATTER **137**

Teacher to Teacher

The lens used in this activity models the compound eyes of many insects. Scientists tell us that the eyes of bees are not only compound, but they also see ultraviolet light. When this light strikes many types of flowers, they glow in a way that's invisible to the human eye — but it's like a neon sign to a hungry bee!

⟨?⟩ WHAT HAPPENED?

A **lens** focuses **light** to produce an **image**. Many devices use lenses (microscope, telescope, camera, etc.) to help us see differently. The device we used is a **kaleidoscope**. It combines several lenses, resulting in multiple images. Look at your partner with and without the kaleidoscope to see the difference between one lens (the one in your eye) and many (the ones in the kaleidoscope).

Some **insects** like flies have eyes with multiple lenses. Scientists call this arrangement a **compound eye**. Compound eyes work well for a fly, but not for you since you don't have the **brain** of a fly! When you tried to catch the ball using the compound eye, your human brain couldn't decide what to do with all those images. This made it nearly impossible to catch the ball.

⟨?⟩ WHAT WE LEARNED

1 What was the name of the device used in this activity? What makes it produce multiple images?

a) a kaleidoscope lens

b) it combines several lenses, it's a compound lens, etc.

2 Describe what your partner looked like in Step 3. What created this effect?

a) answers will vary, but should include multiple images

b) the compound lens

3 Describe Step 4. What made it hard to catch the ball? Why was this a problem?

a) answers will vary

b) it looked like lots of balls!

c) didn't know which image was the real one

4 What is an eye with multiple lenses called? What type of creature has such eyes?

a) a compound eye

b) many insects have compound eyes

5 Name at least two additional devices that use a lens to produce an image. What is each device used for?

camera, telescope, overhead projector, magnifying glass, microscope, etc.

What Happened

Review the section with students. Emphasize bold-face words that identify key concepts and introduce new vocabulary.

*A **lens** focuses **light** to produce an **image**. Many devices use lenses (microscope, telescope, camera, etc.) to help us see differently. The device we used is a **kaleidoscope**. It combines several lenses, resulting in multiple images. Look at your partner with and without the kaleidoscope to see the difference between one lens (the one in your eye) and many lenses (the ones in the kaleidoscope).*

*Some **insects**, like flies, have eyes with multiple lenses. Scientists call this arrangement a **compound eye**. Compound eyes work well for a fly, but not for you since you don't have the **brain** of a fly! When you tried to catch the ball using the compound eye, your human brain couldn't decide what to do with all those images. This made it nearly impossible to catch the ball.*

What We Learned

Answers will vary. Suggested responses are shown at left.

Conclusion

Read this section aloud to the class to summarize the concepts learned in this activity.

Food for Thought

Read the Scripture aloud to the class. Talk about how the things of this world can cause us to lose sight of spiritual things. Discuss ways to stay focused on our relationship with God.

Journal

If time permits, have a general class discussion about notes and drawings various students added to their journal pages. Discuss correct and incorrect predictions, and remind students that this "trial and error" process is part of the scientific process.

A lens focuses light to produce an image. A kaleidoscope combines several lenses, resulting in multiple images. Your brain needs accurate images in order to make the body function properly.

1 John 5:19, 20 When you look through a kaleidoscope, you see many images swirling around. It can be very confusing. All those images can make simple things become difficult.

Sometimes the world can be very confusing, surrounding us with many things that draw us away from God. This Scripture reminds us that keeping close to Jesus can help us find God. The more time we spend with him, the clearer everything becomes.

JOURNAL My Science Notes

Extended Teaching

1. Using the Internet, books, and encyclopedias, research different kinds of eyes. Make a bulletin board comparing human eyes with the eyes of various animals and insects.

2. Invite an optometrist to visit your classroom. Discuss how different lenses (glasses and contacts) can correct different kinds of eye problems. Ask students to write a paragraph about one thing they learn.

3. Have students research color blindness. How does it affect vision? Who is more likely to be affected — boys or girls? Have a class discussion about their findings.

4. Have teams list other devices that use lenses (microscopes, telescopes, cameras, overhead projectors, etc.). Challenge each team to create a poster about one of these items, how it works, and ways it's used.

5. Invite the manager of a store that sells kaleidoscopes to visit your classroom. Ask him/her to bring samples to view and to discuss how kaleidoscopes work. Have students write thank-you letters to the store.

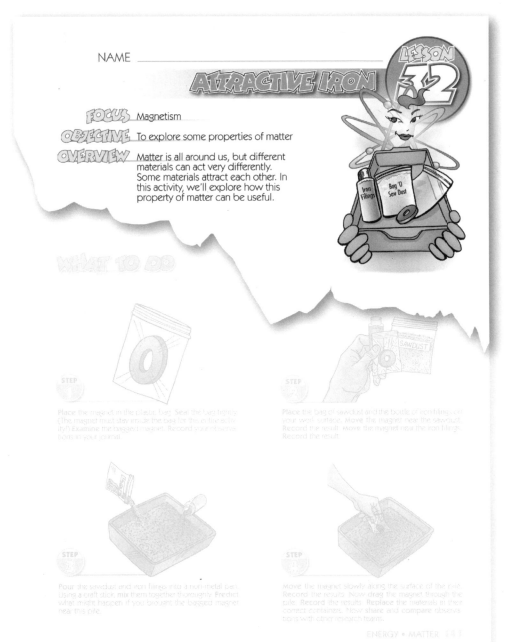

NAME _____

ATTRACTIVE IRON

LESSON 32

FOCUS Magnetism

OBJECTIVE To explore some properties of matter

OVERVIEW Matter is all around us, but different materials can act very differently. Some materials attract each other. In this activity, we'll explore how this property of matter can be useful.

WHAT TO DO

STEP Place the magnet in the plastic bag. Seal the bag tightly. (The magnet must stay inside the bag for this entire activity!) Examine the bagged magnet. Record your observations in your journal.

STEP Place the bag of sawdust and the bottle of iron filings on your work surface. Move the magnet near the sawdust. Record the result. Move the magnet near the iron filings. Record the result.

STEP Pour the sawdust and iron filings into a non-metal pan. Using a craft stick, mix them together thoroughly. Predict what might happen if you brought the bagged magnet near this pile.

STEP Move the magnet slowly along the surface of the pile. Record the results. Now drag the magnet through the pile. Record the results. Replace the materials in their correct containers. Now share and compare observations with other research teams.

ENERGY • MATTER

Category

Physical Science
Energy/Matter

Focus

Magnetism

Objective

To explore some properties of matter

National Standards

A1, A2, B1, B2, B3, D1, E2, E3, F3, F5, G1

Materials Needed

magnet
plastic bag (resealable)
bag of sawdust
bottle of iron filings
craft stick
plastic tray or pan

Safety Concerns

Additional Comments

Make certain the bags with the magnets are securely closed. (Removing filings from a bare magnet can be difficult.) To minimize handling, have students use the craft stick to scrape the filings off the magnet bag and into the bottle. Option: rather than separating materials now, simply use fresh supplies next year.

Overview

Read the overview aloud to your students. The goal is to create an atmosphere of curiosity and inquiry.

WHAT TO DO

Monitor student research teams as they complete each step.

ATTRACTIVE IRON

LESSON 32

FOCUS Magnetism

OBJECTIVE To explore some properties of matter

OVERVIEW Matter is all around us, but different materials can act very differently. Some materials attract each other. In this activity, we'll explore how this property of matter can be useful.

WHAT TO DO

STEP 1

Place the magnet in the plastic bag. **Seal** the bag tightly. (The magnet must stay inside the bag for this entire activity!) **Examine** the bagged magnet. **Record** your observations in your journal.

STEP 2

Place the bag of sawdust and the bottle of iron filings on your work surface. **Move** the magnet near the sawdust. **Record** the result. **Move** the magnet near the iron filings. **Record** the result.

STEP 3

Pour the sawdust and iron filings into a non-metal pan. Using a craft stick, **mix** them together thoroughly. **Predict** what might happen if you brought the bagged magnet near this pile.

STEP 4

Move the magnet slowly along the surface of the pile. **Record** the results. Now **drag** the magnet through the pile. **Record** the results. **Replace** the materials in their correct containers. Now **share** and **compare** observations with other research teams.

ENERGY • MATTER 141

Teacher to Teacher

Scientists sort elements according to chemical and physical properties. An element's chemical properties determine how it reacts to chemical change. An element's physical properties determine whether it's solid, liquid, or gas, if it's a conductor or insulator, if it's attracted by a magnet, and so on. It's also important to remember that magnets can be either permanent (like lodestone) or temporary (like electromagnets).

WHAT HAPPENED?

Some materials are **magnetic**. This means they have the ability to **attract** certain kinds of **metal** like iron, cobalt, and nickel. Scientists call these **ferrous** (magnetic) metals. **Non-ferrous** materials, including some metals like aluminum, are not attracted by magnets. You demonstrated this in Step 4 when you dragged the magnet through the pile. The iron filings were attracted to the magnet, but the sawdust wasn't.

Magnetism is one of the basic **forces** in the universe. Magnets make electric motors run, lock and unlock car doors, operate certain kinds of switches — even check for real coins in a vending machine. Recyclers use huge magnets to help them sort ferrous and non-ferrous materials.

WHAT WE LEARNED

1 Why was it important to keep the magnet in the bag for this activity? What might have happened if you didn't?

a) so the filings wouldn't stick to it

b) the filings would be hard to remove

2 Describe what happened in Step 2. Which material was attracted by the magnet? Why?

a) answers will vary

b) the iron filings

c) because they were ferrous

3 What was your prediction in Step 3? How did this reflect what actually happened in Step 4?

a) answers will vary

b) answers will vary, but should reflect logical comparisons

4 What do scientists call magnetic materials? Is a magnet attracted to all kinds of metal? Why or why not?

a) ferrous

b) no

c) some metals are non-ferrous

5 Recycling centers receive many different materials, often mixed up in piles. How can a magnet be used to sort these materials? What would you label the two piles?

a) it can grab the ferrous metals

b) ferrous/non-ferrous (note: NOT magnetic/non-magnetic)

What Happened

Review the section with students. Emphasize bold-face words that identify key concepts and introduce new vocabulary.

Some materials are **magnetic**. *This means they have the ability to* **attract** *certain kinds of* **metal** *like iron, cobalt, and nickel. Scientists call these* **ferrous** *(magnetic) metals.* **Non-ferrous** *materials, including some metals like aluminum, are not attracted by magnets. You demonstrated this in Step 4 when you dragged the magnet through the pile. The iron filings were attracted to the magnet, but the sawdust wasn't.*

Magnetism is one of the basic **forces** *in the universe. Magnets make electric motors run, lock and unlock car doors, operate certain kinds of switches — even check for real coins in a vending machine. Recyclers use huge magnets to help them sort ferrous and non-ferrous materials.*

What We Learned

Answers will vary. Suggested responses are shown at left.

Conclusion

Read this section aloud to the class to summarize the concepts learned in this activity.

Food for Thought

Read the Scripture aloud to the class. Talk about how God's presence changes our lives. Discuss ways we can make a difference in the world once God fills our hearts.

Journal

If time permits, have a general class discussion about notes and drawings various students added to their journal pages. Discuss correct and incorrect predictions, and remind students that this "trial and error" process is part of the scientific process.

 **CONCLUSION**

Different materials behave differently because of different properties. These properties can help scientists and engineers create useful devices. They also help recyclers sort materials.

 **FOOD FOR THOUGHT**

Acts 4:31 Until the magnet arrived, the iron filings were lifeless. They didn't show any movement or activity. But when the power of the magnet came near, things changed dramatically! The iron filings really became active, and they helped us see the power that was present.

Scripture tells us that something special happens when God fills our lives. We may feel dull, ordinary, and powerless — but when the Spirit of God begins working in our lives, we can begin to make a real difference in the world. Just as the filings made the magnet's power visible, so we can make God's power and love visible to others.

JOURNAL   My Science Notes

Extended Teaching

1. Have teams test other metal objects in the classroom to see if they are ferrous or non-ferrous. (WARNING: Keep magnets away from electronics and computers!) Encourage teams to share and compare findings.

2. Take a field trip to a metal recycler. Ask them to demonstrate the powerful electromagnets they use for sorting metals. Have students write a paragraph about one thing they learn.

3. Repeat this activity adding a bag of salt to the mix. Challenge students to figure out how to separate the three materials.

(Hint: remove the filings, use water to dissolve the salt, drain the water, etc.)

4. Invite a machinist or welder to visit your classroom. Ask him/her to bring samples of different metals and to talk about how each one requires different handling. Have students write a paragraph about one thing they learn.

5. Have teams discuss what life would be like with no metals. After the discussion, have students write a few paragraphs about how their lives would be different in a world without a specific kind of metal.

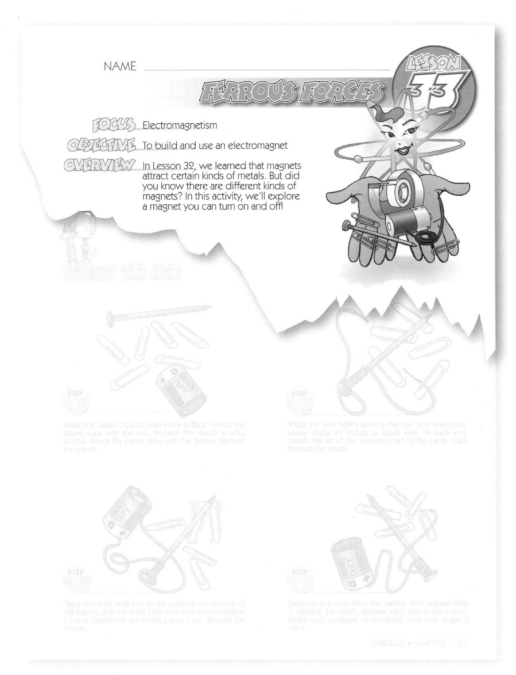

NAME _____

FERROUS FORCES

LESSON 33

FOCUS Electromagnetism

OBJECTIVE To build and use an electromagnet

OVERVIEW In Lesson 32, we learned that magnets attract certain kinds of metals. But did you know there are different kinds of magnets? In this activity, we'll explore a magnet you can turn on and off!

Category

Physical Science
Energy/Matter

Focus

Electromagnetism

Objective

To build and use an electromagnet

National Standards

A1, A2, B1, B2, B3, D1, E3, G1

Materials Needed

paperclips - 5
insulated wire - 18"
nail
D-cell battery
tape

Safety Concerns

2. Thermal Burn
The nail or paperclips may become hot if left connected to the battery for too long.

4. Sharp Objects
A sharp nail poses a possible safety hazard. Monitor to prevent horseplay.

Additional Comments

It's very important to educate students about the dangers of household current. Remind them that, although batteries are relatively safe, electricity coming from a wall plug is very dangerous. Students should never attempt to use it for science experiments!

Overview

Read the overview aloud to your students. The goal is to create an atmosphere of curiosity and inquiry.

WHAT TO DO

Monitor student research teams as they complete each step.

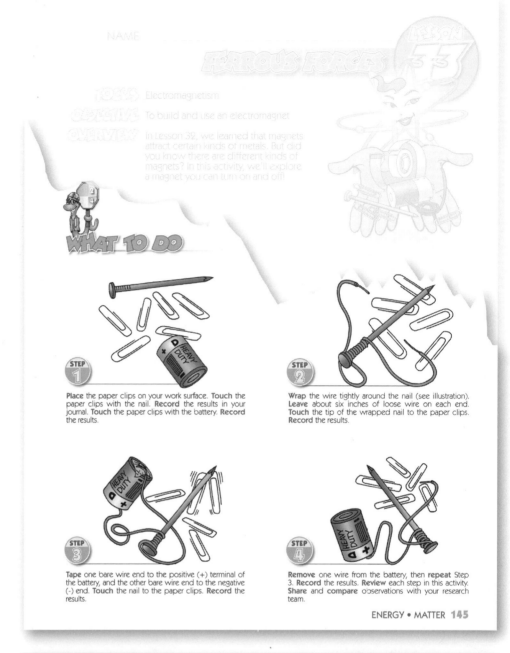

Electromagnetism

To build and use an electromagnet

In Lesson 32, we learned that magnets attract certain kinds of metals. But did you know there are different kinds of magnets? In this activity, we'll explore a magnet you can turn on and off!

WHAT TO DO

STEP 1
Place the paper clips on your work surface. **Touch** the paper clips with the nail. **Record** the results in your journal. **Touch** the paper clips with the battery. **Record** the results.

STEP 2
Wrap the wire tightly around the nail (see illustration). **Leave** about six inches of loose wire on each end. **Touch** the tip of the wrapped nail to the paper clips. **Record** the results.

STEP 3
Tape one bare wire end to the positive (+) terminal of the battery, and the other bare wire end to the negative (-) end. **Touch** the nail to the paper clips. **Record** the results.

STEP 4
Remove one wire from the battery, then **repeat** Step 3. **Record** the results. **Review** each step in this activity. **Share** and **compare** observations with your research team.

ENERGY • MATTER **145**

Teacher to Teacher

Electromagnetism is very versatile. It can not only use magnetism to create electricity, it can also use electricity to make magnetism! Inside power plants, giant turbines spin magnets inside wire coils, creating the electricity we use each day. At a metal recycler, a flip of a switch sends electricity flowing through wire coils, creating a temporary magnet that can lift huge weights. Both are forms of electromagnetism.

?WHAT HAPPENED?

Ferrous (magnetic) **metals** are not only attracted to a **magnet**, but with the addition of electric **current**, they can be turned into magnets themselves. You created a small **electromagnet** by wrapping wire around a nail (ferrous metal) and passing electric current through it. As long as the current was on, the nail was a magnet!

This activity helped us discover that magnetism has a partner. It's called **electricity**! The magnetism/electricity combination is a basic **force** on Earth. Scientists refer to this as **electromagnetic force**. Electromagnets are used in millions of electric motors, performing many different kinds of work.

?WHAT WE LEARNED

1 Describe what happened in the first two steps. What affect did the battery, nail, and wrapped nail have on the paper clips?

a) answers should describe the tests

b) none

2 Describe what happened in Step 3. How was this step different from the previous steps?

a) answers should describe the test

b) a wire was attached to both ends of the battery

146 ENERGY · MATTER

3 Compare Step 3 and Step 4. How were they similar? How were they different?

a) similar: same materials, same test

b) different: paperclips were attracted in Step 3 only; one wire was disconnected in Step 4

4 What happens when current is applied to ferrous metal? What does this create?

current + ferrous metal = electromagnetism, creating a temporary magnet

5 Based on what you've learned, how could the ability to turn a magnet on and off be helpful?

answers will vary, but should include ideas like picking things up and dropping them

ENERGY · MATTER 147

What Happened

Review the section with students. Emphasize bold-face words that identify key concepts and introduce new vocabulary.

*Ferrous (magnetic) **metals** are not only attracted to a **magnet**, but with the addition of electric **current**, they can be turned into magnets themselves. You created a small **electromagnet** by wrapping wire around a nail (ferrous metal) and passing electric current through it. As long as the current was on, the nail was a magnet!*

*This activity helped us discover that magnetism has a partner. It's called **electricity**! The magnetism/electricity combination is a basic **force** on Earth. Scientists refer to this as **electromagnetic force**. Electromagnets are used in millions of electric motors, performing many different kinds of work.*

What We Learned

Answers will vary. Suggested responses are shown at left.

Lesson 33 · **147**

Conclusion

Read this section aloud to the class to summarize the concepts learned in this activity.

Food for Thought

Read the Scripture aloud to the class. Talk about God's power in our lives. How can this attract others? Discuss how we should treat each other when God fills our hearts.

Journal

If time permits, have a general class discussion about notes and drawings various students added to their journal pages. Discuss correct and incorrect predictions, and remind students that this "trial and error" process is part of the scientific process.

CONCLUSION

Magnetism and electricity are related forces. An object made of ferrous metal can be turned into an electromagnet if current is conducted around it.

FOOD FOR THOUGHT

Luke 24:49 The nail was just a nail until the power of the electric current began to flow. Then it suddenly had the amazing ability to attract other metals to the source of power.

In this Scripture, Jesus tells his followers to wait for the Holy Spirit to flow through them. This gave them the power to draw others to God. When we spend time with God each day, the power of his Holy Spirit can fill our lives. As we become more like Jesus, our example can help draw others to God.

JOURNAL My Science Notes

Extended Teaching

1. Take a field trip to a power plant. Encourage students to listen closely as the guide explains how power is made. Have them write a paragraph about one thing they learn.

2. Have teams discuss what the world would be like with no electricity. After the discussion, ask students to write a paragraph or two about how their lives would be different with no electricity.

3. Invite an electrician to visit your classroom. Ask him/her to bring tools and samples of wire and outlets. Talk about the importance of electrical safety. Have students write a paragraph about one thing they learn.

4. Have teams make lists of different devices that use electricity. Challenge them to create a poster about one of these devices, how it works, and how it's used.

5. If any local car dealer carries electric hybrids (Honda Insight and Toyota Prius are two examples), invite them to bring one to your school. Have the dealer "show and tell" how this unique vehicle works.

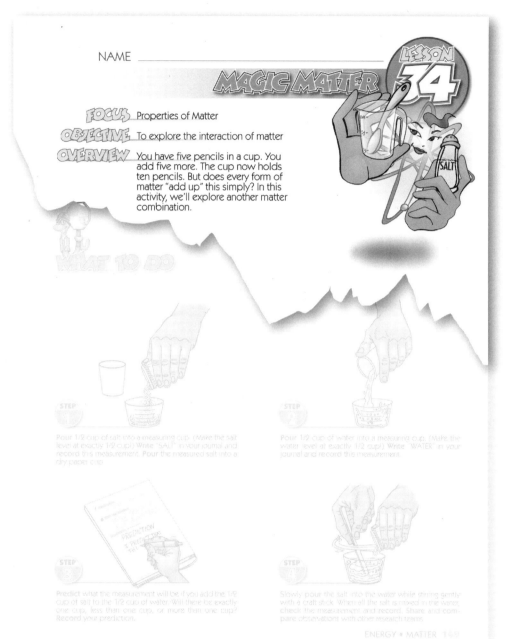

NAME _____

MAGIC MATTER LESSON 34

FOCUS Properties of Matter

OBJECTIVE To explore the interaction of matter

OVERVIEW You have five pencils in a cup. You add five more. The cup now holds ten pencils. But does every form of matter "add up" this simply? In this activity, we'll explore another matter combination.

WHAT TO DO

STEP 1
Pour 1/2 cup of salt into a measuring cup. (Make the salt level at exactly 1/2 cup) Write "SALT" in your journal and record this measurement. Pour the measured salt into a dry paper cup.

STEP 2
Pour 1/2 cup of water into a measuring cup. (Make the water level at exactly 1/2 cup) Write "WATER" in your journal and record this measurement.

STEP 3
Predict what the measurement will be if you add the 1/2 cup of salt to the 1/2 cup of water. Will there be exactly one cup, less than one cup, or more than one cup? Record your prediction.

STEP 4
Slowly pour the salt into the water while stirring gently with a craft stick. When all the salt is mixed in the water, check the measurement and record. Share and compare observations with other research teams.

ENERGY • MATTER 149

Category

Physical Science
Energy/Matter

Focus

Properties of Matter

Objective

To explore the interaction of matter

National Standards

A1, A2, B1, B2, B3, E1, E2, E3, F5, G1

Materials Needed

paper cup
craft stick
salt
measuring cup
water

Safety Concerns

4. Slipping
There is a potential for spills with this activity. Remind students to exercise caution.

Additional Comments

The water surface will be curved, making measuring a bit difficult, but the shortage from a full cup should still be obvious. Warn students not to experiment at home! Mixing common materials can be very dangerous. (For instance, bleach and ammonium combine to create deadly chlorine gas!)

Overview

Read the overview aloud to your students. The goal is to create an atmosphere of curiosity and inquiry.

WHAT TO DO

Monitor student research teams as they complete each step.

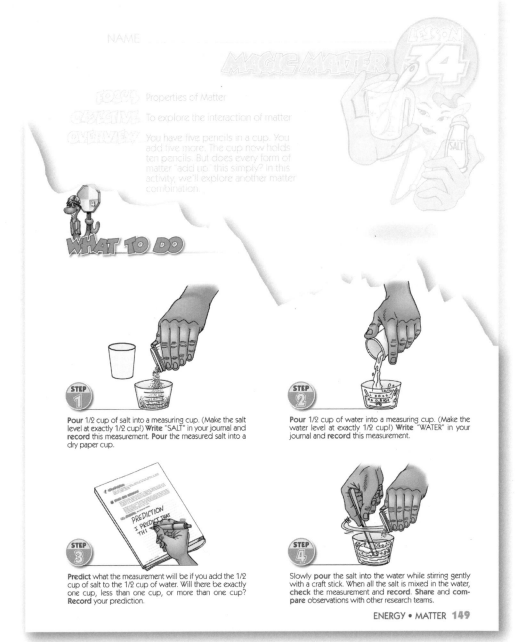

Properties of Matter

To explore the interaction of matter

You have five pencils in a cup. You add five more. The cup now holds ten pencils. But does every form of matter "add up" this simply? In this activity, we'll explore another matter combination.

WHAT TO DO

STEP 1
Pour 1/2 cup of salt into a measuring cup. (Make the salt level at exactly 1/2 cup!) **Write** "SALT" in your journal and **record** this measurement. **Pour** the measured salt into a dry paper cup.

STEP 2
Pour 1/2 cup of water into a measuring cup. (Make the water level at exactly 1/2 cup!) **Write** "WATER" in your journal and **record** this measurement.

STEP 3
PREDICTION
I PREDICT THAT THIS

Predict what the measurement will be if you add the 1/2 cup of salt to the 1/2 cup of water. Will there be exactly one cup, less than one cup, or more than one cup? **Record** your prediction.

STEP 4
Slowly **pour** the salt into the water while stirring gently with a craft stick. When all the salt is mixed in the water, **check** the measurement and **record**. **Share** and **compare** observations with other research teams.

ENERGY • MATTER **149**

Teacher to Teacher

Matter can be divided into three groups: elements, compounds, and mixtures. Mixtures can be divided into two types: homogenous and heterogeneous. Heterogeneous mixtures are like oil and water — no matter how they're mixed, they'll still separate. By contrast, homogenous solutions don't settle or separate easily. Saltwater is a great example.

WHAT HAPPENED?

No, this activity wasn't magic. Like most tricks, it's easy to explain once you understand the science involved. When you poured the salt and **water** together, you made a **mixture**. A mixture is made any time different kinds of **matter** are combined.

As you stirred the mixture, water **dissolved** some of the **salt** breaking it into tiny particles. The water completely surrounded these particles, replacing all the **air** space that had been between the larger particles. This space was part of your measurement in Step 1. Since the air was replaced by water from Step 2, the mixture's final **volume** was less than one cup.

WHAT WE LEARNED

1 Describe the table salt in Step 1. What state of matter is it?

a) hard, chunky, grainy, etc.

b) solid

2 Describe the water in Step 2. What state of matter is it?

a) wet, drippy, liquid, etc.

b) liquid

3 What did you predict in Step 3?
How did this prediction reflect what actually happened in Step 4?

a) answers will vary

b) answers will vary, but should reflect logical conclusions

4 Explain why adding 1/2 cup of salt to 1/2 cup of water didn't result in 1 cup of salt water.

the water dissolved the salt, eliminating the air space that was measured in Step 1

5 Unlike salt and water, cooking oil and water don't mix. Based on what you've learned, what would the final volume be if you repeated this activity with oil and water?

it should be one full cup since oil and water won't mix together like salt and water

What Happened

Review the section with students. Emphasize bold-face words that identify key concepts and introduce new vocabulary.

*No, this activity wasn't magic. Like most tricks, it's easy to explain once you understand the science involved. When you poured the salt and **water** together, you made a **mixture**. A mixture is made any time different kinds of **matter** are combined.*

*As you stirred the mixture, water **dissolved** some of the **salt,** breaking it into tiny particles. The water completely surrounded these particles, replacing all the **air** space that had been between the larger particles. This space was part of your measurement in Step 1. Since the air was replaced by water from Step 2, the mixture's final **volume** was less than one cup.*

What We Learned

Answers will vary. Suggested responses are shown at left.

Conclusion

Read this section aloud to the class to summarize the concepts learned in this activity.

Food for Thought

Read the Scripture aloud to the class. Talk about how God can fill the emptiness in our hearts. Discuss some ways we can increase our personal devotional time.

Journal

If time permits, have a general class discussion about notes and drawings various students added to their journal pages. Discuss correct and incorrect predictions, and remind students that this "trial and error" process is part of the scientific process.

CONCLUSION

A mixture is made when two different forms of matter are combined. The volume of a combination can vary depending on the types of matter combined.

FOOD FOR THOUGHT

Psalm 16:11 Combining the salt and water seemed like simple addition at first glance. You probably didn't think about all the empty space inside matter. The cup didn't fill up quite like you expected!

This Scripture talks about filling up the empty places in our lives. By learning to trust God, we can fill our hearts with joy and peace. Without God, the emptiness results in anger, pain, and sorrow. Which would you like to fill your heart with? The choice is yours!

JOURNAL My Science Notes

Extended Teaching

1. Repeat this activity mixing various materials with water (drink mix, oil, liquid soap, etc.). Use only one material each time! Have students compare the results with the original activity and draw conclusions.

2. Take a field trip to a local bakery. Discuss the ingredients that go into making various baked goods. Find out what solutions are involved and how they work. Have students write a paragraph about one thing they learn.

3. Discuss the difference between solutions and solvents. Encourage students to conduct a "Solution Safari" at home. Have them list the solutions they find (soft drinks, cleaning fluids, furniture polish, ice tea, etc.).

4. Invite a cook or chef to class. Have him/her talk about the ingredients in various dishes. Find out how he/she uses solutions. Have students write a paragraph about one thing they learn.

5. Using the Internet, have teams research simple solutions. Challenge each team to create a poster depicting one solution, what it's made from, and how it's used.

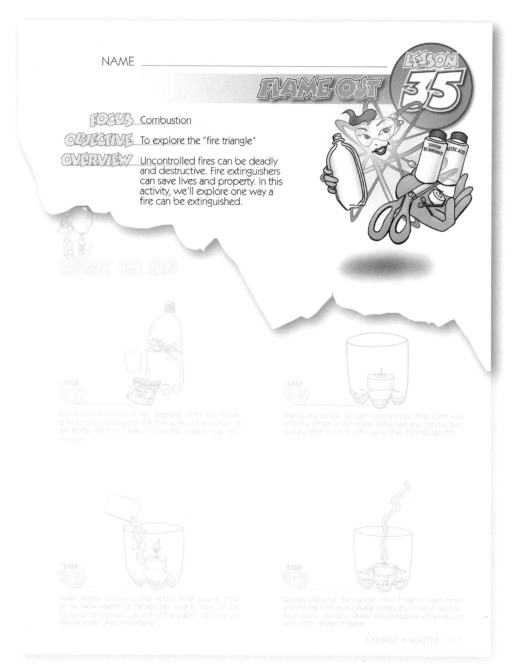

NAME _____

FLAME OUT

LESSON 35

FOCUS Combustion

OBJECTIVE To explore the "fire triangle"

OVERVIEW Uncontrolled fires can be deadly and destructive. Fire extinguishers can save lives and property. In this activity, we'll explore one way a fire can be extinguished.

WHAT TO DO

ENERGY • MATTER

Category

Physical Science
Energy/Matter

Focus

Combustion

Objective

To explore the "fire triangle"

National Standards

A1, A2, B1, B2, E1, E2, E3, F5, G1

Materials Needed

paper cup
candle
sodium bicarbonate
acetic acid
lighter
scissors
two-liter bottle

Safety Concerns

2. Open Flame
Remind students to exercise caution around the open flame of the candle.

4. Sharp Objects
Remind students to exercise caution when using scissors.

Additional Comments

Turn off any fans before beginning. Avoid unnecessary movement (you or the students) during Steps 3 and 4, as air currents will whisk the carbon dioxide right out of the container, ruining the experiment! Tea candles work well for this activity. Keep a fire extinguisher handy in case of emergencies.

Overview

Read the overview aloud to your students. The goal is to create an atmosphere of curiosity and inquiry.

WHAT TO DO

Monitor student research teams as they complete each step.

FLAME OUT

LESSON 35

IDEA Combustion

OBJECTIVE To explore the "fire triangle"

OVERVIEW Uncontrolled fires can be deadly and destructive. Fire extinguishers can save lives and property. In this activity, we'll explore one way a fire can be extinguished.

WHAT TO DO

STEP 1

Cut a two-liter bottle in half. **Dispose** of the top half as directed by your teacher. **Fill** the dents in the bottom of the bottle half full of baking soda. **Fill** a paper cup with vinegar.

STEP 2

Watch as your teacher lights your candle. **Drip** a little wax onto the center of the bottle. **Blow out** your candle, then quickly **stick** it in the soft wax so that it stands upright.

STEP 3

Make notes in your journal about what you've done so far. Now **watch** as the teacher relights your candle. Gently **pour** the acetic acid from the paper cup onto the baking soda. (Avoid the flame!)

STEP 4

Quietly **observe** the candle. (Don't talk or even move around the container.) **Make notes** about what you see. After a few minutes, **share** and **compare** observations with other research teams.

ENERGY • MATTER **153**

Teacher to Teacher

In chemical terms, here's what happened: $NaHCO_3 + CH_3COOH$ resulted in $CO_2 + H_2O + CH_3COONa$. (Not very helpful, is it?) In layman's terms, one result of baking soda + vinegar = carbon dioxide.

Since carbon dioxide is more dense than air, it sank to the bottom, pushing the air up and out. This removed one of the essential components from the fire triangle, stopping combustion.

154 · Lesson 35

?WHAT HAPPENED?

Fires need three things for **combustion** (burning) to occur — **oxygen, fuel,** and **heat.** Firefighters call this the **fire triangle.** Remove one or more parts of the fire triangle and the fire will go out!

This fire started when you supplied heat from a match. The air supplied oxygen, and the candle wax was fuel. In Step 3 you combined acetic acid and baking soda, producing **carbon dioxide** gas. The heavy gas began to fill the container, **pushing** the air with its oxygen out the top. If left undisturbed, this gas soon replaced so much oxygen that the fire went out.

?WHAT WE LEARNED

1 What are the three parts of the fire triangle?
What was the source of each part in this activity?

a) oxygen, fuel, heat

b) oxygen from the air, fuel from the candle wax, heat from the flame

2 Describe what happened in Step 3.
What did the acetic acid and baking soda combination produce?

a) answers will vary, but should be a logical description of the process

b) carbon dioxide gas

3 Based on what you learned in earlier lessons, which has the greater density: oxygen or carbon dioxide? How do you know this?

a) carbon dioxide

b) the air left and the flame went out

4 Explain why the reaction between the baking soda and vinegar extinguished the fire.

Carbon dioxide is heavier than air, so it sank to the bottom, replacing the oxygen. Without oxygen, combustion ceased.

5 Firefighters sometimes remove brush and trees from an area. What part of the fire triangle does this involve? They also spray water on fires. How does this relate to the fire triangle?

a) fuel

b) Water removes the "heat" part of the triangle. Enough water even removes some of the air.

What Happened

Review the section with students. Emphasize bold-face words that identify key concepts and introduce new vocabulary.

Fires need three things for **combustion** *(burning) to occur —* **oxygen, fuel,** *and* **heat.** *Firefighters call this the* **fire triangle.** *Remove one or more parts of the fire triangle and the fire will go out!*

This fire started when you supplied heat from a match. The air supplied oxygen, and the candle wax was fuel. In Step 3, you combined acetic acid and baking soda, producing **carbon dioxide** *gas. The heavy gas began to fill the container,* **pushing** *the air with its oxygen out the top. If left undisturbed, this gas soon replaced so much oxygen that the fire went out.*

What We Learned

Answers will vary. Suggested responses are shown at left.

Conclusion

Read this section aloud to the class to summarize the concepts learned in this activity.

Food for Thought

Read the Scripture aloud to the class. Talk about the meaning of faith, hope, and love. How does God's love cause us to reach out to those around us? Discuss practical ways to serve others.

Journal

If time permits, have a general class discussion about notes and drawings various students added to their journal pages. Discuss correct and incorrect predictions, and remind students that this "trial and error" process is part of the scientific process.

 CONCLUSION

Fires need three things for combustion: oxygen, fuel, and heat. This is known as the fire triangle. Remove any part of the fire triangle, and there won't be a fire.

 FOOD FOR THOUGHT

1 Corinthians 13:13 The fire triangle is a good way to remember what's important when trying to put out a fire! Although each of the parts is different, they are all necessary for combustion to occur.

This Scripture talks about faith, hope, and love. Although each of these is important, Paul reminds us that God's love is the most important of all. When God's love is in our hearts, we think more about the needs of others than our own desires. Reach out to others and share the fire of God's love!

JOURNAL My Science Notes

Extended Teaching

1. Have a class discussion about the fire triangle. Challenge each team to create a poster illustrating the fire triangle. Have them use pictures from magazines or student drawings.

2. Invite a representative from the local fire department to visit your classroom. Talk about the importance of fire drills, both at school and at home. Have students create mini-posters about fire safety.

3. Have your class sponsor a "fire protection week" at your school. Local fire departments can provide ideas, and often even literature to distribute.

4. Research the common causes of household fire. Using this information, challenge each team to select a specific hazard and create one section of a fire safety bulletin board.

5. Take a field trip to a local fire station. Have the firefighters demonstrate the use of various types of equipment and fire protection gear. Have students write a paragraph about one thing they learn.

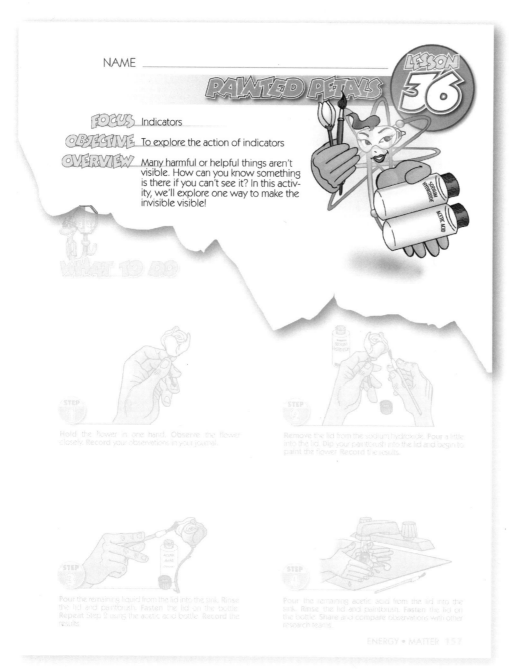

Focus

Indicators

Objective

To explore the action of indicators

National Standards

A1, A2, B1, E1, E2, E3, F1, F4, F5, G1

Materials Needed

silk flower (treated)
paintbrush
sodium hydroxide
acetic acid

Safety Concerns

2. Chemical Burn
Avoid contact of sodium hydroxide with skin.

3. Poison
Keep all chemicals away from mouth and eyes.

4. Slipping
Liquids create a potential for slipping. Remind students to use extra caution.

Additional Comments

Always use the chemical in the lid, not in the bottle! (This helps avoid contamination of chemical in the bottle.) Even though solutions are dilute, goggles and gloves are a good option for this activity to help students develop proper chemical safety habits. Sodium hydroxide can burn skin with prolonged contact. Clean up any spills immediately, using a paper towel and cold water.

Overview

Read the overview aloud to your students. The goal is to create an atmosphere of curiosity and inquiry.

WHAT TO DO

Monitor student research teams as they complete each step.

Indicators

To explore the action of indicators

Many harmful or helpful things aren't visible. How can you know something is there if you can't see it? In this activity, we'll explore one way to make the invisible visible!

WHAT TO DO

STEP 1
Hold the flower in one hand. **Observe** the flower closely. **Record** your observations in your journal.

STEP 2
Remove the lid from the sodium hydroxide. **Pour** a little into the lid. **Dip** your paintbrush into the lid and begin to **paint** the flower. **Record** the results.

STEP 3
Pour the remaining liquid from the lid into the sink. **Rinse** the lid and paintbrush. **Fasten** the lid on the bottle. **Repeat** Step 2 using the acetic acid bottle. **Record** the results.

STEP 4
Pour the remaining acetic acid from the lid into the sink. **Rinse** the lid and paintbrush. **Fasten** the lid on the bottle. **Share** and **compare** observations with other research teams.

ENERGY • MATTER **157**

Teacher to Teacher

Scientists are not the only ones who use chemical indicators. Environmentalists use them to check lakes and streams for signs of acid rain; homeowners use them to check pH levels in hot tubs; recreation directors use them to make sure public swimming pools are safe, and so on. One of the most common uses of chemical indicators is the soil testing kits found at garden centers.

❓ WHAT HAPPENED?

A chemical can be an **acid**, a **base**, or **neutral**. Some chemicals (called **indicators**) change colors around acids or bases. The flower was coated with **phenolphthalein**, an indicator that's colorless around acid. But phenolphthalein turns bright pink in the presence of a base. In Step 2, this helped you see that **sodium hydroxide** is a base. In Step 3, painting on **acetic acid** (vinegar) helped **neutralize** the base, so the indicator became colorless again.

Common acids include vinegar, citrus juice, and soda pop. Common bases include ammonia, detergents, and antacids. Pure water is neutral. Indicators help us check everything from blood sugar levels to swimming pool conditions to soil fertility.

❓ WHAT WE LEARNED

1 Describe what happened to the flower when you painted it with sodium hydroxide in Step 2.

it turned pink where the paintbrush touched it

2 Describe what happened to the flower when you painted it with acetic acid in Step 3.

it changed back to its original color

3 Most chemicals can be divided into three groups. What are they? Give an example of each.

acid: vinegar: citrus juice, or soda pop
base: ammonia: detergents, antacids
neutral: pure water

4 What is an indicator? How are indicators helpful?

a) a chemical that changes colors around an acid or base

b) helps us detect acids or bases we can't see

5 Some berries thrive in acid soil. A farmer buys a field where he wants to plant this kind of berries. Based on what you know, how could an indicator help the farmer?

it would let the farmer know the soil pH so he could add materials to raise or lower the acidity

What Happened

Review the section with students. Emphasize bold-face words that identify key concepts and introduce new vocabulary.

*A chemical can be an **acid**, a **base**, or **neutral**. Some chemicals (called **indicators**) change colors around acids or bases. The flower was coated with **phenolphthalein**, an indicator that's colorless around acid. But phenolphthalein turns bright pink in the presence of a base. In Step 2, this helped you see that **sodium hydroxide** is a base. In Step 3, painting on **acetic acid** (vinegar) helped **neutralize** the base, so the indicator became colorless again.*

Common acids include vinegar, citrus juice, and soda pop. Common bases include ammonia, detergents, and antacids. Pure water is neutral. Indicators help us check everything from blood sugar levels to swimming pool conditions to soil fertility.

What We Learned

Answers will vary. Suggested responses are shown at left.

Conclusion

Read this section aloud to the class to summarize the concepts learned in this activity.

Food for Thought

Read the Scripture aloud to the class. Talk about ways to stay close to God. Discuss way to begin applying these ideas during the summer break.

Journal

If time permits, have a general class discussion about notes and drawings various students added to their journal pages. Discuss correct and incorrect predictions, and remind students that this "trial and error" process is part of the scientific process.

CONCLUSION

A chemical can be an acid, a base, or neutral. Indicators help us identify substances by changing colors.

FOOD FOR THOUGHT

John 1:29 Your flower petals were pure white until the sodium hydroxide came along. Although it looked as clear and harmless as water, it quickly stained the petals pink. But covering the petals with the base removed the stain and made the flowers white again.

Sin is like that. It can look harmless at times, but can really stain your life. Selfish deeds, harmful words, things we do to hurt others — all can leave their mark. This Scripture reminds us that Jesus came to take away the stain of sin. Trust in Jesus and he can give you a clean, new heart.

JOURNAL My Science Notes

160 ENERGY · MATTER

Extended Teaching

1. Invite a lab technician or similar medical professional to visit your classroom. Ask him/her to talk about how medical testing uses indicators. Have students write a paragraph about one thing they learn.

2. Using the Internet, have teams research acid rain. What are its causes? Students can help reduce the problem by looking for ways to reduce energy use at home and school. Encourage teams to list possibilities.

3. Continue discussing acid rain. Challenge teams to create a poster that shows problems associated with acid rain, or a map of areas in the U.S. where acid rain levels are high.

4. Repeat this activity, painting the flower with safe household chemicals. Based on the results, make a list of which ones are acids and which are bases. (Note: Flower will probably need replacement after this activity.)

5. Take a field trip to a municipal swimming pool. Ask a lifeguard to show the materials he/she uses to test for proper pH and to demonstrate their use. Have students write a paragraph about one thing they learn.

True/False (Circle T for true, F for false.)

T   F   **1.** Hard, dry seeds are not alive.

T   F   **2.** If the weather is too cold or too dry, seeds will not sprout.

T   F   **3.** Most seeds sprout best in a very cold area.

T   F   **4.** Seeds are the way that many plants reproduce.

T   F   **5.** Seeds are a major source of food for humans and animals.

Multiple Choice (Fill in the circle beside the best answer.)

6. Which of the following is not an important function of seeds?
- ○ **a.** making more plants
- ○ **b.** emitting oxygen so people can breathe
- ○ **c.** providing food for people
- ○ **d.** providing food for animals

7. In this activity, the towel in the petri dish served what purpose?
- ○ **a.** regulated oxygen
- ○ **b.** regulated water
- ○ **c.** regulated food
- ○ **d.** regulated sunlight

8. Scientists call the "sprouting" process . . .
- ○ **a.** sproutation
- ○ **b.** reproduction
- ○ **c.** regulation
- ○ **d.** germination

9. Scientists call the "baby plant" in a seed . . .
- ○ **a.** a germin
- ○ **b.** an embryo
- ○ **c.** a stem-root
- ○ **d.** an embargo

10. Which of the following are found in every seed?
- ○ **a.** a baby plant and water
- ○ **b.** food and oxygen
- ○ **c.** a baby plant and food
- ○ **d.** oxygen and leaves

SATURATION SITUATION

True/False (Circle T for true, F for false.)

T   F   **1.** Skin helps preserve the water in a creature's body.

T   F   **2.** If an animal loses too much water it could die.

T   F   **3.** The only purpose of skin is to preserve water.

T   F   **4.** Your skin is your body's largest organ.

T   F   **5.** Different body coverings serve different functions.

Multiple Choice (Fill in the circle beside the best answer.)

6. The chemical that produces color in human skin is called . . .
- **a.** water
- **b.** lanolin
- **c.** melanin
- **d.** carbon dioxide

7. Scientists call the "purpose" of something its . . .
- **a.** function
- **b.** structure
- **c.** covering
- **d.** energy

8. The way something looks or how it's built is its . . .
- **a.** function
- **b.** structure
- **c.** covering
- **d.** energy

9. Why did the uncovered sponge dry faster than the covered sponge?
- **a.** The uncovered sponge was exposed to more sunlight.
- **b.** The plastic wrap on the uncovered sponge kept its moisture in.
- **c.** The covered sponge was exposed to more sunlight.
- **d.** The plastic wrap on the covered sponge kept its moisture in.

10. Increased amounts of melanin makes your skin . . .
- **a.** lighter
- **b.** more yellow
- **c.** darker
- **d.** Melanin does not affect skin color.

11

True/False (Circle T for true, F for false.)

T F **1.** A complex eye can only detect the difference between dark and light.

T F **2.** The Tube Eye is a model of a simple eye.

T F **3.** The human eye uses a lens to bend or focus light.

T F **4.** The deli paper in the Tube Eye modeled the lens in a human eye.

T F **5.** The human brain is an important component of vision.

Multiple Choice (Fill in the circle beside the best answer.)

6. Which of the following structures is found in human eyes?

   ○ **a.** deli paper
   ○ **b.** visionary fluid
   ○ **c.** lenses
   ○ **d.** tubes

7. Human vision requires all of the following except . . .

   ○ **a.** light
   ○ **b.** lens
   ○ **c.** brain
   ○ **d.** pictures

8. When you look at an object, what do scientists call the picture you see in your brain?

   ○ **a.** a lens
   ○ **b.** visionary fluid
   ○ **c.** an image
   ○ **d.** an object

9. Simple eyes found in some creatures are used primarily to tell . . .

   ○ **a.** right from wrong
   ○ **b.** left from right
   ○ **c.** light from dark
   ○ **d.** up from down

10. Simple eyes and complex eyes both need which of the following to function?

   ○ **a.** light
   ○ **b.** dark
   ○ **c.** lenses
   ○ **d.** tubes

True/False (Circle T for true, F for false.)

T   F   **1.** Seeds from different kinds of plants are identical.

T   F   **2.** An important function of seeds is to allow plants to reproduce.

T   F   **3.** All plants use identical methods to spread their seeds.

T   F   **4.** Another name for a baby plant is an embryo.

T   F   **5.** Wind, water, and animals all help to spread seeds.

Multiple Choice (Fill in the circle beside the best answer.)

6. Which of the following is not vital to plant survival?
- ○ **a.** light
- ○ **b.** warmth
- ○ **c.** rocks
- ○ **d.** water

7. What might happen if a plant could not scatter its seeds?
- ○ **a.** The new plants would grow close and support the parent plant.
- ○ **b.** The new plants would provide extra nutrients for the parent plant.
- ○ **c.** There would be no noticeable effect.
- ○ **d.** The new plants would be too crowded and die.

8. Which of the following seeds are most likely to be spread by wind?
- ○ **a.** light, fluffy seeds
- ○ **b.** seeds that float
- ○ **c.** seeds with hooks
- ○ **d.** large, seed-filled fruit

9. Which of the following seeds are most likely to be spread by water?
- ○ **a.** light, fluffy seeds
- ○ **b.** seeds that float
- ○ **c.** seeds with hooks
- ○ **d.** large, seed-filled fruit

10. Which of the following is least likely to be spread by an animal?
- ○ **a.** light, fluffy seeds
- ○ **b.** nuts
- ○ **c.** seeds with hooks
- ○ **d.** seed-filled fruit

True/False (Circle T for true, F for false.)

T   F   **1.** A plant's leaves have only one function.

T   F   **2.** A falling raindrop has kinetic energy.

T   F   **3.** Leaves help spread rain evenly to a plant's roots.

T   F   **4.** A plant with fewer leaves can absorb more kinetic energy.

T   F   **5.** Leaves help keep the soil around plants from eroding.

Multiple Choice (Fill in the circle beside the best answer.)

6. When leaves absorb the kinetic energy of raindrops, they protect the . . .
- ○ **a.** light
- ○ **b.** soil
- ○ **c.** water
- ○ **d.** seeds

7. Scientists call the loss of soil . . .
- ○ **a.** kinetics
- ○ **b.** potential
- ○ **c.** erosion
- ○ **d.** energy

8. Leaves direct rain toward what part of a plant?
- ○ **a.** roots
- ○ **b.** soil
- ○ **c.** flowers
- ○ **d.** seeds

9. What is one function of a plant's roots?
- ○ **a.** to repel soil
- ○ **b.** to absorb soil
- ○ **c.** to repel water
- ○ **d.** to absorb water

10. Plants can be planted on a hillside to . . .
- ○ **a.** help increase soil erosion.
- ○ **b.** help decrease soil erosion.
- ○ **c.** make soil drier and harder.
- ○ **d.** increase kinetic energy of falling rain.

True/False (Circle T for true, F for false.)

T   F   **1.** Only a very small portion of most food is water.

T   F   **2.** Micro-organisms (like bacteria and mold) need water to grow.

T   F   **3.** Removing water or warmth slows the decomposition process.

T   F   **4.** Dehydration is the process of adding water to food.

T   F   **5.** Raisins are an example of a dehydrated food.

Multiple Choice (Fill in the circle beside the best answer.)

6. Bacteria must have which of the following to grow?
- ◯ **a.** mold
- ◯ **b.** warmth
- ◯ **c.** light
- ◯ **d.** salt

7. Dehydration helps preserve food by . . .
- ◯ **a.** removing water
- ◯ **b.** removing warmth
- ◯ **c.** both of the above
- ◯ **d.** neither of the above

8. All of the following are ways to preserve food except . . .
- ◯ **a.** washing
- ◯ **b.** freezing
- ◯ **c.** dehydration
- ◯ **d.** refrigeration

9. When something absorbs water, it usually . . .
- ◯ **a.** shrinks.
- ◯ **b.** dehydrates.
- ◯ **c.** expands.
- ◯ **d.** doesn't change.

10. Without preservation, food quickly . . .
- ◯ **a.** dehydrates
- ◯ **b.** freezes
- ◯ **c.** expands
- ◯ **d.** spoils

True/False (Circle T for true, F for false.)

T   F   **1.** Jumping when you hear a loud noise is an example of stimulus/response.

T   F   **2.** Your nervous system helps you react to things in your environment.

T   F   **3.** Everyone responds in the same way to the same kind of stimulus.

T   F   **4.** Your brain, eyes, nerves, and muscles always work independently.

T   F   **5.** A sudden loud noise can be a stimulus.

Multiple Choice (Fill in the circle beside the best answer.)

6. Each of the following is a kind of stimulus except . . .
- ○ **a.** light
- ○ **b.** noise
- ○ **c.** jumping
- ○ **d.** heat

7. Each of the following is a kind of response except . . .
- ○ **a.** smiling when you see a friend
- ○ **b.** stopping at a red traffic light
- ○ **c.** fireworks exploding in the sky
- ○ **d.** crying when something sad happens

8. Which of the following were not involved in catching the frog?
- ○ **a.** eyes and ears
- ○ **b.** nerves and muscles
- ○ **c.** hand and brain
- ○ **d.** teeth and hair

9. Jerking your hand away from a hot surface is . . .
- ○ **a.** a stimulus
- ○ **b.** a response
- ○ **c.** both stimulus and response
- ○ **d.** neither stimulus or response

10. Which of the following can affect a person's stimulus/response times?
- ○ **a.** age
- ○ **b.** ability
- ○ **c.** health
- ○ **d.** all of the above

True/False (Circle T for true, F for false.)

T   F   **1.** Your heart beats much slower immediately after exercising.

T   F   **2.** The faster your heart beats, the faster your pulse.

T   F   **3.** Your heart pushes blood through your entire body.

T   F   **4.** Your heart is a kind of muscle.

T   F   **5.** You need less oxygen and energy while you're exercising.

Multiple Choice (Fill in the circle beside the best answer.)

6. The rhythmic bumping you can feel on your wrist is called your . . .
- ○ **a.** purse
- ○ **b.** heart pump
- ○ **c.** pulse
- ○ **d.** wart

7. Your heart beats . . .
- ○ **a.** only when you are awake.
- ○ **b.** only when you exercise.
- ○ **c.** every moment you are alive.
- ○ **d.** unless you are really scared.

8. Your pulse is caused by . . .
- ○ **a.** your heart signaling nerves in your wrist.
- ○ **b.** your arm muscles flexing in rhythm.
- ○ **c.** your heart pumping blood through your body.
- ○ **d.** your fingers bumping against your wrist.

9. When you are exercising, your heart . . .
- ○ **a.** slows down until you are finished.
- ○ **b.** speeds up.
- ○ **c.** keeps pumping at a steady rate.
- ○ **d.** is not affected in any way.

10. What does blood carry to all parts of the body?
- ○ **a.** oxygen
- ○ **b.** food
- ○ **c.** brain cells
- ○ **d.** nerves

True/False (Circle T for true, F for false.)

T   F   **1.** Scientists call the body's framework of bones a skeleton.

T   F   **2.** Only human beings have skeletons.

T   F   **3.** Human bones come in many shapes and sizes.

T   F   **4.** The human skeleton is composed of less than 100 bones.

T   F   **5.** Unlike skin and tissue, bones are not alive.

Multiple Choice (Fill in the circle beside the best answer.)

6. Bones do all of the following except . . .
- ○ **a.** protect vital organs.
- ○ **b.** protect the nervous system.
- ○ **c.** store nutrients like calcium.
- ○ **d.** pump blood through the body.

7. Which of the following are not connected to bones?
- ○ **a.** tendons
- ○ **b.** ligaments
- ○ **c.** blood vessels
- ○ **d.** muscles

8. What organ does the skull protect?
- ○ **a.** heart
- ○ **b.** brain
- ○ **c.** lungs
- ○ **d.** pancreas

9. A broken bone hurts because . . .
- ○ **a.** bones are alive.
- ○ **b.** bones are not alive.
- ○ **c.** bones store nutrients.
- ○ **d.** bones are like fingernails.

10. Bones produce special blood cells to . . .
- ○ **a.** strengthen ligaments.
- ○ **b.** fight disease.
- ○ **c.** clean blood vessels.
- ○ **d.** weaken tissue.

LESSON 10

True/False (Circle T for true, F for false.)

T　F　**1.** There are five states of matter.

T　F　**2.** Whenever something changes states, energy is involved.

T　F　**3.** Matter is the name scientists use for everything that surrounds us.

T　F　**4.** Stirring salt into water creates a solution.

T　F　**5.** An example of physical change is water evaporating.

Multiple Choice (Fill in the circle beside the best answer.)

6. What states of matter were involved in this activity?
- ○　**a.** solid, solution, and gas
- ○　**b.** plasma, solution, and gas
- ○　**c.** solution, solid, and liquid
- ○　**d.** solid, liquid, and gas

7. Which of the following is NOT a physical change?
- ○　**a.** water boiling
- ○　**b.** water freezing
- ○　**c.** a match burning
- ○　**d.** breaking a match

8. When something evaporates, which state of matter does it become?
- ○　**a.** gas
- ○　**b.** liquid
- ○　**c.** solid
- ○　**d.** plasma

9. A physical change always results in the material changing . . .
- ○　**a.** form
- ○　**b.** temperature
- ○　**c.** color
- ○　**d.** solution

10. Dry salt is what state of matter?
- ○　**a.** gas
- ○　**b.** plasma
- ○　**c.** solid
- ○　**d.** liquid

True/False (Circle T for true, F for false.)

T F **1.** Water is made of molecules.

T F **2.** Surface tension can be described as water molecules "holding hands".

T F **3.** The force of gravity was not involved in this activity.

T F **4.** The needle floated because the surface tension was less than the pull of gravity.

T F **5.** Surface tension is what makes falling raindrops round.

Multiple Choice (Fill in the circle beside the best answer.)

6. Surface tension is . . .

    ○ **a.** a force.

    ○ **b.** a form of gravity.

    ○ **c.** extremely powerful.

    ○ **d.** a form of matter.

7. Falling flat on the surface of a swimming pool hurts because . . .

    ○ **a.** your body only has to break the connection between a few water molecules.

    ○ **b.** your body must connect a huge number of water molecules.

    ○ **c.** your body must break the connection between a huge number of water molecules.

    ○ **d.** swimming pools usually contain "hard" water.

8. The surface of the water in a bucket is not completely flat because of . . .

    ○ **a.** gravity

    ○ **b.** surface tension

    ○ **c.** disconnected molecules

    ○ **d.** water tension

9. The water around the floating needle looked . . .

    ○ **a.** perfectly flat

    ○ **b.** round like a ball

    ○ **c.** dented

    ○ **d.** peaked

10. Which of the following is not a force?

    ○ **a.** the weight of the needle

    ○ **b.** surface tension

    ○ **c.** the shape of the molecules

    ○ **d.** gravity

LESSON 12

GREAT DECEIVER

True/False (Circle T for true, F for false.)

T F **1.** Some materials can absorb water.

T F **2.** Dehydration means removing the water from something.

T F **3.** When water changes from liquid to gas, the process is called absorption.

T F **4.** A paper towel cleaning up spilled water is an example of absorption.

T F **5.** Some materials, like glass or plastic, do not absorb water.

Multiple Choice (Fill in the circle beside the best answer.)

6. The dry gel used in this activity is highly . . .
○ **a.** repellent
○ **b.** hygroscopic
○ **c.** evaporative
○ **d.** saturated

7. This type of gel would be good for . . .
○ **a.** making materials wetter because it releases water so well.
○ **b.** making materials drier because it absorbs water so well.
○ **c.** making materials wetter because it absorbs water so well.
○ **d.** making materials drier because it repels water so well.

8. Why is this type of gel helpful for shipping plants long distances?
○ **a.** It keeps the water in a very liquid condition.
○ **b.** It makes the water evaporate very quickly.
○ **c.** It heats the soil and keeps the plants warm.
○ **d.** It absorbs water, keeping it near the plant's roots.

9. How would this type of gel work in disposable diapers?
○ **a.** very poorly because chemicals should not be used around infants
○ **b.** very poorly because the gel gives off large amounts of water
○ **c.** very well because the gel absorbs moisture quickly
○ **d.** very well because the gel can help keep skin soft

10. A dry cracker is an example of what kind of material?
○ **a.** evaporated
○ **b.** hygroscopic
○ **c.** dehydrated
○ **d.** boiled

True/False (Circle T for true, F for false.)

T   F   **1.** During this activity, gravity was removed from the cup.

T   F   **2.** Gravity constantly pulls on things like people, pets, and buildings.

T   F   **3.** Gravity is a force.

T   F   **4.** On Earth, gravity pulls on some objects but not on others.

T   F   **5.** The water in this activity was unaffected by gravity, but the cup was.

Multiple Choice (Fill in the circle beside the best answer.)

6. Gravity is which kind of force?
- ○ **a.** pull
- ○ **b.** push
- ○ **c.** both push and pull
- ○ **d.** neither push nor pull

7. Which of the following best describes what happened in this activity?
- ○ **a.** The cup fell faster.
- ○ **b.** The water fell faster.
- ○ **c.** The cup and water fell at the same rate.
- ○ **d.** The cup fell fastest in Step 2, but the water fell faster in Step 4.

8. Gravity is considered . . .
- ○ **a.** a theory
- ○ **b.** a hypothesis
- ○ **c.** a natural law
- ○ **d.** an observation

9. Gravity . . .
- ○ **a.** causes objects to fall.
- ○ **b.** keeps us from floating off into space.
- ○ **c.** makes rivers and streams run downhill.
- ○ **d.** all of the above

10. Which of the following is true about gravity?
- ○ **a.** Gravity does not affect things on the Moon.
- ○ **b.** Gravity only functions close to Earth.
- ○ **c.** Gravity affects only small objects like cups and water.
- ○ **d.** Gravity affects all matter.

RUNNY MONEY

True/False (Circle T for true, F for false.)

T   F   **1.** Inertia only affects small objects like coins.

T   F   **2.** When the flicked coin struck the stack of coins, inertia caused the stack to fall over.

T   F   **3.** Because of inertia, an object that is stopped stays stopped.

T   F   **4.** Because of inertia, an object that is moving stays moving.

T   F   **5.** Forces can cause objects to move.

Multiple Choice (Fill in the circle beside the best answer.)

6. What causes a flicked penny to stop, even if it doesn't hit something?
- ◯   **a.** heat
- ◯   **b.** friction
- ◯   **c.** gravity
- ◯   **d.** light

7. For every action, there is . . .
- ◯   **a.** a reaction
- ◯   **b.** a second action
- ◯   **c.** flicked inertia
- ◯   **d.** an inertia action

8. At the start of this activity, what helped keep the stack of pennies motionless?
- ◯   **a.** friction
- ◯   **b.** gravity
- ◯   **c.** inertia
- ◯   **d.** all of the above

9. Forces can _____ between objects.
- ◯   **a.** be completely removed
- ◯   **b.** never be transferred
- ◯   **c.** be transferred
- ◯   **d.** only be actions, never reactions

10. Wearing a seat belt . . .
- ◯   **a.** uses inertia because when the car stops, you stop.
- ◯   **b.** does not use inertia because cars are too large to have inertia.
- ◯   **c.** is a dangerous thing to do when riding in a car.
- ◯   **d.** is a kind of force that keeps everything moving during a collision.

NAME_____ DATE_____

TEETER TOTTER PENNIES

LESSON 15

True/False (Circle T for true, F for false.)

T F **1.** An object is considered "balanced" when it has the same amount of force on both sides.

T F **2.** Opening a paint can with a screwdriver is an example of a balanced force.

T F **3.** Your arm can act like a lever.

T F **4.** A teeter-totter on the playground is an example of a lever.

T F **5.** A balanced lever has more force on one side than on the other.

Multiple Choice (Fill in the circle beside the best answer.)

6. In this activity, what was added to both sides to balance the ruler?
- ○ **a.** light
- ○ **b.** friction
- ○ **c.** heat
- ○ **d.** force

7. Which of the following could not be a lever?
- ○ **a.** a teeter-totter
- ○ **b.** a wheel
- ○ **c.** a ruler
- ○ **d.** your arm

8. When the ruler had more pennies on one side than the other . . .
- ○ **a.** there were equal amounts of force on both sides.
- ○ **b.** there were balanced forces on both sides.
- ○ **c.** there was no gravity on either side.
- ○ **d.** there was more force on one side than the other.

9. To balance two students of unequal weight on a teeter-totter, you must . . .
- ○ **a.** move the lighter student closer to the middle.
- ○ **b.** move both students to the same side.
- ○ **c.** move the heavier student closer to the middle.
- ○ **d.** place both students the exact same distance from the center.

10. What is the "pivot point" of a lever called?
- ○ **a.** the middle
- ○ **b.** the fulcrum
- ○ **c.** the lever point
- ○ **d.** the teeter point

True/False (Circle T for true, F for false.)

T   F   **1.** There were no forces involved in this activity.

T   F   **2.** Gravity did not play a role in this activity.

T   F   **3.** Forces were transferred in this activity.

T   F   **4.** Buoyancy is what made the dropper in this activity float.

T   F   **5.** The force to make the dropper "dive" came from your muscles.

Multiple Choice (Fill in the circle beside the best answer.)

6. A term that is similar to buoyancy is . . .
- ○ **a.** falling
- ○ **b.** gravity
- ○ **c.** sinking
- ○ **d.** floating

7. When you squeezed the bottle, it caused the air bubble in the dropper to . . .
- ○ **a.** expand
- ○ **b.** compress
- ○ **c.** float
- ○ **d.** escape

8. How does buoyancy relate to gravity?
- ○ **a.** Buoyancy opposes gravity.
- ○ **b.** Buoyancy pulls in the same direction as gravity.
- ○ **c.** Buoyancy is the same thing as gravity.
- ○ **d.** The action of buoyancy is identical to gravity.

9. Liquids . . .
- ○ **a.** have nothing to do with buoyancy.
- ○ **b.** are never used to move things.
- ○ **c.** can't be compressed.
- ○ **d.** are unable to make objects float.

10. What force made the dropper float?
- ○ **a.** gravity
- ○ **b.** sinking
- ○ **c.** compression
- ○ **d.** buoyancy

True/False (Circle T for true, F for false.)

T   F   **1.** Molecules are tiny invisible particles.

T   F   **2.** As air begins to cool, the space between molecules begins to contract (shrink).

T   F   **3.** Water always pours smoothly from any kind of bottle.

T   F   **4.** Moving gasses (like hot air) can create movement in other objects.

T   F   **5.** Air pressure on Earth always remains constant.

Multiple Choice (Fill in the circle beside the best answer.)

6. Another name for "squeezing together" is . . .
- ○ **a.** expanding
- ○ **b.** evolving
- ○ **c.** contracting
- ○ **d.** depressurizing

7. When you pushed on the balloon, why wouldn't it go into the jar?
- ○ **a.** The air in the bottle pushed back.
- ○ **b.** There was too much friction in your hand.
- ○ **c.** You simply weren't strong enough.
- ○ **d.** Air pressure pushed up more than you could push down.

8. The purpose of the straw in this activity was to . . .
- ○ **a.** place a huge amount of force on the balloon.
- ○ **b.** squeeze the air in the room so the balloon could come out.
- ○ **c.** squeeze the air in the jar so the balloon could come out.
- ○ **d.** allow air into the jar to equalize the pressure.

9. When the fire went out and the balloon popped into the jar, . . .
- ○ **a.** the forces were exactly equal.
- ○ **b.** there was more force outside the jar than inside.
- ○ **c.** there was more force inside the jar than outside.
- ○ **d.** there were no longer any forces present.

10. The pushing and pulling force of air is called . . .
- ○ **a.** air pressure
- ○ **b.** air forces
- ○ **c.** air gravity
- ○ **d.** air friction

True/False (Circle T for true, F for false.)

T F **1.** Forces can make objects move.

T F **2.** The upward force demonstrated in this activity is called gravity.

T F **3.** The direction of a force can never be changed.

T F **4.** One thing that helped the Spinning Wing fly was the shape of the wing.

T F **5.** Torque is a twisting force.

Multiple Choice (Fill in the circle beside the best answer.)

6. In this activity, the Spinning Wing flew because . . .
- ○ **a.** lift was greater than gravity.
- ○ **b.** gravity was greater than lift.
- ○ **c.** there were no forces present.
- ○ **d.** forces were balanced on both sides of the wing.

7. As the Spinning Wing flew, air pressure . . .
- ○ **a.** was greater on the wing's top than on its bottom.
- ○ **b.** was greater on the wing's bottom than on its top.
- ○ **c.** was balanced equally on the wing's top and the bottom.
- ○ **d.** was identical on all parts of the wing.

8. Which of the following is not a form of torque?
- ○ **a.** a spinning propeller
- ○ **b.** a spinning wheel
- ○ **c.** a dropping ball
- ○ **d.** a swinging bat

9. What did the Spinning Wing do with the force provided by your hands?
- ○ **a.** changed the direction of force
- ○ **b.** changed the force into light and heat energy
- ○ **c.** made the force move only in a straight line
- ○ **d.** removed the presence of any force

10. What device is the Spinning Wing most similar to?
- ○ **a.** a lever
- ○ **b.** a helicopter
- ○ **c.** a baseball bat
- ○ **d.** a teeter-totter

True/False (Circle T for true, F for false.)

T   F   **1.** Everything around us is made of matter.

T   F   **2.** Gas is not a matter since we cannot see it.

T   F   **3.** The air that surrounds Earth is called the atmosphere.

T   F   **4.** Matter is a type of push or pull.

T   F   **5.** Weather is created by the constant movement of air.

Multiple Choice (Fill in the circle beside the best answer.)

6. In this activity, it was hard to pour water into the second bottle because . . .
- ○ **a.** air was trapped inside.
- ○ **b.** air was trapped outside.
- ○ **c.** water is not a form of matter.
- ○ **d.** air is not a form of matter.

7. Which of the following is not an example of air creating movement?
- ○ **a.** wet laundry drying on a clothesline
- ○ **b.** a gently blowing wind
- ○ **c.** a hurricane
- ○ **d.** the air inside a balloon

8. Which of the following is not a state of matter?
- ○ **a.** a solid
- ○ **b.** a liquid
- ○ **c.** a gas
- ○ **d.** All of the above are states of matter.

9. What state of matter was trapped in the second bottle?
- ○ **a.** a solid
- ○ **b.** a liquid
- ○ **c.** a gas
- ○ **d.** none of the above

10. What state of matter was poured into the first bottle?
- ○ **a.** a solid
- ○ **b.** a liquid
- ○ **c.** a gas
- ○ **d.** none of the above

True/False (Circle T for true, F for false.)

T F **1.** Air pressure is all around us.

T F **2.** Air pressure is a kind of force.

T F **3.** Air pressure only has enough power to move very small objects.

T F **4.** Air pressure in the atmosphere affects the weather.

T F **5.** Air pressure can keep a basketball from going flat.

Multiple Choice (Fill in the circle beside the best answer.)

6. Which of the following does not illustrate air pressure?
- **a.** the space inside car tires
- **b.** the water trapped in a full bottle
- **c.** the space inside a basketball
- **d.** the air used to run commercial tools

7. When it wasn't sealed with your thumb, why didn't the straw go into the potato?
- **a.** potatoes are too hard for straws to pierce
- **b.** one of the two straws was much weaker
- **c.** without the trapped air, the straw was too weak
- **d.** removing the wrapper made the straw much weaker

8. What made the sealed straw stronger?
- **a.** trapped air compressed, supporting the straw
- **b.** trapped air expanded, supporting the straw
- **c.** sealing removed all the air from the straw
- **d.** sealing removed all the air from the potato

9. How did this activity prove that air is a form of matter?
- **a.** the potato could not be pierced
- **b.** the straw with the trapped air penetrated the potato
- **c.** it showed the straw supplied the strength to pierce the potato
- **d.** air is not a form of matter

10. What would happen if there was no air pressure?
- **a.** human beings could not breathe
- **b.** weather systems would move more rapidly
- **c.** weather systems would move more slowly
- **d.** the atmospheric moisture would be much higher

a reason for
Science

True/False (Circle T for true, F for false.)

T F **1.** Everything on Earth is made of matter.

T F **2.** Matter on Earth comes in three forms.

T F **3.** The three forms (states) of matter are animal, mineral, and vegetable.

T F **4.** Matter does not have volume or mass.

T F **5.** Matter is anything that takes up space and has substance.

Multiple Choice (Fill in the circle beside the best answer.)

6. In this activity, why didn't the cotton in the cup get wet when you pushed it under water?

○ **a.** Because water is not matter, it couldn't make the cotton wet.

○ **b.** Because air is matter, the trapped air's volume kept the water out of the cup.

○ **c.** Because air is not matter, the water and cotton could not bond.

○ **d.** This kind of cotton is extremely water repellent.

7. Which of the following is a gas?

○ **a.** sugar

○ **b.** gasoline

○ **c.** air

○ **d.** light

8. Which of the following is a solid?

○ **a.** sugar

○ **b.** gasoline

○ **c.** air

○ **d.** light

9. Which of the following is a liquid?

○ **a.** sugar

○ **b.** gasoline

○ **c.** air

○ **d.** light

10. Which of the following is not a form of matter?

○ **a.** sugar

○ **b.** gasoline

○ **c.** air

○ **d.** light

LESSON
22

WAVE WATCHER

True/False (Circle T for true, F for false.)

T F **1.** Water is more dense than oil.

T F **2.** Oil floats on water because it is more dense than water.

T F **3.** Oil and water are both liquids.

T F **4.** Waves can contain powerful amounts of energy.

T F **5.** Liquids always mix easily and never form layers.

Multiple Choice (Fill in the circle beside the best answer.)

6. Moving water . . .
- ○ **a.** can cause erosion.
- ○ **b.** can never cause erosion.
- ○ **c.** does not contain energy.
- ○ **d.** always contains layers of oil.

7. The energy for this activity came directly from . . .
- ○ **a.** the heat of the sun on the bottle.
- ○ **b.** the shape of the bottle.
- ○ **c.** chemicals in the oil.
- ○ **d.** your muscles.

8. When you pour liquid more dense than water into water . . .
- ○ **a.** the dense liquid will float on the water.
- ○ **b.** the water will float on the dense liquid.
- ○ **c.** the dense liquid and water will blend together.
- ○ **d.** no liquid is more dense than water.

9. A major source of energy for ocean waves is . . .
- ○ **a.** rain.
- ○ **b.** shells.
- ○ **c.** salt.
- ○ **d.** wind.

10. Ocean waves carry an enormous amount of . . .
- ○ **a.** energy.
- ○ **b.** light.
- ○ **c.** oil.
- ○ **d.** chemicals.

True/False (Circle T for true, F for false.)

T   F   **1.** It takes energy to make anything move.

T   F   **2.** When moving water shifts materials, it is called erosion.

T   F   **3.** Because it is a natural force, it is impossible to stop erosion.

T   F   **4.** Although locally severe, soil erosion is only a minor problem worldwide.

T   F   **5.** Barriers along lake shores can help absorb or divert wave energy.

Multiple Choice (Fill in the circle beside the best answer.)

6. The energy of moving water can be . . .
- ○ **a.** destroyed
- ○ **b.** ignored
- ○ **c.** absorbed
- ○ **d.** deflated

7. What might happen if soil erosion were not controlled?
- ○ **a.** It would affect plants, but not people or animals.
- ○ **b.** There could be food shortages because plants need soil.
- ○ **c.** Water in streams and rivers would become crystal clear.
- ○ **d.** There would be no serious problem since soil is just dirt.

8. Erosion takes place . . .
- ○ **a.** along the ocean's shore.
- ○ **b.** on the edge of rivers.
- ○ **c.** along streams.
- ○ **d.** all of the above

9. When you placed your hand in front of the sand, it modeled a . . .
- ○ **a.** beach
- ○ **b.** blanket
- ○ **c.** barrier
- ○ **d.** barometer

10. Which of the following might help control erosion?
- ○ **a.** planting grass
- ○ **b.** cutting down trees
- ○ **c.** killing weeds
- ○ **d.** bare ground

True/False (Circle T for true, F for false.)

T   F   **1.** Moving water can hold and carry sediments.

T   F   **2.** The heaviest materials are usually in the top layers of sediment.

T   F   **3.** As water slows down, it loses energy.

T   F   **4.** Sediments can be deposited by either wind or water.

T   F   **5.** Gravity is the force that keeps sediments suspended.

Multiple Choice (Fill in the circle beside the best answer.)

6. If moving water holds and carries materials, it is called a . . .
- **a.** solution
- **b.** suspension
- **c.** sediment
- **d.** Water can not carry materials.

7. What force pulls sediments down?
- **a.** gravity
- **b.** suspension
- **c.** waves
- **d.** shaking

8. The waters of a major flood are a form of . . .
- **a.** solution
- **b.** suspension
- **c.** sediment
- **d.** none of the above

9. To keep a material suspended in water takes constant . . .
- **a.** light
- **b.** heat
- **c.** air
- **d.** energy

10. Which of the following would a flood probably carry the farthest?
- **a.** ping-pong balls
- **b.** sand
- **c.** wood
- **d.** nails

Copyright ©2003 The Concerned Group, Inc.

True/False (Circle T for true, F for false.)

T   F   **1.** Light is a form of matter.

T   F   **2.** Light can pass through some things, but not all things.

T   F   **3.** Light bounces off some materials.

T   F   **4.** The protein and fat molecules in milk are smaller than water molecules.

T   F   **5.** Blue light scatters easily because of its wavelength.

Multiple Choice (Fill in the circle beside the best answer.)

6. The light from the flashlight was . . .
- ○ **a.** a form of energy.
- ○ **b.** a form of matter.
- ○ **c.** a form of material.
- ○ **d.** none of the above

7. The process scientists call "scattering" explains why . . .
- ○ **a.** bad weather occurs.
- ○ **b.** the sky looks blue.
- ○ **c.** rainbows require sunlight.
- ○ **d.** light passes through milk.

8. If light can pass through a material, that material is . . .
- ○ **a.** scattered
- ○ **b.** transparent
- ○ **c.** reflective
- ○ **d.** not matter

9. All of the following materials are transparent except . . .
- ○ **a.** clear glass
- ○ **b.** pure water
- ○ **c.** contact lenses
- ○ **d.** fresh milk

10. What affect did the milk in this activity have on light?
- ○ **a.** The milk absorbed the light.
- ○ **b.** The milk passed through the light.
- ○ **c.** The milk scattered the light.
- ○ **d.** The milk did not affect the light.

True/False (Circle T for true, F for false.)

T F **1.** When animals die, their bones always become fossils.

T F **2.** Any preserved part of an ancient living thing is called a fossil.

T F **3.** The preserved footprint of an ancient creature is also a fossil.

T F **4.** A mold fossil is an actual bone from an ancient creature.

T F **5.** A cast fossil bears little resemblance to the original object.

Multiple Choice (Fill in the circle beside the best answer.)

6. Another word for rotting or spoiling is . . .
- ○ **a.** decreasing
- ○ **b.** increasing
- ○ **c.** decomposing
- ○ **d.** composing

7. Which body part is most likely to have become a fossil?
- ○ **a.** muscle
- ○ **b.** stomach
- ○ **c.** hair
- ○ **d.** bone

8. An animal track made in soft mud resembles . . .
- ○ **a.** a mold fossil
- ○ **b.** a cast fossil
- ○ **c.** a bone fossil
- ○ **d.** none of the above

9. Why are teeth more likely to become fossils than muscle?
- ○ **a.** they are more likely to decompose
- ○ **b.** they are less likely to decompose
- ○ **c.** they are just as likely to decompose
- ○ **d.** none of the above

10. What is one problem with studying ancient life through fossils?
- ○ **a.** Fossils only provide certain kinds of information.
- ○ **b.** Fossils are always much too heavy to transport.
- ○ **c.** Fossils are usually fakes, created by scientists.
- ○ **d.** Fossils are only found in one location on Earth.

True/False (Circle T for true, F for false.)

T   F   **1.** Groups of stars that have a certain shape when viewed from Earth are called constellations.

T   F   **2.** The constellations we see are exactly the same as those seen by ancient people.

T   F   **3.** Constellations were used by ancient people to determine directions after dark.

T   F   **4.** Every star in a constellation is identical to every other star in that group.

T   F   **5.** All stars stay in exactly the same place and never move.

Multiple Choice (Fill in the circle beside the best answer.)

6. Ancient people named constellations after . . .
- **a.** animals
- **b.** people
- **c.** objects
- **d.** all of the above

7. If you were millions of miles out in space, the constellations would . . .
- **a.** look identical to what we see from Earth.
- **b.** look much different than what we see from Earth.
- **c.** be harder to see because you would be too far from Earth.
- **d.** look more like planets.

8. The stars in the constellations we studied were . . .
- **a.** all exactly the same distance from Earth.
- **b.** all identical in every way.
- **c.** different colors and distances from Earth.
- **d.** all very, very tiny.

9. What we call stars are actually far away . . .
- **a.** suns
- **b.** moons
- **c.** planets
- **d.** solar systems

10. A thousand years ago, the constellations seen from Earth were . . .
- **a.** identical to what we see today, because stars do not move.
- **b.** somewhat different from what we see today, because stars move over time.
- **c.** much smaller than what we see now, because stars grow over time.
- **d.** There is no way to know because this was too long ago.

True/False (Circle T for true, F for false.)

T   F   **1.** Waves transfer energy from one place to another.

T   F   **2.** It takes energy to make anything move.

T   F   **3.** Many forms of energy travel in waves.

T   F   **4.** Light is a form of energy that travels in waves.

T   F   **5.** When a wave bounces back, scientists call this "reflection."

Multiple Choice (Fill in the circle beside the best answer.)

6. All of the following can travel in waves except . . .
- ○ **a.** light
- ○ **b.** darkness
- ○ **c.** sound
- ○ **d.** heat

7. Which of the following is an example of reflection?
- ○ **a.** looking directly at a candle
- ○ **b.** waves bouncing back from a rocky shore
- ○ **c.** dropping a slinky on the floor
- ○ **d.** throwing a ball

8. When you wiggled one end of the slinky, what was transferred to the other end?
- ○ **a.** sound
- ○ **b.** heat
- ○ **c.** energy
- ○ **d.** light

9. Which of the following devices uses waves to transfer energy?
- ○ **a.** a television
- ○ **b.** a radio
- ○ **c.** a cellular phone
- ○ **d.** all of the above

10. Which of the following activities does not use waves to transfer energy?
- ○ **a.** sunlight striking the surface of a leaf
- ○ **b.** hammering a nail into a board
- ○ **c.** talking to your teacher on the phone
- ○ **d.** cooking a pizza in the oven

MILK JUG MEGAPHONE

LESSON 29

True/False (Circle T for true, F for false.)

T F **1.** Sound is a form of energy that travels in waves.

T F **2.** Making sound louder is called amplification.

T F **3.** Tapping the slinky with a pencil created a form of energy.

T F **4.** Amplification is used to weaken sound energy.

T F **5.** Waves prevent sound from traveling from one place to another.

Multiple Choice (Fill in the circle beside the best answer.)

6. In this activity, the slinky . . .
- ○ **a.** destroyed the energy transferred to it.
- ○ **b.** carried sound energy away from the milk jug.
- ○ **c.** transferred sound energy to the milk jug.
- ○ **d.** absorbed sound energy from the milk jug.

7. Banging on a pan with a spoon . . .
- ○ **a.** transfers energy to the surface of the pan.
- ○ **b.** destroys the energy supplied by your muscles.
- ○ **c.** transfers energy from the pan to the spoon.
- ○ **d.** does not create sound energy.

8. Sound is a form of . . .
- ○ **a.** light
- ○ **b.** energy
- ○ **c.** transfer
- ○ **d.** heat

9. The milk jug made the sound from the slinky seem . . .
- ○ **a.** softer.
- ○ **b.** louder.
- ○ **c.** unable to be heard.
- ○ **d.** exactly the same.

10. A device that makes a sound louder is called . . .
- ○ **a.** an amplifier
- ○ **b.** a sounder
- ○ **c.** an acoustic
- ○ **d.** a softener

True/False (Circle T for true, F for false.)

T   F   **1.** Energy comes in many different forms.

T   F   **2.** Changing energy from one form into another is never a good idea.

T   F   **3.** In this activity, the string absorbed light energy from the sun.

T   F   **4.** Food providing energy for exercise is an example of energy changing forms.

T   F   **5.** A material that can absorb and release light is called phosphorescent.

Multiple Choice (Fill in the circle beside the best answer.)

6. Which of the following would be a good use for phosphorescent material?

○   **a.** safety clothing for people who work at night
○   **b.** a form of upholstery to make a chair softer
○   **c.** special insulation to make a room much quieter
○   **d.** an ingredient in cooked or baked food

7. Why was it important to begin this activity by placing the string in a dark area?

○   **a.** to be certain the string was not broken
○   **b.** to be certain the string was not releasing sound energy
○   **c.** to be certain the string was not absorbing heat energy
○   **d.** to be certain the string was not absorbing or releasing light energy

8. What was the purpose of placing the string in direct sunlight?

○   **a.** to allow it to absorb heat energy
○   **b.** to allow it to release sound energy
○   **c.** to allow it to absorb light energy
○   **d.** to allow it to release light energy

9. Recharging a cellular phone battery is an example of . . .

○   **a.** destroying energy
○   **b.** storing sound and heat energy
○   **c.** transferring energy from one place to another
○   **d.** using heat energy only

10. Scientists call a material "phosphorescent" if it can absorb and release . . .

○   **a.** sound
○   **b.** light
○   **c.** water
○   **d.** heat

BUG'S EYE VIEW

True/False (Circle T for true, F for false.)

T F **1.** Insects eyes have exactly the same structure as human eyes.

T F **2.** Most insect's eyes produce a single image of what they're looking at.

T F **3.** Insects have simple eyes; humans have compound eyes.

T F **4.** A kaleidoscope makes multiple images of what you're looking at.

T F **5.** A lens focuses light to produce an image.

Multiple Choice (Fill in the circle beside the best answer.)

6. The device used in this activity is called . . .
- ○ **a.** a lightscope
- ○ **b.** a lens maker
- ○ **c.** a kaleidoscope
- ○ **d.** a compondoscope

7. What does a lens do?
- ○ **a.** focuses sound to produce an image
- ○ **b.** focuses light to produce an image
- ○ **c.** focuses images to produce light
- ○ **d.** focuses images to produce sound

8. Scientists call an eye with many lenses a . . .
- ○ **a.** multiple eye
- ○ **b.** compound eye
- ○ **c.** intelligent eye
- ○ **d.** kaleidoscope

9. The "picture" a lens creates is called . . .
- ○ **a.** a kaleidoscope
- ○ **b.** a multiple eye
- ○ **c.** a focus
- ○ **d.** an image

10. Why would a compound eye work for an insect but not for a human?
- ○ **a.** The human brain is not designed to work with a compound eye.
- ○ **b.** The human brain is designed to work with only with compound eyes.
- ○ **c.** A compound eye does not allow enough light for vision.
- ○ **d.** A compound eye focuses too much light for vision.

True/False (Circle T for true, F for false.)

T   F   **1.** Magnets are sometimes used to help separate materials in a recycling center.

T   F   **2.** A magnet is attracted to wood.

T   F   **3.** All three states of matter (solid, liquid, and gas) are magnetic.

T   F   **4.** Ferrous metals are attracted to a magnet.

T   F   **5.** Aluminum is an example of a non-ferrous metal.

Multiple Choice (Fill in the circle beside the best answer.)

6. Iron, cobalt, and nickle are attracted to a magnet. They are . . .
- ○ **a.** non-ferrous metals
- ○ **b.** ferrous metals
- ○ **c.** non-ferrous woods
- ○ **d.** ferrous woods

7. A material that has the ability to attract ferrous metals is called . . .
- ○ **a.** unmagnetic
- ○ **b.** attractive
- ○ **c.** unattractive
- ○ **d.** magnetic

8. Aluminum and copper are not attracted to a magnet. They are . . .
- ○ **a.** non-ferrous metals
- ○ **b.** ferrous metals
- ○ **c.** non-ferrous woods
- ○ **d.** ferrous woods

9. Magnetism is . . .
- ○ **a.** a non-ferrous metal found only on Earth.
- ○ **b.** a ferrous metal found only in space.
- ○ **c.** a basic force in the universe.
- ○ **d.** a basic force found only on Earth.

10. Which of the following would not need a magnet to work?
- ○ **a.** an electric motor
- ○ **b.** an electric door lock
- ○ **c.** a bicycle wheel
- ○ **d.** a vending machine

True/False (Circle T for true, F for false.)

T   F   **1.** An electromagnet is a magnet you can turn on or off.

T   F   **2.** Applying current to a piece of non-ferrous metal can turn it into an electromagnet.

T   F   **3.** Magnetism has a "partner" that is called electricity.

T   F   **4.** Unlike battery current, electricity from household current can be very dangerous.

T   F   **5.** A "D cell" battery can be used as a small electrical power source.

Multiple Choice (Fill in the circle beside the best answer.)

6. In this activity . . .
  ○   **a.** the electrical current made the nail magnetic.
  ○   **b.** the nail made the electrical current magnetic.
  ○   **c.** the nail kept the electrical current from becoming a magnet.
  ○   **d.** the nail was already magnetic before electrical current was applied.

7. Electricity . . .
  ○   **a.** is unable to work with magnetism because they are opposing forces.
  ○   **b.** works with magnetism to create an important kind of force.
  ○   **c.** works with magnetism to attract materials like wood and plastic.
  ○   **d.** is not related to magnetism in any way.

8. Scientists call the combination of magnetism and electricity . . .
  ○   **a.** magnoelectricity
  ○   **b.** electromagnetism
  ○   **c.** electrocurrent
  ○   **d.** magnocurrent

9. An electromagnet could be used to . . .
  ○   **a.** open and lock a car door.
  ○   **b.** help an electric motor to run.
  ○   **c.** sort different metals at a recycling center.
  ○   **d.** all of the above

10. Electromagnets are helpful because . . .
  ○   **a.** they can charge batteries.
  ○   **b.** they can make nails sharper.
  ○   **c.** they can be turned on and off.
  ○   **d.** they can attract wood and plastic.

True/False (Circle T for true, F for false.)

T   F   **1.** When different kinds of matter are combined, it is called a mixture.

T   F   **2.** Matter can be a solid, a liquid, or a gas.

T   F   **3.** In this activity, the salt was a solid and the water was a gas.

T   F   **4.** All solids will dissolve in water.

T   F   **5.** When added to a mixture, liquid matter has no volume.

Multiple Choice (Fill in the circle beside the best answer.)

6. In this activity, adding 1/2 cup of water to 1/2 cup of salt resulted in . . .
- ○ **a.** a mixture of exactly one cup.
- ○ **b.** a mixture of less than one cup.
- ○ **c.** a mixture of more than one cup.
- ○ **d.** two layers because water and salt do not mix.

7. Adding water to salt, then stirring, will cause the salt to . . .
- ○ **a.** dissolve
- ○ **b.** expand
- ○ **c.** melt
- ○ **d.** evaporate

8. The salt and water mixture bubbled when stirred because . . .
- ○ **a.** water squeezed the air out of the salt crystals.
- ○ **b.** salt squeezed the air out of the water molecules.
- ○ **c.** salt and water squeezed the air out of the craft stick.
- ○ **d.** air in the spaces between the salt crystals was escaping.

9. When we say that the water "dissolved" the salt, it means . . .
- ○ **a.** the water squeezed and compressed the salt crystals.
- ○ **b.** the water surrounded the salt crystals, breaking them into tiny pieces.
- ○ **c.** the water melted the salt crystals, producing heat.
- ○ **d.** the water melted the salt crystals, producing light.

10. Since water and oil do not mix, adding 1/2 cup of oil to 1/2 cup of water results in . . .
- ○ **a.** exactly one cup of liquid.
- ○ **b.** less than one cup of liquid.
- ○ **c.** more than one cup of liquid.
- ○ **d.** a mixture of one cup.

True/False (Circle T for true, F for false.)

T   F   **1.** Uncontrolled fires can be destructive and dangerous.

T   F   **2.** When vinegar and baking soda are mixed, it produces carbon monoxide.

T   F   **3.** Carbon dioxide is lighter than air.

T   F   **4.** A fire must have oxygen to continue burning.

T   F   **5.** When the baking soda reacted with the vinegar, it started a fire.

Multiple Choice (Fill in the circle beside the best answer.)

6. Another name for combustion is . . .
- ○ **a.** burning
- ○ **b.** carbon dioxide
- ○ **c.** fire triangle
- ○ **d.** flame out

7. Which of the following does not help a fire keep burning?
- ○ **a.** oxygen
- ○ **b.** heat
- ○ **c.** fuel
- ○ **d.** carbon dioxide

8. Removing one or more parts of the fire triangle will cause the fire to . . .
- ○ **a.** burn brighter
- ○ **b.** burn faster
- ○ **c.** go out
- ○ **d.** explode

9. This activity showed a difference in density between carbon dioxide and air because . . .
- ○ **a.** the heavier air sank to the bottom, replacing the lighter carbon dioxide.
- ○ **b.** the heavier carbon dioxide sank to the bottom, replacing the lighter air.
- ○ **c.** the heavier air caused the candle flame to go out.
- ○ **d.** none of the above

10. Clearing brush and small trees helps remove which part of the fire triangle.
- ○ **a.** oxygen
- ○ **b.** heat
- ○ **c.** fuel
- ○ **d.** all of the above

True/False (Circle T for true, F for false.)

T   F   **1.** An indicator is a chemical that changes color because of a neutral substance.

T   F   **2.** A chemical can be an acid, neutral, or base.

T   F   **3.** Acetic acid is a good example of a chemical indicator.

T   F   **4.** Sodium hydroxide is a good example of a chemical indicator.

T   F   **5.** In this activity, the flower had been coated with an indicator in advance.

Multiple Choice (Fill in the circle beside the best answer.)

6. Another name for acetic acid is . . .
- ○ **a.** vinegar
- ○ **b.** sodium hydroxide
- ○ **c.** phenolphthalein
- ○ **d.** water

7. What does adding acedic acid to sodium hydroxide do?
- ○ **a.** dissolves
- ○ **b.** colors
- ○ **c.** neutralizes
- ○ **d.** burns

8. Which of the following is not a common household base?
- ○ **a.** ammonia
- ○ **b.** vinegar
- ○ **c.** detergent
- ○ **d.** antacids

9. Which of the following is not a common household acid?
- ○ **a.** ammonia
- ○ **b.** vinegar
- ○ **c.** soda pop
- ○ **d.** orange juice

10. Pure water is . . .
- ○ **a.** acid
- ○ **b.** base
- ○ **c.** neutral
- ○ **d.** part acid, part base

Assessment Answer Key
LIFE

Lesson 1
Sprout Science

1. F
2. T
3. F
4. T
5. T
6. b
7. b
8. d
9. b
10. c

Lesson 2
Saturation Situation

1. T
2. T
3. F
4. T
5. T
6. c
7. a
8. b
9. d
10. c

Lesson 3
Tube Eye

1. F
2. T
3. T
4. F
5. T
6. c
7. d
8. c
9. c
10. a

Lesson 4
Special Delivery

1. F
2. T
3. F
4. T
5. T
6. c
7. d
8. a
9. b
10. a

Lesson 5
Leaf Umbrella

1. F
2. T
3. T
4. F
5. T
6. b
7. c
8. a
9. d
10. b

Lesson 6
Swell Creature

1. F
2. T
3. T
4. F
5. T
6. b
7. a
8. a
9. c
10. d

Lesson 7
Reaction Response

1. T
2. T
3. F
4. F
5. T
6. c
7. c
8. d
9. b
10. d

Lesson 8
Pumping Pulse

1. F
2. T
3. T
4. T
5. F
6. c
7. c
8. c
9. b
10. a

Lesson 9
Bare Bones

1. T
2. F
3. T
4. F
5. F
6. d
7. c
8. b
9. a
10. b

Lesson 10
Three States

1. F
2. T
3. T
4. T
5. T
6. d
7. c
8. a
9. a
10. c

Lesson 11
Needle Boat

1. T
2. T
3. F
4. F
5. T
6. a
7. c
8. b
9. c
10. c

Lesson 12
Great Deceiver

1. T
2. T
3. F
4. T
5. T
6. b
7. b
8. d
9. c
10. b

Lesson 13
Gravity Stopper

1. F
2. T
3. T
4. F
5. F
6. a
7. c
8. c
9. d
10. d

Lesson 14
Runny Money

1. F
2. F
3. T
4. T
5. T
6. b
7. a
8. d
9. c
10. a

Lesson 15
Teeter Totter Pennies

1. T
2. F
3. T
4. T
5. F
6. d
7. b
8. d
9. c
10. b

Lesson 16
Diving Dropper

1. F
2. F
3. T
4. T
5. T
6. d
7. b
8. a
9. c
10. d

Lesson 17
Balloon Gobbler

1. T
2. T
3. F
4. T
5. F
6. c
7. a
8. d
9. b
10. a

Lesson 18
Spinning Wing

1. T
2. F
3. F
4. T
5. T
6. a
7. b
8. c
9. a
10. b

Lesson 19
Reluctant Water

1. T
2. F
3. T
4. F
5. T
6. a
7. d
8. d
9. c
10. b

Lesson 20
Potato Stabber

1. T
2. T
3. F
4. T
5. T
6. b
7. c
8. a
9. b
10. a

Lesson 21
Waterproof Cotton

1. T
2. T
3. F
4. F
5. T
6. b
7. c
8. a
9. b
10. d

Lesson 22
Wave Watcher

1. T
2. F
3. T
4. T
5. F
6. a
7. d
8. b
9. d
10. a

Lesson 23
Wash Away Waves

1. T
2. T
3. F
4. F
5. T
6. c
7. b
8. d
9. c
10. a

Lesson 24
Flood In A Jar

1. T
2. F
3. T
4. T
5. F
6. b
7. a
8. b
9. d
10. a

Lesson 25
Sky In A Jar

1. F
2. T
3. T
4. F
5. T
6. a
7. b
8. b
9. d
10. c

Lesson 26
Fast Fossil

1. F
2. T
3. T
4. F
5. F
6. c
7. d
8. a
9. b
10. a

Lesson 27
Star Search

1. T
2. F
3. T
4. F
5. F
6. d
7. b
8. c
9. a
10. b

Lesson 28
Wave Maker

1. T
2. T
3. T
4. T
5. T
6. b
7. b
8. c
9. d
10. b

Lesson 29
Milk Jug Megaphone

1. T
2. T
3. T
4. F
5. F
6. c
7. a
8. b
9. b
10. a

Lesson 30
Sunshine String

1. T
2. F
3. T
4. T
5. T
6. a
7. d
8. c
9. c
10. b

Lesson 31
Bugs Eye View

1. F
2. F
3. F
4. T
5. T
6. c
7. b
8. b
9. d
10. a

Lesson 32
Attractive Iron

1. T
2. F
3. F
4. T
5. T
6. b
7. d
8. a
9. c
10. c

Lesson 33
Ferrous Force

1. T
2. F
3. T
4. T
5. T
6. a
7. b
8. b
9. d
10. c

Lesson 34
Magic Matter

1. T
2. T
3. F
4. F
5. F
6. b
7. a
8. d
9. b
10. a

Lesson 35
Fire Triangle

1. T
2. F
3. F
4. T
5. F
6. a
7. d
8. c
9. b
10. c

Lesson 36
Painted Petals

1. F
2. T
3. F
4. F
5. T
6. a
7. c
8. b
9. a
10. c

Shopping List

This **"Shopping List"** is provided for your convenience. It contains all the items that are not common classroom supplies (paper, pencil, scissors, etc.) or components found in your Materials Kit.

Please note: There are a few items (like tissue paper rolls) that require advance planning for effective collection.

Lesson 1
Paper towels

Lesson 2
Plastic wrap
Aluminum pie plate

Lesson 3
Cardboard tube

Lesson 4
Apple

Lesson 6
Bowl
Pie pan or tray

Lesson 8
Stopwatch

Lesson 10
Disposable pie pan
Black construction paper

Lesson 11
Needle
Pointed tweezers

Lesson 13
Bucket
Paper towels

Lesson 16
Soft drink bottle (2 liter)

Lesson 17
Glass jar (1 gallon, wide mouth)
Lighter

Lesson 19
Soft drink bottles (2)

Lesson 20
Fresh potato

Lesson 21
Aquarium
Paper towels

Lesson 22
Soft drink bottle (2 liter)
Blue food coloring
Cooking oil

Lesson 23
Container

Lesson 24
Small glass jar

Lesson 25
Clear glass jar
Flashlight
Milk

Lesson 26
Petroleum jelly

Lesson 29
Milk jug (1 gallon)

Lesson 30
Shoebox

Lesson 32
Plastic tray/pan

Lesson 34
Measuring cup

Lesson 35
Lighter
Bottle (2 liter)